The Sum of Things

THE SUM OF THINGS

by

David Wilson

Foreword by
The Right Honourable The Viscount Slim OBE DL

SPELLMOUNT
Staplehurst

British Library Cataloguing in Publication Data:
A catalogue record for this book is available
from the British Library

ISBN 1-86227-134-8

First published in the UK in 2001 by
Spellmount Limited
The Old Rectory
Staplehurst
Kent TN12 0AZ

Tel: 01580 893730
Fax: 01580 893731
E-mail: enquiries@spellmount.com
Website: www.spellmount.com

1 3 5 7 9 8 6 4 2

Typeset in Palatino by MATS, Southend-on-Sea, Essex
Printed in Great Britain by
TJ International Ltd, Padstow, Cornwall

Contents

List of Maps

For my Grandchildren
Alice, Kingsley, Cosmo and Sylvia
and in Memory of
Sylvia Marianna and Alison Mary

Thanks and Acknowledgements

The idea for this book started at some party on the Island of Islay, at which I was not present. A cousin by marriage, but with contacts in the book trade, Janey Wilks, and other members of the family, seemed to think I ought to write something down about what I had done and where I had been. She got on to me and together we concocted a synopsis and a specimen chapter which she very kindly sent round to various contacts, alas with little success, but somehow she and others persuaded me to go on with what I had started. And with the help of many others this is the result.

I owe especial thanks to those who have read and criticised individual chapters, Lieutenant General Sir John MacMillan, Brigadier Miles Marston, Major Gerald Hadow, all of my Regiment; Gordon Graham (late of the Camerons and a distinguished member of the publishing trade), Lieutenant Colonel John Cormack, once with me in BRIXMIS under my command, and Colonel Peter Cook, late Royal Australian Regiment.

And then follow a whole lot of people, who have had nothing to do with the army but who have plodded through chapters and given all sorts of advice, Roma Ogilvy Watson, Theo Harris, my sister Prudence, Maggie my daughter, my son Sandy, my granddaughter Alice and a very old friend from Australia whose husband was killed with the 2/19 AIF in Malaya, Carmel Quinlan.

Then there are my Editors, Lionel Browne of Sandhurst Editorial Consultants, and Jamie Wilson of Spellmount Publishers.

Finally there is my own Regiment, who have allowed me to use the old 91st and 93rd Highlanders' Crests and the coloured drawing of the map of Korea by the late Captain Robin Fairrie on the jacket. And I must thank Viscount Slim for his Foreword which I do not think I deserve.

Foreword

by The Right Honourable The Viscount Slim OBE DL

Within the close family of our Regiment David Wilson is a bit of a legend. None can compete with his memory and knowledge of our history over the centuries, together with the names of men and events that have made The Argyll and Sutherland Highlanders a great Regiment. He is the third generation of his immediate family to serve in the Argylls, previously his grandfather and father, with great distinction.

The reader will discover that David Wilson has lived an exciting, international and eventful life. His leadership and mettle were forged and tested in the harshness of battle from early youth on the Northwest Frontier of India, coming to terms with retreat and defeat in Malaya, victory in Burma after the close run battle for Kohima, a terrorist war in Palestine and then Korea.

David Wilson has two wonderful families, the Regiment and his own, in that order. Unstintingly both have had his complete loyalty, dedication and love and this is reciprocated in large measure. All of us have found it exhilarating to serve with him. David's enthusiasm combined with his strong and sensible leadership and his single determination in battle to hammer the enemy has assured admiration.

The near destruction of the Regimental System and the attitudes and policies of our Government to political correctness and human rights is sadly damaging the vital and special military ethos so essential to the Army to ensure that when we fight, we win. The reader may care to reflect on this and to thank his lucky stars that there have always been soldiers like the author who have devoted their lives to their Regiment and the Nation.

SLIM
House of Lords
2001

xi

Introduction

First toast

I had a delightful piece of parchment once: my commission. It was written in precise heraldic language, and addressed to me by the then King, Edward the Eighth by the Grace of God of Great Britain, Ireland and the British Dominions beyond the Seas, King, Defender of the Faith, Emperor of India. I was his Trusty and well beloved Alexander David Robin Graham Wilson, and he bid me Greeting. He also reposed especial Trust and Confidence in my Loyalty, Courage and Good Conduct, and did by these presents Constitute and Appoint me to be an Officer in his Land Forces from the twenty sixth day of August 1936.

There was much more, but there was a constitutional hiccup that year, and when I received my commission some months later in India I found that it had been signed by his brother, then King George the Sixth. It was in my baggage in Singapore when the surrender came, and disappeared along with all my worldly goods in the smoke, flames and disgrace of that surrender. This was a pity: there could not have been many commissions that had both kings' names on them. It would have been worth quite something today.

I was now an officer, but – like others of my generation – I had never actually sworn an oath to defend anyone. (From 1939 onwards everyone started their service in the ranks, and swore an oath of loyalty when they first joined up.) So strictly speaking my contemporaries, my forebears and I were mercenaries. We served for pay, and should we be posted to India, we would be paid by the Indian Exchequer. We were hired out to the Indian government, paid for by the Indian taxpayer, and lived in India at his expense to support British rule and justice over him in his own country. But we were young, and never actually thought of it in these terms. We just got on with the job, and in so doing enjoyed ourselves immensely, made numerous friends, and saw many places that even today's tourists cannot visit.

Sir Francis Hastings Doyle wrote a poem called 'The Red Thread of Honour' about a minor skirmish in Sind, when eleven men of the 13th Foot – which became the Somerset Light Infantry – mistook their orders, attacked a small hill fort, and were all killed. Their gallant conduct so impressed the tribesmen of those parts that, in accordance with their ancient tribal custom, they tied a red thread to each of the dead soldiers' wrists – the highest honour they could bestow.

There still runs through all our fighting services a red thread of tradition, duty and honour: perhaps the Royal Navy and the Royal Air Force might prefer a different hue, but they will know what I mean. What follows is the story of how I came to follow in my family's tradition: how I was slowly absorbed into a regimental family, how I was trained in its ways, and how – in my time – I passed some of that thread on to those who came after.

It used to be traditional for Indian cooks to refer to the course that started a meal as 'first toast'; the savoury at the end was called 'second toast'. This is just the appetiser. I hope you will enjoy the courses that follow.

Glossary of Abbreviations and Military Terms

Honours and Awards
KCB	Knight Commander of the Order of the Bath
CB	Commander of the Order of the Bath
DSO	Companion of the Distinguished Service Order
CBE	Commander of the Order of the British Empire
OBE	Officer of the Order of the British Empire
MBE	Member of the Order of the British Empire
DCM	The Distinguished Conduct Medal
MM	The Military Medal

Organisations and Units
AVG	American Volunteer Group (A volunteer organisation of airmen from the US)
ADC	Aide de Camp (a General's personal Staff Officer)
BOAC	British Overseas Airways Corporation (now British Airways)
BAOR	British Army of the Rhine
BRIXMIS	British Commanders in Chief Mission
GSFG	Group of Soviet Forces, Germany
GHQ	General Headquarters
GDR	German Democratic Republic (East Germany in those days)
GSO	General Staff Officer
MA	Military Assistant (a senior Staff Officer to a Commander)
OCTU	Officer Cadet Training Unit
RAR	Tbe Royal Australian Regiment
RAC	Royal Armoured Corps (tank units)
SACEUR	Supreme Commander Allied Powers Europe
SHAPE	Supreme Headquarters Allied Powers Europe
SE IAPEX	The Annual Exercise and Study carried out at SHAPE

IZL	Irgun Zvi Leumi (a hardline Jewish terrorist organisation)

Korean abbreviations

CLM	Commonwealth Liaison Mission
DMZ	The demilitarised zone between North and South Korea
KPA	Korea People's Army (North Korea)
ROK	Republic of Korea
CCF	Chinese Communist Forces
MAC	The Military Armistice Commission (UN, based on Panmunjom)

Miscellaneous

Basha	A jungle hut
Bhatti	The common oil lamp used everywhere in the East
Lat Sahib	Urdu for a General Officer
Ghora Pultan	White soldiers, i.e. a British battalion or detachment
DAA&QMG	A Staff Officer on a Brigade or Divisional Staff dealing in administration
DIS	Detailed Issue Section
FSD	Field Supply Depot
GPT	General Purpose Transport

} units located on Kohima Ridge

CHAPTER 1
Sylvia

My father, mother, sister and I left Edinburgh in January 1935. I was to go to Sandhurst, and my father had gone with the Battalion to Tidworth for his last few months in command. Then he would leave the Army. For too long he had been so uncompromising and so critical of those in authority that they had decided he had reached his ceiling. So we moved to my mother's home, Court Lodge in Lamberhurst, as a temporary base until the future was a bit clearer.

There were one or two newcomers in the village, and one afternoon I was summoned to tea with a family who had bought one of the many oast houses that were no longer required for the diminishing hop trade. Colonel E.L. Mackenzie CIE DSO had served with distinction in the Royal Sussex Regiment, and he and his wife Rennie had spent their retirement buying up old and disused oasts, doing them up, getting their gardens in order, and selling them when all was ready, before moving on to their next conversion.

They were a nice couple, and we struck up a friendship with them almost as soon as we arrived. The Colonel was one of the first to hold the rank of Colonel Commandant, which the British Army had invented in (I think) 1917, when they did away with the rank of Brigadier General. (The title was soon changed to that of mere 'Brigadier'. The badges of rank – the crown and three stars – remained the same.)

I am not sure why I was invited that day, but I put on the accustomed garb of an off-duty Sandhurst cadet of those days – green pork pie hat, tweed jacket, and corduroy trousers – and appeared on time. There were two other guests, their two nieces. Sylvia, the elder, was dark, and Rosemary very fair. I suppose they were aged 13 and 11, and they spoke English with a marked French accent, as they had just come back to England from France, where they had previously lived all their lives in the French Alps. They were nice girls, but there was a world of difference between a 13-year-old and a Sandhurst cadet, pork pie hat and all. The only thing I remember about that party was that I made some remark that sent Rosemary into a fit of giggles, which resulted in her doing what was called the 'nose trick' when gobbets of cake somehow choked her, with

1

dreadful results, and she was sent out of the room to clean up the mess on her dress.

It was a pleasant enough party, but at the proper time I said goodbye and left, and thought no more about it. The two girls made friends with my sister, who was five years younger than me, and from time to time we came across each other.

Years later, in letters from my mother, there was mention of Sylvia, who was then working on one of the women's glossy magazines, staying at Sydney Street, which became our home in 1937, and sharing the cellar during the blitzes in 1941 and 1942, but I could not really put a face to her; the tea party had faded into the past.

On 1 January 1945 I arrived at 28 Sydney Street, en route to the Staff College. I had seen the New Year in rather too well in the Divisional Mess at Tunbridge Wells with Marcus Linton and other chums, and was not feeling my best. I had three nights to go before getting myself down to Camberley. My mother had arranged for Sylvia, who was then in the WRAF, to stay for two of them, and I had managed to get tickets to a very good play by Terence Rattigan for the evening and planned to take her out to dinner. Luckily the journey from Tunbridge Wells West to Victoria had dissipated some of the previous night's potations, but it was rather like appearing on the television in one of Cilla Black's *Blind Date* parties. I really had no idea who I was going to meet, but my mother and sister had assured me that I would get on well with her.

I humped my baggage out of the taxi and into my room, which was on the ground floor, and walked upstairs into the drawing room. There I got a sort of electric shock – a feeling I had never had before in my life. On the sofa was a handsome, rather tall, dark girl, with very direct grey eyes looking at me as if I was some sort of comic act on a music hall stage. (She told me later she realised very well the state I was in. She herself was recovering from a party she had had at Durrington, her RAF station, the night before.) No one had ever looked at me quite like that before, and I suddenly realised she was something very special, and quite out of the ordinary.

Six months later we were married.

For twenty-five years she held my career together, raised a family, made a home wherever I was posted, and apart from a great deal of stability and common sense, brought a legacy of adventure and art into our somewhat conservative and stuffy family. This came down through her very remarkable Russell grandparents.

John Peter Russell, Sylvia's grandfather, came from an Australian family of ironmasters, who had emigrated there from Scotland at the beginning of the 1800s and had done very well indeed: many of the lovely balconies and railings in Sydney and Melbourne were the products of the

Sydney Iron Foundry set up by Sir Peter Nicol Russell. But John Peter, having inherited a considerable fortune, came to England, and studied at the Slade and at Fernand Cormon's academy in Paris, where he made great friends with Van Gogh. His other friends and contemporaries were Matisse, Rodin and Robert Louis Stevenson! He married Marianna, Rodin's model (and some say mistress), who was Italian and a most beautiful person in every way, and set up in an enormous house in Belle Ile, off the coast of Brittany. He became perhaps Australia's leading Impressionist. Sylvia inherited much of her grandmother's good looks and her grandfather's artistic talent, and passed them down through her children.

She very much took the place of my sister – lost, in those days, to the church – and my father adored her. When he first met her and she was still in the WRAF, he enquired what rank she held – he had little idea of RAF ranks or organisation – and when she explained that a leading aircraftwoman was roughly the equivalent of an army corporal, he looked at me and said: 'A corporal? Couldn't you have done a bit better than that?' He had no idea that she was in fact employed in a very highly secret job, and to this day I have no idea what she was doing. And they say that women are gossips!

We got ourselves a lovely little farmhouse in Crowborough, Sussex, and kept it all our married life together, but in true Army style we were bundled around from one quarter to another. The coldest was 9 Clarendon Place, Stirling, where the north wind howled through the double front door, and we froze solid at times. There was Balliabruaich at Dunoon, facing the Clyde, with the hill and 'jungle' almost coming through the back bathroom window, but wonderful in the summer. When I was an instructor at the Staff College, Camberley, we lived in what would be a pretty clapped-out council house in 97 Kings Ride, but then all our friends did too – no garages, only a bicycle and tool shed!

The most attractive residence we ever had was Le Blanc Moulin at Seraincourt, about forty miles out of Paris. This was a lovely old water-mill, which we rented from Monsieur Français, late Adjutant Chef (RSM) of the 6ème Chasseurs Alpins in World War I, who had done well in the business of *assurances*, and was charmed by Sylvia who spoke near-perfect French. Then there was our grand villa in Berlin, but nobody knew who the owners were, or had been. They had disappeared during the war.

I lost count of how many times we moved – all the packings and unpackings, the sorting-out of schools, the organisation of holidays and clothes, the visits to prize-givings and speech days, and the inevitable illnesses and sicknesses that hit families – always when things seemed to be going well. Being an Army wife is no joke. Then there are all the extra duties of looking after the soldiers' wives and families, and trying to help them with *their* problems.

Looking back now I don't know how she stuck it. There were times when I could have murdered her, and I am sure there were times when she could have murdered me! But she had trained herself to live by the old saying 'Never explain – never complain!' and she got on with the job. For twenty-five years.

And just when the time came that we thought we could relax, and I had left the service, came cancer.

It had started in Korea, but all seemed well until one day in December 1970 I found her sitting in the kitchen by a half-peeled bowl of potatoes, and she asked me to finish them, as she said she felt too weak, and could not carry on. She looked old and tired, and grey.

Our local GP, a very old friend of the family, got her into our local hospital next day for a very thorough examination, and the verdict was not good – cancer of the liver. She had perhaps six weeks to live: they held no hope of any recovery. She would be dead some time in the middle of January, but we could look after her at home. Nursing help was available – she need not go into hospital. The question was, could I cope?

There was no choice. Maggie – our daughter, teaching in Australia – came back to lend a hand, and cope we did. Until about ten days before she died Sylvia could get around the house and come for drives in the car. Life went on fairly normally: friends would call in, there were parties, eventually in her bedroom when she could not get around, but still life went on, until finally she got too weak to move, and we had to do every-thing for her.

In the middle of January 1971 she got weaker and weaker, and one night she was very disturbed, and I had to sit up with her. Early next morning I felt she had little time left, so I walked across to the Catholic church and asked our great friend the parish priest if he would come over and give her the last sacraments. She was quite conscious at the time, and much calmer than she had been at night.

It was Maggie's turn to sit with her, and I went downstairs to get a few things organised, when Maggie came down, and very calmly said: 'Daddy, she gave a sort of choking noise. I think she is dead.'

I went upstairs. She was lying quite still in her bed. Her eyes were still open, so I closed them, and kissed her for the last time, but she was far, far away by then.

There was a mass of things to be done. Peter, my friend, trustee and solicitor was ready to take the weight off my shoulders, and was expecting my telephone call. There was not much either of us could say, but I had a lot to do, and this deadened the shock for a while.

A part of my life was finished for ever.

What follows is a story of people and places, of the way we lived, and of the way we behaved. Society is different today: communications are quicker and better, and the Services bear little relationship to their forebears between the two World Wars, but certain things have not changed, and I hope never will.

CHAPTER 2
Slow boat to Karachi

We had an early lunch on 31 December 1936 at my grandmother's house in Broadwater Down, Tunbridge Wells. I said goodbye to my grandmother, father, mother and sister shortly after one o'clock, climbed into my little and very elderly Austin Seven saloon, and set off for Tidworth via Camberley. It was to be almost eight years before I saw them again (and nine years before I saw my father).

It was a lovely afternoon as I puttered down the long road. My journey was broken by a stop for tea with an old Regimental comrade of my father, Colonel G.W. Muir, and his wife. They had asked me to call in to collect a small parcel, which I was to take out to Kenny, their son, who was serving with the 93rd (or to give them their proper title, the 2nd Battalion, the Argyll and Sutherland Highlanders), who were then stationed at Rawalpindi.

I got to Tidworth at about 6.30 pm and immediately changed into mess kit as it was Hogmanay, and we were due for the traditional visit to the Sergeants' Mess bearing the Atholl Brose – that innocuous-looking mixture of whisky, oatmeal and cream – to see the New Year in. I was very young (just over 20), and had no idea of the hidden power of the brew. Later that night I had some difficulty in getting my mess boots off and my pyjamas on!

Next morning, with Douglas Clarke as passenger, I set off in the Austin for Southampton. Douglas, who was the son of Harry Clarke, CO 1st Battalion, had bought the machine off me for £25, I think, and was to take possession of it at Southampton Docks. It is just as well that the present drink-drive laws had not been invented then: that Atholl Brose was powerful stuff, and I was still suffering from its after-effects. But we made it to the docks alongside HMT *Dorsetshire* without any problems.

Dorsetshire was some 10,000 tons, white hulled, with a wide green line down the side and a single yellow funnel. She was run by the Bibby Line for the War Office. Rumour had it that she had once been a pilgrim ship, carrying the faithful to Red Sea ports for Mecca, squashed into the accommodation space like sardines in a can. In her present role, after a bit of conversion, she carried British soldiers to and from their distant

6

stations, also squashed in her holds like sardines. Officers and their ladies travelled in style, in very comfortable accommodation in the after-part of the ship. With luck and a following wind, she could stagger along at perhaps 12 knots. In the Red Sea with a following wind, she turned into an airless oven. I was to find this out in due course.

Not many people today have ever seen the departure of a troopship in peacetime. It was always quite an occasion. There would be a military band playing; red tabbed and brassarded staff officers and their minions would strut about officiously, bearing files and clipboards; and for the final goodbye some sort of 'High Heid Yin' – a Brigadier or perhaps a General – would be alongside to give a final salute as the ship edged away from the quay and the band played 'Auld Lang Syne'. I cannot remember if we rated a General that day, but it was an impressive piece of stage management.

As we edged our way out to sea I sought my cabin, which I was to share with three other officers. It was a roomy affair, with four bunks and a basin, plenty of cupboard space, and a chest of drawers for each of us. We needed this as, for the whole of the voyage, uniform was worn, and mess kit for weekday dinners. The four of us shared one cabin steward, a charming elderly gentleman who told us he was an Arakanese, and had served with the Bibby Line for thirty years. As a young man he had been a steward on one of the ships that took part in the Gallipoli landing. He was charming, extremely efficient, and a mine of information.

Soon it was time to change for dinner and meet our other companions. There were two other Argylls on the boat: Ian Stonor and Gordon Campbell Colquhoun. I was technically the senior, as I had amassed more marks in the Sandhurst passing-out exam (not that that really meant much). The Senior Officer on board was Lieutenant Colonel G.B. Henderson of the 11th Royal Ludhiana Sikhs, who had been at Wellington College with my father. His son Robert, also of the 11th Sikhs, was at Wellington with me, and not for the first time I experienced that interesting bond of friendship that the much derided 'old school tie' can bring.

After dinner Bob Laird of the East Yorkshires and I put on our great-coats and went right forward to the eye of the ship. We sat and watched the lights of the coastal towns pass on the starboard side: Bournemouth, Swanage, Weymouth, and dropping astern now the Needles light. I don't know how Bob felt, but I was excited to be really on my own, aged just 20 years and 4 months, with prep school, Wellington and Sandhurst all behind me. The first day of January 1937 had been an exciting day, a milestone in my life.

Next morning all the officers were assembled in the dining saloon. We were detailed off for various duties, and training programmes were arranged. For example there was a course in Urdu run in the afternoons by

7

senior officers of the Indian Army, who were travelling with us. Small arms training was not neglected: we fired at a towed target over the stern. Before breakfast there was physical training for all. There were lectures on India, on the Indian Army, and on all sorts of other subjects. Whatever else might happen, we were not going to be allowed to sit around in idle boredom.

There was one unpleasant but important duty, that of ship's Orderly Officer. This was a twenty-four-hour assignment, but for our first turn we, the very young, were taken in charge by an older and more experienced mentor. The Orderly Officer of the day had to attend each troops' mealtime, and inspect the mess decks three times a day. This needed a strong stomach. Things were not too bad by day, but at night the hammocks were slung, and the smell of unwashed bodies was over-powering. In rough weather there was also vomit all over the place. I had the misfortune to draw the duty when we were lurching slowly through heavy weather in the Bay of Biscay some three days out. I have a strong seagoing stomach, and have never actually been seasick, but it was touch and go. At the end of the period of duty the orderly officer had to complete a formidable form, which went to the OC Troops. It was my bad luck to have three terms of duty as Orderly Officer: the Bay of Biscay was the worst, but the Red Sea with a following wind was nearly as bad.

It gave me some idea of how Nelson's Navy must have lived – but instead of just three and a half weeks at sea he and his officers and men spent years under those sort of conditions. They were tough!

We made Port Said in ten days or so. There were the gully gully men (local magicians) and their chickens, and – best of all – Simon Artz's store, where we all bought our Bombay Bowlers (the genuine article) and much else, and then we were off that evening down the Suez Canal. For this we had a small searchlight in the bows, which made the journey even more fascinating, and soon we came to Lake Timsah, and here I must digress and go back to 1915 when my grandfather was around these parts.

Major General Alexander Wilson CB was posted from India in November 1914 to take charge of the Suez Canal defences, which at that time consisted of just one Indian infantry brigade. During November, December and January work commenced on a number of defensive posts, most of them on the western (Egyptian) side of the Canal, in what he described in his despatch as 'a systematic development of the naturally strong line of defence afforded by the Canal'. The Canal Company's tugs and barges were mobilised, the water supply was improved, arrangements were made for hospitals and the evacuation of sick and wounded, and a system of police intelligence and surveillance was installed.

In the first fortnight of 1915 reports from Syria suggested that the Turkish Army was on the move south, but in what strength and with what intention was not clear. By 15 January it was known that Turkish forces had entered Sinai, and on 18 January a French hydroplane discovered a force of some 8,000–10,000 Turks near Bir es Saba. British forces' mounted patrols into the desert were also making contact with Turks. There was a small engagement near Kantara on 26 January, and the New Zealand Infantry Brigade, newly arrived, were sent to Ismailia. HMS *Swiftsure*, *Clio*, *Ocean* and *Minerva* took station in the Canal at Kantara, Ballah, El Shatt and Shalouf, ready to add to the firepower.

The General Officer in Command was then Lieutenant General Sir John Maxwell, and I have two letters from him during this period to my grandfather. The first, dated 8 January 1915, ends as follows:

> Are you confident that your posts are strong enough? We have plenty of time and men to improve them.
>
> I know a purely passive defence does not commend itself to everyone, but where you have a desert and a strong line like the Suez Canal it would be folly to folly to set these aside, either for a scrap or to follow up a defeat. I mean the Turks to have all the enjoyment they can get out of the desert and I don't intend our people to go into it beyond the range of their water bottles.
>
> I have seen General Younghusband today and have talked this over with him.

And on 28 January another letter, this time typed and marked 'SECRET', was addressed as follows:

The General Officer Commanding Canal Defences

> I do not wish to tie your hands as regards attacking isolated advance posts of the enemy. You can use your discretion as to this; I merely point out that it is the enemy's game to lure us out of our lines and our game to induce them to attack our lines; you must also bear in mind that any reverse will have serious consequences in Egypt, perhaps Europe; therefore before any attack you must be reasonably sure that the force you attack is not within reach of support, and that your force is if anything more than adequate for the task.
>
> At present the information brought to us by aerial reconnaissance has hardly been sufficiently accurate to depend on, especially in regard to numbers.

CAIRO
J.G. MAXWELL
28 January 1915 Lieutenant General
Commanding the Force in Egypt

There in a nutshell were very specific instructions to my grandfather: the Canal was to be the line of defence. And so it proved.

In the last few days of January 1915 the Turkish Army closed the gap, and despite desultory actions at the end of January, launched a determined attack on the night of 3 February at Toussum and Kantara. HMS *Hardinge* was struck by two 6 inch shells, and had to be towed into Lake Timsah near Serapeum. The Ismailia ferry post was overrun. HMS *Swiftsure* and *Hardinge*, together with the French ships *Requin* and *D'Entrecasteau* and numerous torpedo boats and armed launches all took part, with the New Zealand Brigade, and the 22nd, 28th, 29th and 32nd Brigades.

Engagements continued for some thirty-six hours, but by 5 February our aircraft reported that the Turks were in retreat, though further desultory firing took place all along the line. The battle was over and the Canal safe.

In his Despatch No. 2 of 19 August 1915, General Maxwell forwarded my grandfather's own despatch to the War Office, adding one or two remarks of his own, and ending:

> In conclusion I would like very specially to bring to the notice of the Secretary of State for War, the eminent services of Major General A. Wilson CB, who has commanded the Canal Defences, with ability, tact and resource since November 16th 1914.

That final paragraph got my grandfather a KCB; he was made Lieutenant Governor of Jersey, and Colonel of the Argyll and Sutherland Highlanders. He died in July 1937.

There were questions in Parliament about the affair: were we defending the Canal, or was the Canal defending Egypt?

In January 1937, as I watched *Dorsetshire* plod her way along past the marker boards, and the navigation lights of Lake Timsah and the Kantara Bridge, I never realised the family link with these places. I had not read enough history, and had never seen the family papers that my grandfather had kept. It was all too exciting, and I was too young in those days. When I woke up the next morning we were past Suez and into the Red Sea.

We stopped at Aden for a whole day, and a party of us were taken ashore and around Crater, where a young Colonel known as 'Mad Mitch' and the 91st were later to make their name. All I remember was the strange smell of the East, and the heat, and then it was back on board and onwards to Karachi. We got there on 23 January.

Hardly had the ship tied up and the gangway been raised than a horde of Indian servants appeared. One of them, immaculately dressed, and wearing the yellow and green cummerbund of the 93rd, came towards me with a letter. It was from the Adjutant, John Tweedie. It was quite short, and read:

2/Lieutenant A.D.R.G.WILSON

This is your bearer, Nawab Khan; he will look after you.

His wages will be Rs30 monthly.

J.W. TWEEDIE
Captain and Adjutant

And look after me he did for the next three years. He came from Poonch, a small native state in the foothills of the Himalayas. He was responsible for linen, uniform and all my own kit. He also held what one might call the personal purse, and could at any time produce money if I needed it. But at the end of each month he gave me a meticulous account of all his spending, and I would pay him what I owed. He was about my height, good looking, intelligent, smart and scrupulously honest. Sadly, when we were posted to Singapore in August 1939, I lost touch with him. I am ashamed of that, but the war intervened.

We stayed on board for one more night, but the next evening we disembarked to board our train, which was bound eventually for Peshawar. It was a typical Indian troop train, with the special stock designed for transporting the BORs (British Other Ranks), as the Jocks were now known. Their carriages were fitted with long and – I suspect – uncomfortable bunks, and lavatories at both ends. There were no corridor connections. In the middle of the train was a kitchen car where their meals were prepared, and dished out at various stops en route.

There were standard Indian second class carriages for families, first class for officers and their 'ladies', and a double restaurant car. The train seemed bigger than trains at home, and with reason: the gauge was 5 ft 6 in, rather than the 4 ft 8 in that we were used to. But the thing that interested me most was the engine. She was a big 4-6-0, and if you took away the cowcatcher and the searchlight, she could have looked quite at home in the UK (or more accurately Scotland), for that was where she had been built. Her class was known throughout India as a 'mail engine', because she was designed to work the fastest mail trains.

She jogged my memory back some twelve years to when we were stationed in Allahabad. About a mile from my father's married quarters was the East Indian Railway and its engine shed: a main depot filled with many machines, pouring out smoke. Our nurse in those days, Anne Howard, had a father who was high up in the engineering department of the South Indian Railway, and sometimes used to take me (my sister was

11

too young) to the sheds among those enormous machines, painted green, with the big letters E.I.R. on their tenders in shining brass. This engine was different: it was black, with four steel bands round the boiler, and N.W.R. (for North Western Railway) on its tender. But somehow I felt suddenly as if it were a familiar friend from the past.

When I got to my carriage, which was at the end of the train, I found that Ian and Gordon, my two fellow Argylls, were with me, together with an officer from the Hampshires, also Rawalpindi bound.

There were two bunks below, two up above them, two cane chairs, a large lavatory/shower, and an assortment of lights and fans. Our bearers had laid out our bedding rolls on our bunks. They themselves had a servants' compartment at the end of the coach, and would appear for orders at each major stop. There was some discussion as to which of the three window selections we should use. We decided on the gauze to keep the dust out, plus the slats, rather than the glass. It was a wise choice.

Dinner was about to be served in the restaurant car, and so we congregated there. The service was excellent, but the selection of food was not quite up to Bibby Line standards! There would be a good curry at midday, and then in the evening lentil soup (*dhal*), followed by boiled or roast chicken, or occasionally an omelette, and bread and butter pudding – plus of course first and last toast! After we had finished our meal the train stopped to allow the troops to feed, and we returned to our compartments, and got into our sleeping bags. Night had fallen, and I dozed off, to awake to a babble of noise outside.

We had stopped at a small station called Jungshahi. The place was alive with activity, and under pressure lamps and hurricane *bhattis* sellers of all sorts were shouting out their wares: *garam chai* (hot tea), *pani Mussulman* (water for Mohammedans), *pani Hindu* (water for Hindus), *sag alu* (potato curry), and a great deal more, but we had been strictly told not to deal with them for fear of dreadful infection from every possible disease. It seemed a pity: some of the sweetmeats looked very tempting.

This was my first experience of an Indian railway station at night. I was to have many more such experiences all over the continent in the years to come. And then the train pulled out, and I went to sleep.

Next morning our bearers entered with a mug of tea for our *chota hazri* ('little breakfast'), and warned us that breakfast itself would be in the dining car. We got changed and ready, and when the next stop came walked alongside the train to the car. We were in a siding, and the troops were parading outside their kitchen car for their breakfast. It seemed that we were in the middle of a desert. The countryside was flat, with little cultivation: it was very sandy, with just a few desolate trees somehow managing to exist. We were indeed at the edge of the Scinde Desert, which was to accompany us for the rest of that day and some of the next.

The train rolled on and on through dusty, boring country, with here and there a small oasis of trees, houses and sparse fields, and from time to time a major station or passing point. It was hot and dusty. We mostly lay on our bunks with our fans on, drinking soda water!

From time to time we stopped at garrison towns such as Multan and Lahore, and various individuals, families and drafts of men left the train, which was getting emptier as we went along. I felt the loss of my *Dorsetshire* companions as a slow severing of links with home, and on the morning of the third day there was only the Rawalpindi and Peshawar lot left. The restaurant car seemed very empty for the last lunch. We were due to arrive at 4 pm, so we all changed into our best uniform: kilt, red-and-white diced hose, spats, the lot. At least we were going to arrive smart and properly dressed. All except me, that was.

For years my family have dealt with a famous tailor, who had better remain nameless. Thanks to my father's eagle eye my outfit was complete, and properly built and fitted, all except for one item – my khaki Wolseley helmet (there was a white one too for ceremonial occasions, but I never wore it). Each helmet had a length of white or khaki cloth called a *pagri* wound round it, with between five and seven folds. Ours had seven; on the left-hand side of the *pagri* was a square tartan flash with A&SH in yellow capital letters, and stuck into the lot was a white hackle. My tailor (or his assistant who did it) had made a complete mess of the *pagri*. It was in the wrong material, and most inexpertly wound. Knowing nothing about these things I had accepted it without question at home, but as I compared it with my companions' headgear, I began to get worried. Would it pass muster? I was soon to find out.

We reached Rawalpindi on time, and got out onto the platform, to find quite a delegation waiting for us. It was headed by John Tweedie, the Adjutant, and amongst my particular friends was Peter Winstanley, late of the Lynedoch at Wellington and the New Buildings at Sandhurst. He was completing his year's attachment to the Regiment for the Unattached List Indian Army, when he would join the 5th Royal Gurkha Rifles (Frontier Force). That would not be until September, and in the meantime he was to be my 'wet nurse' and show me round. While all this was going on our bearers were collecting our belongings, and a small army of *tongas*[1] was being mobilised to carry us up to our barracks, which were about a mile away.

But nemesis was on the way towards me in the shape of John Tweedie. He was an old friend of many years when I had been a schoolboy, brought up with his brother Giles. Our two families had served together for three generations now. He was a man of striking good looks and explosive temper, and his welcome to the 93rd was typical:

'Christ Almighty, David, what a bloody awful hat! Take it to the *darsi* [tailor] and get him to tie a proper *pagri* on by first parade tomorrow!'

I had arrived.

NOTES

1   The *tonga* was a small, two-wheeled horse-drawn carriage, the staple transport of all India. It could go faster than the bullock cart, but could not carry anything like the load. It was designed to carry one driver in front and two passengers behind, but usually ended up carrying a great deal more.

CHAPTER 3
The frontier

My Wolseley helmet was soon put to rights by the regimental tailor, but I never wore it again. British soldiers in the late 1930s wore the pith helmet, which was a lighter and much more serviceable affair.

The Army of those days still clung to all sorts of outmoded traditions, one of which was the need to avoid incurring sunstroke. From dawn until 6.00 pm or thereabouts it was mandatory to wear a *topi* (or pith helmet), but at the magic hour of 6.00 pm the risk of sunstroke was passed, and it was permissible to wear forage caps, or in our case glengarries. This was despite the fact that in Rawalpindi it could be freezing cold in the winter months. Still, at least the cholera belts and spine pads[1] that I remembered from my youth had thankfully passed into oblivion.

I did not know very much about being a soldier, let alone an officer, in those days. Sandhurst had taught me little. I could clean a rifle spotlessly, and shoot reasonably straight with it. I could drill with precision on the square. I could ride a horse – but I could do that before I went to Sandhurst's riding school, with its legendary riding instructors and their marvellous repartee. I could polish a bayonet blade until I could see my eyebrows in it. I could bull up my boots, and fumble my way through the manual of military law, but I had no idea of how to command a platoon. In short I was thoroughly wet behind the ears, and I picked up my trade from many patient and long-suffering NCOs, who I was nominally supposed to be commanding; from the Jocks themselves; and from the senior officers of the battalion, who had the ill luck to have me serving under them.

For example, one of the things we learnt at Sandhurst was how to ride a bicycle in proper military fashion: you treated it like a horse. The drill was exactly the same. First you lined up and numbered off, and then the command was given:

'By half sections – right.' You turned your handle bars half right.

'Walk march.' You marched off in step in pairs in a long line.

'Prepare to mount.' This was the tricky bit: you put your outside foot on the pedal, and hopped along using the bicycle like a scooter.

'Mount.' You swung yourself into the saddle, and the column moved off. This was fine until someone in the leading front files had a puncture or hit a stone, and then you all piled into him and landed in an undisciplined heap.

So you were master of your machine, but no one had taught you how to manage a bicycle at night, in mess dress, as Orderly Officer carrying a slung claymore, which somehow you had to carry in your left hand. If you put the scabbard on the handle bars, the sword would fall out backwards. Therefore you had to hold the beastly thing in your left hand, which left you just your right hand to steer the machine, and if you did not take care, the scabbard would insert itself into either the front wheel spokes, spelling instant disaster, or the rear wheel spokes, which produced much the same result. The Orderly Sergeant, riding alongside you, would not be amused.

It was one night when I was Orderly Officer that I learnt I had acquired a nickname that was to haunt me all my service – and still does.

The lines at Rawalpindi consisted of a series of platoon-sized huts, but they had no running water or sanitation in them. Baths and lavatories were in separate buildings, sometimes as far as 100 yards or so away. The lavatories consisted of large buckets under wooden seats, with earth sanitation. The buckets were some 4 ft or more high, and, like Ali Baba's jars for forty thieves, could easily accommodate a man. And of course the young soldiers on first arrival were regaled with dreadful tales of wily Pathans, who would hide at night with their wickedly curved and dreadfully sharp knives, waiting to snick off the tender parts of anyone rash enough to venture out!

The answer was not to venture out at night: you could pee in your boot, chuck it out of the window, and collect it the next morning. If by chance it hit or near missed the Orderly Officer on his rounds, that was a bonus! So we soon learnt to keep well out of boot range of the barrack blocks. But occasionally there were odd disturbances, with young men larking about when they should have been in bed. On one such occasion, I heard the voice of a corporal shout out:

'Get back to youse beds – that fucker Chuckles is on the prowl!'

At first I couldn't think who he was referring to, but then the truth burst on me in a flash. It is a name that has stuck to me all over the world for some sixty years or more now.

They took us young in hand very gently. There was much to learn, for in some ways it was an army of another age that we had joined. Except for the modern rifles and the Vickers Berthier light machine guns (which were pretty useless), the 93rd were not all that much different from the 93rd that had marched and fought in the Indian Mutiny of 1857.

We were horse drawn (or more accurately mule carried), and organised into three rifle companies, each of four platoons. Each platoon had one mule, which carried its one light machine gun, reserve ammunition, and chagals[2] of water. Then there was a machine gun company, of four platoons, each with four Vickers MMGs. Our signals consisted of flag, heliographs, lamps for night, and telephones. There was no such thing as a wireless set in those days; they belonged to Brigade Headquarters, but on operations we would get No. 1 Set,[3] complete with its mule, leader and two signallers, which joined Battalion Headquarters, to provide communications to the Higher Command – when it worked, that is. At night it usually did not work, emitting instead a series of hisses and splutters of static, to the fury of senior officers who were trying to get through to each other.

If they did manage to get through, the result was sometimes memorable as neither would have any idea of proper wireless procedure. Conversations would end in classic style with such remarks as 'Don't you say OVER to me, dammit; I'm saying OVER to you'!

One thing that *had* improved since Mutiny, Crimean and Monsieur Soyer's day was the food. M. Soyer's patent stove[4] was still in use, but we had the petrol burner and its nest of black dixies (oval cooking pots), which could cook up a meal almost anywhere in no time at all. The welcome roar of the cookhouse flashing up its burners at Stand To is something I'll never forget.

Towards the end of 1936 an individual called the Fakir of Ipi had been causing problems in Waziristan, and the Army had been called in to help. There had been some quite severe engagements, one near a place called Bicche Kashkai, where a brigade had been severely handled at night. Things escalated, and at the beginning of April 1937 the 93rd were ordered to mobilise and proceed, first to Bannu, and then to Mir Ali. We did not all go; a rear party had to be left behind to deal with pay and administration, and this was established in our hill station about forty miles from Rawalpindi at Gharial. There was a small pool of officers and men as reinforcements: I was lucky not to have been left behind with it.

So one afternoon we marched out of our lines to Rawalpindi Station, mules and all, and boarded our train (broad gauge), which was to take us to Mari Indus. There we had to change from one broad gauge train into two metre-gauge trains, and this at 2.00 am. You can imagine the scene: there were men, stores and mules all over the place, and our cooks in the centre of the platform with burners going full blast for a meal. Luckily there was a full moon that night, which made things easier. By dawn the two trains were loaded, and we set off to Bannu, in what was known as the 'Heatstroke Express'. If we reached as much as 20 mph at any stage we would have been doing well.

We spent one night under canvas at Bannu, being looked after by one of the Indian regiments of the garrison. Next morning the tents came down, we fell in in column facing north towards the hills, and the pipes and drums of the same regiment that had acted as our host for the night played us out of town, to the tune of 'The Midlothian Pipe Band'. After about three miles they left us and returned to Bannu, and we were left with just our own pipers, six in front and six halfway down the column.

I was near the front of the column, and looked back to see the 93rd Highlanders marching to war in the kilt (for the last time, but I did not realise it then). There was the long dusty column in threes, led by our own pipers, and in front of us a low purple ridge that was the high mountains of Waziristan, still some way off. But the pipes were leading us there in the long, rather slow step of the tunes they play, and I wondered just where they were leading me: to all the places I had never imagined, and where so many friends were to die.

We camped that night at Saidgi, where we found two graves of the 1897 Tochi Valley expedition, belonging to the 93rd. One of them was the grave of Sergeant Major Macdonald, who had died of heat apoplexy on the march from Bannu on 9 July. The Battalion had marched all the way from Miranshah in the hottest of hot weathers!

Next day we marched to Mir Ali, a fortified camp where we were to stay for two weeks, polishing up our battle drills and acting as road-opening pickets for the road to Isha Corner and Razmak. For five days of this period I was given my first command.

Between Mir Ali and Saidgi the road went through a defile known as Shinki. It was guarded by a considerable Scouts post half way through, and another, called Khajuri, at the Mir Ali (northern) end. The whole was garrisoned by a company, Headquarters and two platoons at Shinki Fort, and the other two platoons at Khajuri. I was given command of the latter, with two Vickers MMGs as well.

By day we took to the hills, in a series of *ghashts* – a Pathan word meaning an armed patrol – but at night we manned the parapet of the fort, to keep the evildoers out. Nothing moved on the road by night!

On our first night there was great excitement at Shinki Fort, which burst into a blaze of action, with Verey lights, tracer and MMG fire exploding like a Brocks benefit night. We were perhaps two miles away, and watched excitedly. Who could have survived such a battle? Next morning we found out. One wretched camel had been killed. Nothing else: no bodies, no blood, no abandoned weapons, indeed no trace of any enemy. But there had been some sniping earlier on that evening, and inevitably some sentries had replied. Bullets striking stone rocks make a sort of spark, which to the untrained soldier's eye can be mistaken for someone firing back, which leads to more musketry. In total, about 200 rounds were fired at nothing. Years later, in Bill Slim's Army, the principle was drummed into us all that 'the answer to noise is silence'. Clearly the 93rd still had a lot to learn.

After a week the Battalion was ordered to concentrate at Mir Ali, and

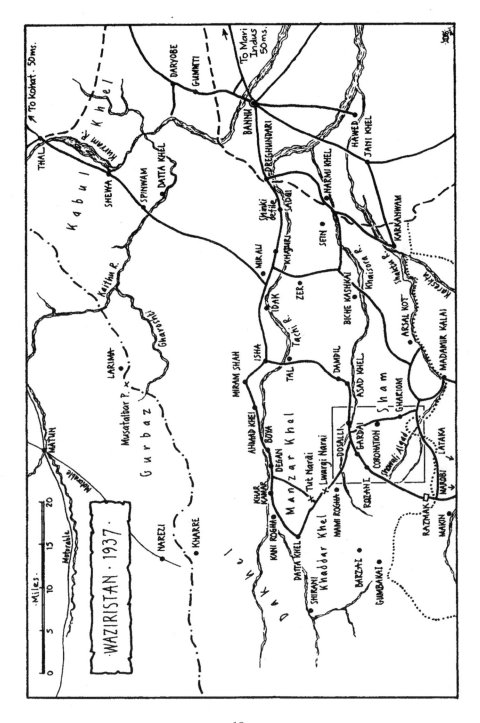

take part in an operation to Bicche Kashkai. About five miles from Mir Ali we had to cross the Tochi River, which was easily forded at that time of year, and beyond it was a long ridge called Zer. It was held in some strength by the enemy.

At that time I was employed as Intelligence Officer, a sort of dogsbody to the Adjutant, John Tweedie. I suspect it was because I knew very little, but could do no harm under his eagle eye. Battalion Headquarters was marked by a green regimental flag carried by one of our drummers, a host of signallers with flags, lamps and helios, and another drummer carrying a large red flag. This was not a banner of political import, but for use if and when it was time to act as rearguard. In addition, Piper Rodham carried a small black wooden case containing message forms and code sheets. These three important gentlemen – the two drummers and the piper – were known, rather like the officers of Parliament, as Green Flag, Red Flag and Black Box.

Shortly after we had forded the river, there was a curious 'crack, thump' sound, followed by others in quick succession. A spout of dust rose from the ground near one of our signallers' legs. Johnnie Hay Young, our Colonel, quietly said: 'Spread out, we are under fire.' It did not seem to worry him in the least. I cannot say I was all that happy.

Almost immediately the section of Vickers MMGs opened up on the ridge of Zer, and from behind us the 3.7 mountain guns started firing in support. I think it was 'C' Company under Captain Frank Elliot, who was leading the advance, that immediately went for the hill and – supported by the guns and machine guns – captured it without loss. It had been a copybook attack, but it was my first introduction to battle – a very gentle introduction, as none of us had been hit, but we had polished off a score of the enemy. It all seemed deceptively easy.

That evening we linked up with another Brigade who had captured Bicche Kashkai, and settled down for the night to be properly sniped at. It was most uncomfortable. One or two of our mules were hit, but luckily no humans. The next morning was spent in clearing up the remaining opposition, and I was sent on the back of a Mk 2 Light Tank with a message to the force in Bicche Kashkai some three miles down the dirt track that passed for a road.

The Mk2 Light Tank was very elderly, with a two-man crew – driver and gunner – and one Vickers MMG in the turret. I suppose it might just have kept the rain out, but I would not have thought it was really bullet proof. On its own it stuck out like a sore thumb, and made excellent practice for the Pathan marksmen on the surrounding hills. Unfortunately there was no room for me inside, and stuff was whistling past me as I sat on the engine cover! Luckily the enemy seemed to be out of practice at moving targets, and I delivered the message without incident. By the time we returned the marksmen had disappeared.

That evening we marched some seven miles north to a big Scouts post called Idak, where we stayed for a week, picketing the road to Isha Corner. This was routine stuff: we were up before dawn and got back at dusk, by which time the Razmak and Miranshah convoys had got through in both directions.

After a week, we moved forward by stages past Isha Corner to Damdil, a large camp where the 5th Gurkhas had had a particularly vicious fight for one of their camp pickets a week or so before, and then to Dosalli, a large brigade camp based on another Scouts post. Here there were actually two Brigades, the 1st and ours, which was called TOCOL (an abbreviation for Tochi Column). We consisted of the 1st Battalion the Royal Ludhiana Sikhs, and the 2nd Battalion of the 4th Gurkha Rifles. We had our own Sappers and a mountain battery, but in addition there was a battery of 18 pounders, and another of 4.5 inch howitzers.

All this gathering of troops was for the purpose of getting up to and holding the Sham Plain. This was only six miles or so from Dosalli, but more than twice that distance by foot, as it was protected by some very steep and jagged mountains, which formed a natural defensive position. It was held in strength by the Wazirs – so much so that a direct attack up the Sre Mela Algad by 1st Brigade, with a bit of help from us, never got anywhere. (It was during that operation that I saw a sight from World War I: a battery of horse-drawn 18 pounders firing shrapnel in support of one part of the operation.)

It was now the first week of May, and it was beginning to get hot. We were attended by a myriad flies by daylight: they got into everything, and it was difficult to drink a mug of tea without swallowing at least one of the pests. The medics provided us with Flit guns, which were of limited use, and in any case you couldn't use them on the march or when you were moving, and the flies were crawling round your eyes and the back of your neck, and your arms were black with them. But we got used to it all.

On the afternoon of 11 May there was an Order Group, held in conditions of some secrecy. We, TOCOL, were going to get to the Sham Plain by night, up the mountain called Iblanke. It was a formidable barrier: only the Scouts had been up it and knew just how steep and precipitous it was. Eight platoons of them were to lead the attack. They would be followed by the 2/11th Sikhs, then the 2/4th Gurkha, and then us. The mountain guns would follow as best they could.

There was to be no move or activity before dark, which I think must have been at about 8 pm. All tents were to be left standing and normal lights shown, so that enemy watchers could have no idea that anything was amiss. To help in recognition officers wore special white patches on their backs so that they could be followed in the dark. And there was one special point about the plan.

Next day – 12 May 1937 – was Coronation Day (the coronation of

George VI), and the Wazirs no doubt assumed that the British/Indian Army would be taking some sort of holiday to celebrate it. Luckily for us they were wrong, and we caught them unprepared: clearly they had never reckoned for one minute that anyone could get up Iblanke at all, let alone by night.

The Scouts started at about 9 pm, wading across the Sre Mela Algad followed by the rest of the Brigade. It had been a dry summer, and the water barely came up to our knees. It meant that we had to go up the hill with cold, wet boots, but exertion soon warmed them up.

My job was to maintain contact with the 2/4th Gurkhas, and in particular with my opposite number, Jack Masters.[5] He and I knew each other pretty well: he had been two years ahead of me at Wellington and Sandhurst. As we scrambled in virtually single file up the slopes, his battalion would leave small posts of three to four men as guides to the route, and guards in case of attack; we – the 93rd – would pass through them, and they would then become the rearguard. It was all very simple on paper, but difficult on a dark night on a steep mountainside. Down below you could hear the bangings and crashes as mules or men slipped and fell, and their loads went tumbling back down.

A curious phenomenon occurs at night time. No matter how slowly the leading men are going, somehow the column concertinas, and those in the rear are either left sitting down or running as hard as they can to keep up. I got caught in this way: suddenly I was all alone, with no one to be seen in front, and – apart from the noises of men and mules falling about – nothing behind. And somewhere along the ridge that we were climbing would be a 4th Gurkha picket of men, fully alert, who could easily mistake me for an enemy. What was I to do?

I decided that blundering about on my own would get me nowhere, so I took the coward's way out and sat down, in the hopes that someone would find me, which they did: my Battalion Headquarters, led by John Tweedie in one of his more explosive moods. What the hell did I think I was doing? Where had the 4th Gurkhas got to? Why had I allowed myself to get out of touch with them?

There is a great way of getting out of that sort of military situation. It involves repeating – in the right order – three stock answers to such questions: 'My fault, Sir'; 'Very sorry, Sir'; 'Won't occur again, Sir'. Interjected at the right moment they are normally guaranteed to take the steam out of an angry senior officer. The trouble was that none of them fitted this case. Luckily, just as John was about to explode, Jack Masters arrived. He was most apologetic for the fact that he had lost his way up a secondary spur, but confident that all was now well and under control.

We scrambled on upwards, and after a while a faint light started on the eastern horizon: dawn was upon us, and as far as I knew the leading Scouts had not yet got up to the *narai*, or pass. If they had not we would be in trouble. The Wazirs could reinforce it very quickly, surprise would be lost, and TOCOL would be caught in single file trying to get up the mountain.

In fact the Scouts did make it, surprising the opposition. After the battle they told us that there had been an exchange of verbal ruderies between themselves and the enemy, who thought they were quite unsupported, and were confident they could hold the pass. But a combined attack by the Scouts and the Sikhs, supported by artillery, gained the pass. It was as just well that it did: as light broke, I could see the whole Brigade strung out, right down to Dosalli Camp far below. If we had not gained complete surprise, we would have been sitting ducks, virtually defenceless.

There were not many casualties. We were onto the plain, and we set about making our camp and putting *sangars*[6] on the surrounding hills. Writing it all down now it seems so simple. At the time I was too tired and too involved to feel frightened, although the few minutes for which I found myself all alone on the mountainside in the dark, and not knowing where to go or what to do, was quite an experience. That experience was put to good use thirteen years later in December 1950, when I found myself commanding two companies of our first battalion some fifty miles north of Pyongyang in North Korea. We had run off the map, the wireless was out, I had no idea where the rest of the Battalion was, it was freezing cold, there was the sound of shooting somewhere ahead, and somehow we had to join up with the rest of the Battalion, who could have been on the moon for all I knew. Moreover, the mantle of command and responsibility sat very heavily on my shoulders. By good fortune, we made it. It was a dreadful night, but nothing like as bad as that climb up Iblanke.

As it was Coronation Day, we called the camp Coronation. TOCOL had done well, and we were justly pleased with ourselves. There was even a rumour that, as the only soldiers of the Empire actually in action on 12 May 1937, we would all be given a Coronation Medal in addition to our Frontier gong. But then the truth came that they had all been given away, and there were none to spare!

Once we had established our camp, our next priority was to build a road down the Sham Algad, initially to get mules and camels up, then widening to a jeep track (although we didn't have jeeps in those days), and finally a full motor road, capable of taking 30-cwt lorries.

We built new *sangars* for pickets, and laid what seemed like miles of barbed wire round them. It was during one such day's work that I fell backwards into a barbed wire fence, lacerating my shorts and my posterior. It was quite a deep cut, which required a stitch or two. It wasn't really very serious, but it was to have a bearing on the future.

The 1st Brigade came up and relieved TOCOL, and we moved five miles down the plain to establish another camp called Ghariom, where the same

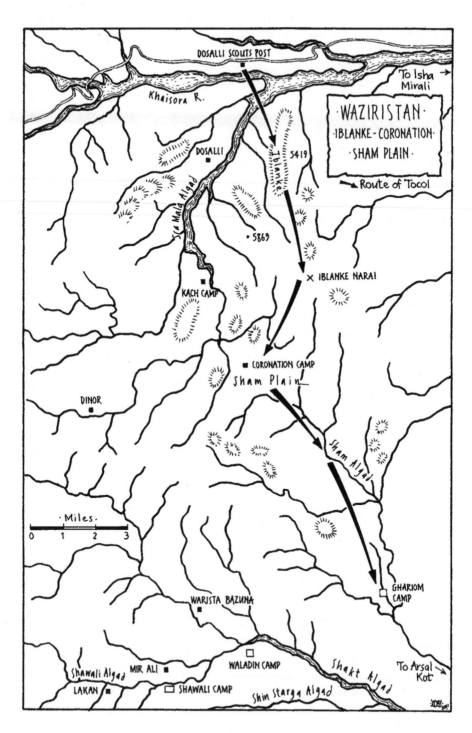

drill took place: perimeter fence, *sangars*, water points, roads and so forth. During this time we had one sharp engagement with some Wazirs, who attacked one party: during this Ted Snowball, one of our MMG platoon commanders, was quite seriously wounded.

The whole point of the exercise was to get within striking distance of the sordid little village called Ipi, where lived the redoubtable Faqir. It was thought that if we occupied that, we could bring him to heel. In the meantime other villages on the edge of the Sham Plain were searched by patrols, bombed from the air, and shelled. All this was to prevent the tribesmen from grazing their flocks in the area that had the best summer grass, and hence bring them to their senses. The tribes depended on their sheep and cattle for milk, meat, hides and wool; they were their only source of livelihood apart from their sparse crops. We were in fact threatening them with starvation unless they resumed a quiet life.

One day an enormous gun arrived at Ghariom, a 6 inch howitzer, which was to shell a particularly recalcitrant village, whose inhabitants were making a real nuisance of themselves, sniping at us by night and laying ambushes by day. They were to be taught a lesson, and my platoon and I were involved.

In order to range accurately on the village, we had to set up an observation post on one of the many hills surrounding Ghariom. My platoon were detailed to capture it early one morning, to make it safe for the generals and staff officers who wished to see the action, and also for it to serve as a base for the Royal Air Force signals detachment that was coming along for communications with the aircraft that was to do the spotting.

Before first light we set off: myself, thirty or so assorted Jocks, my platoon mule and its leader, and the RAF signals detachment, who clearly thought the whole affair was a total waste of time. Their judgement proved to be correct. They consisted of a pilot officer, who would much rather have been in his aeroplane, two signallers, and a mule with its leader, carrying an enormous RAF wireless set. It would be an understatement to describe the detachment as being thoroughly pissed off with the job.

Without much trouble, and with no opposition, we established ourselves on our mountain and waited for the High Heid Yins, who arrived in good order. I had never seen so much top brass together before. They trained their glasses on the offending village, far away, and consulted their watches. The aircraft, a Wapiti from Miranshah, was supposed to be overhead at 0830, but 0900 came and there was still not a sound. There were mutterings and consultations among the Brass. Eventually, some forty minutes late, a far-off buzzing was heard, and soon we saw the machine flying in our direction.

It was now the turn of the RAF signals detachment to get in touch with the machine, which it did, but at some length. Eventually the senior general could stand it no longer.

'For God's sake, Man,' he addressed the young RAF pilot, 'Find out why he is late!'

So the following exchange took place:

'Charlie Able, why are you late? Why are you late, over to you? Over.'

Typically the aircraft set and the ground set suddenly worked like a dream, and very clearly, so that everyone could hear the pilot's reply:

'Charlie Able, that's partly my business but bugger all of yours. Over.'

The Jocks thought this was the funniest thing they had heard for years, the staff officers looked apoplectic, and the RAF crew were beside themselves with mirth. For the first time that day they were enjoying themselves. The Wapiti droned off to its position over the village, and attention shifted to Ghariom Camp, where the monster gun was getting ready to fire.

The gun drill for a 6 inch howitzer would do justice to a corps de ballet. It is very complicated and stately with, as a final *pièce de résistance*, the ramrod being tossed backwards to the No. 1 behind the trail. I had never seen it before, and I found it all very impressive. Eventually the shell was rammed home, hands were raised and lowered to acknowledge commands, and with an enormous bellow the monster fired.

The shell missed us by inches, and landed some 2,000 yards short of the target. There was consternation. Down below at the gunsite, there was clearly something wrong. People were anxiously looking up the gun barrel, and poking about with the ramrod: all was not well. Then we got a message that the gun was out of action. Somehow the driving band of the shell had completely removed what is known as a 'land' – a piece of the rifling – and the gun could not be safely fired again. So we all went home: the staff in high dudgeon, the Wapiti because it was running out of fuel, and the RAF signals team, who had greatly enjoyed seeing the pongos, brown jobs, or whatever they called us in those days, making what can only be described as a howling balls of things. As my very first example of Army/RAF interservice cooperation it was a memory to be treasured.

We spent many days improving the camp and building roads. The bulldozer and JCB had not been invented in those days, and it was pick and shovel work initially until the track was wide enough to take a grader. We got extra pay – I think I rated one rupee an hour – but my barbed wire injury was playing up, and nothing our regimental doctor could do seemed to have any effect. I was put on the sick list, and woke up one morning with a raging temperature thanks to blood poisoning. I was ignominiously shipped back to the hospital at Razmak, the main base for our operations.

TOCOL was ordered to Arsal Kot, the village HQ of the Fakir of Ipi, but by the time it got there he had flown the nest (or rather his flea-ridden caves). Our engineers blew some caves in and destroyed a tower or two; after twenty-four hours the force withdrew, and it was then that they ran into trouble. A letter written by me to my father survives and describes the events:

> As 15 platoon was coming off their hill, they were followed up and suffered two casualties. They immediately went back up the hill to get them off, and suffered more on the way, and charged the enemy off the top. Charlie Anderson threw two bombs after them, one of which failed to explode, but the other did a lot of damage.
>
> More casualties were suffered by the platoon, and few might have survived if Sergeant Morrison and his platoon [had not] then come to their help without orders from anyone.
>
> We lost six killed and seven wounded, but reckoned we had accounted for over thirty of the enemy, mostly Mahsuds. We also lost two rifles.
>
> So far we had had twelve killed and sixteen wounded.

From another letter a month later:

> Rumour has it that we are to be relieved on the 20th of July, but I don't suppose it will come to anything.
>
> So far we have collected one Military Cross and four MMs as immediate awards. The MC was won by our Doctor, who did wonders in the Arsal Kot battle; he was stunned by a rock and grazed by a bullet at almost point blank range, but continued to help the wounded off the hill under fire. Sergeant Morrison got one of the Military Medals (he was actually put in for a DCM but didn't get it). We all thought Charlie Anderson should have had a Military Cross, but he had to be content with a Mention.

While all this was going on I was laid up with a ridiculous but badly poisoned leg. It was my company in that action, and I should have been with them. There was no penicillin in those days, but the medics stuffed me full of all sorts of drugs in the hospital at Razmak, and I returned in time for a second expedition to Arsal Kot, which went off without any real interference and little shooting.

That was really the end of my frontier experience. Along with Bill Forbes and Charlie Anderson I was ordered back to our hill depot at Gharial, to be taught the mysteries of the Vickers machine gun before going to the Machine Gun School at Ahmednagar for a two-month course.

I had served out my apprenticeship as a young officer. I had found some sort of place in the Regiment, and had proved I was of some use. I had been sent off on jobs on my own in charge of parties of Jocks; for two days

I had even been in charge of a whole Company (at least I *thought* I was in charge; the NCOs did the job for me). Best of all, I had got to know the Jocks, whom my father's generation called the 'Warriors'. When you are up a hill in a round stone *sangar* for four days with some twenty or so of them, the differences between officer, NCO and men tend to shrink: stories are swapped, food is shared, and everyone depends on everyone else, particularly at night.

Quite the most unpleasant experience is being sniped at from a higher hill in the dark. You have the feeling that you personally are the target, but you have so many other things to think about that you are too busy to feel afraid. Even so you still count the days and hours until your relief's arrival, and the chance to have some sort of decent meal and a wash.

I suppose I learnt more in six months on the frontier than I might have picked up in six years on an ordinary peacetime station.

I had grown up.

NOTES

1   The spine pad was a padded piece of material worn down the back. It was supposed to keep the rays of the sun off, and hence prevent heatstroke. In fact it was as good as useless, and served only to promote prickly heat.

2   A *chagal* was a small water carrier, borne on the shoulder. It was made of thick khaki material, rather like the shape of a bagpipe bag. It carried about eight pints of water, which – thanks to evaporation – was kept marvellously cool.

3   The No. 1 set was the standard Royal Signals piece of equipment, which provided the rear link from battalions to Brigade Headquarters. It was replaced by the No. 9 and No. 11 sets when war started.

4   Monsieur Soyer invented his stove at about the time of the Crimean War. It was portable, could burn wood or coal, and was the backbone of Army cookery until the advent of the petrol burner in the late 1920s.

5   If you want to read a proper account of Iblanke, read his *Bugles and a Tiger* (Michael Joseph, 1956; republished by Buchan & Enright in 1986), pp. 234–236.

6   A *sangar* is the equivalent of a section (or larger) position, built of large rocks in mountainous country where it is not possible to dig. It is waist high with a firing step.

CHAPTER 4
India

I was taken from Ghariom Camp in Waziristan in a brother officer's limousine. I have no idea how it had got to Ghariom; strange things happened in 1937. We drove down the road that we had originally marked out as a camel track, down Iblanke, past Shinki and Bannu, over the Kohat Pass, through Peshawar to Rawalpindi, and then turned up the hills to Murree.

At Tret, where we stopped to fill up the radiator, there was an old man with a wonderful Indian instrument – a sort of many-stringed violin, with sounding strings – who would entertain the sahibs with music, both Indian and Scottish. He could play the most marvellous pipe tunes, grace notes and all; he knew the marches of all the regiments that had passed by: and reels and strathspeys came naturally to him. We all knew him well.

I don't know how many miles we had covered, but late that evening we came to the little cantonment of Gharial, nestling on its own ridge about 1,000 feet below Murree. It was designed by our Victorian predecessors as a hill station for just one battalion, and was hewn out of the ridge. It had a parade ground and football field, a rifle range, barrack huts, messes, married quarters for officers and other ranks, a tiny little garrison church, and a village where local traders lived with their families. Surrounded by pine trees it offered the most marvellous view wherever one looked: we were some 6,000 feet up.

In those days when a unit such as an infantry battalion was sent on active service to the frontier, it left behind a nucleus of staff and reinforcements to see to the administration and look after the families. There were usually three officers, a warrant officer, some assorted NCOs, and maybe as many as 100 men, either medically unfit or, having been discharged from hospital, awaiting return to active duty. In addition, all the pay and allowance records were kept at this depot.

There were three of us from the Battalion – Bill Forbes, Charlie Anderson and myself – all destined for the Machine Gun School at Ahmednagar in the South. Peter Winstanley – my friend and contemporary from Wellington and Sandhurst – who was awaiting posting to the 5th Gurkha Rifles, was due to depart for Waziristan and the Battalion next day, leaving his red setter Paddy with me. Captain Thomas Dickson was in command.

It was nice to be back in civilisation, even though by today's standards it was not of even the one-star hotel variety. I think my bungalow had electric light, but I had a hurricane lamp as standby. Our bungalows were designed for two people: I had a living room, a bedroom and a *guselkhana*, or bathroom. Furniture was virtually non-existent: a tin bath, a *charpoy* (bed), a chest of drawers, two cupboards, two easy chairs, a bedside table, a desk and another table. For a small sum you could hire from the regimental contractor more chairs and tables, rugs and more besides. With all these things, a piano and my HMV portable gramophone I was very comfortable.

Attached to the officers' bungalows were the *bhisti*, or water carrier, who every evening brewed up the hot water for your tin bath in a used kerosene tin, and the *jemadar*, or sweeper, who emptied your thunderbox (as the commode that rested in your *guselkhana* was commonly known). I also had my personal bearer, Nawab Khan.

Bill, Charlie and I had no actual duties with the depot. We took our turns at orderly officer and other matters, but from early morning to late evening we were trained hard in the Vickers machine gun. We had some six weeks to become proficient in it before we presented ourselves at Ahmednagar, where we would be put through a stringent passing-in test. If we failed we could find ourselves RTUd (Returned to Unit) – in other words sent back in disgrace – so we worked. We were under the personal instruction of one John Hood Smith, then a sergeant, but later a major at the end of the war. He made sure that we learnt all we had to.

There are not many of us left now who can boast of being a 'machine gunner', but I am one of that rare species. Pacifists and others will say that it was nothing but a scientific way of killing at long range, but then so was the longbow in its heyday at Crécy and Agincourt. In World War I it had proved itself master of the battlefield, and we were still using it in Korea in 1950. So what was the magic of the Vickers/Maxim?

I think it was the teamwork. The Vickers required a crew of three to operate it successfully: it was too big for one man to carry. It devoured ammunition, and it was temperamental. It had a myriad working parts, and if any one of them failed or broke you were in trouble. There was a drill for everything you did. There were the four positions of stoppages and the means of clearing them. There were the lessons on mechanism, which had to be learnt by heart, and which I can still recite – Lesson 6, for example:

When the force of explosion is expended, the fusee spring takes command by unwinding the chain around the fusee; it imparts a circular and forward movement to the crank handle, forcing the lock forward, and inserting a new round into the breech.

In this way we had the operation of the gun firmly implanted in our brains. If anything went wrong, or broke, we were trained to deal with it, in those vital seconds that could mean the difference between life and death. Day by day, we learnt our drills and learnt to handle the guns, until the day when John Hood Smith would reckon that we were up to the standard required for Ahmednagar.

There was not much time for social life: there were no girls in Gharial. Murree was a very different place – there were lots of them up there – but that meant money, and I had little to spare. In any case I was due to go to Kashmir for two weeks as my father was there and it was my 21st birthday.

So one day a hired car arrived (I think it was an open Chevrolet tourer with the hood down), and I loaded my luggage onto it. The bedding roll always went on the nearside mudguard behind the headlamp, and the camp basin and chair went on the offside to balance it. Nawab Khan sat with the rest of the baggage in the back, and I sat next to the driver as we left Gharial in state for Srinagar.

This was the first time I had been driven down a mountain road by an Indian driver. It was rather like a ride on a mountainous helter skelter, and even after all these years my heart still pounds at the memory. Any owner of a taxi (for that is what the car was) wishes to save fuel, but the drivers in the foothills of the Himalayas had it down to a fine art. At the top of every hill our driver stopped the engine and freewheeled down the other side, relying solely on the car's brakes and bulb horn, and on his superb local knowledge of the road ahead. We flew down the straights, and careered round corners with a whoosh of air and a screech of tyres. It was not so bad when I was on the inside of the bend, but on the outside, with thousands of feet of rock and *khud*[1] below me, I felt as though my last hour had come.

On we rushed: chickens and pedestrians leapt for their lives, oncoming buses and cars squeezed past, and the milestones flashed by. At last we reached the bottom, where we joined the meandering Jhelum River, and followed its course to the vale of Kashmir. The engine was turned on once more, and although the cornering was still nerve-racking, at least there were no terrible precipices below threatening to gobble us up. It was some seven hours' drive to Srinagar; what I remember so clearly was the smell of woodsmoke and the poplar trees that lined the final twenty miles or so.

My father was taking Robert Morgan Grenville[2] on a trip round the world, and was then halfway through his itinerary, and we all stayed at the Nedous Hotel in Srinagar. They had just returned from Ladakh via the Deosai plateau. My father was temporarily ensconced in a little nursing home on the outskirts of Srinagar, recovering from some sort of fever that had laid him low. Robert was in the Nedous with me. My father was clearly struck by the way I had matured in the eight months since I had last seen him, and I felt he had aged somewhat; he was not at his best anyway, owing to whatever fever he had caught. He was surprised at the speed at which I climbed up the Takt-i-Suleiman, a landmark behind the nursing home about 1000 feet high, but it was a piddling affair compared with some of the places that I had had to scale in Waziristan (and that was with weapons as well).

There was an interesting description in one of my father's letters of an Indian family who were great friends, the Purbis. He was Director of Customs, a Kashmiri Dogra of very good family and very highly connected; she was English and a great friend of my mother. They had a daughter, Lynette, aged about 12 or 13 then, very pretty indeed, and who, according to my father's description, could not take her eyes off me for one minute. I must have been very insensitive then; I never noticed. Six and a half years later I was to come across the nursing home and Lynette under very different circumstances.

It was soon time to go back to Gharial, pack up my things, and report to the Machine Gun School at Ahmednagar. I had not done badly for my 21st birthday: a lovely Mk 1 Leica camera from my father, and a beautiful Rigby 12 bore from my Uncle William, were the highlights, but sadly both were lost in Singapore.

This time I was making the journey by train. Travel by rail in India was marvellous, but in true Indian fashion there was a complicated procedure to be followed. If you were on duty (as I was) you first obtained what was known as a Form D, which had your name and destination on it. Armed with this you went to the unit accountant (an Indian member of the administrative staff), who had every rule and regulation at his finger tips. He detached part of the form, which you signed, and then gave you an advance of one and a half times the first class fare. On arrival at the station of departure you handed the form into the ticket office, and for just half the first class fare you were given your ticket. You now were the proud possessor of your ticket, a somewhat mutilated Form D, and whatever sum of rupees made up the first class fare – this was your travel allowance for food and necessaries on the way. Your servant had a similar sort of form, but for third class.

On arrival at your destination (your new unit), you had the form signed by the adjutant, as proof of arrival, and then gave it to your new unit accountant, who put it in the filing system that balanced all the accounts. Woe betide you if you tried to short-circuit or in any way bypass this interesting but cumbrous system. This was babuism at its best and most efficient; the Indian accounting staff and the railways loved it.

It was a long journey: the North Western Railway to Delhi, and then the Mail towards Bombay, with a very early morning change at Manmad for Ahmednagar. I had a first class coupé all to myself, while Nawab Khan was in the servants' quarters at the end of the carriage, for three nights and

32

two days, including the change at Delhi. So began my love affair with the Indian railways (up until then my only previous experience had been with troop trains). I was to travel many miles and spend many hours on them in the next few years, and I became quite knowledgeable about railway working, and about engines in particular. I had managed trips on the footplate on every mail train and every main line, both broad gauge and metre gauge, by the end of 1944, some seven years later – and all for free, as I was on duty.

On the second day we were going south, hauled by a Great Indian Peninsula Atlantic 4-4-2. At Bina I went up to the engine and talked to the driver, a Scot, ex Caledonian Railway from Motherwell. He asked me whether I would like to 'come aboard' for the next section of the run, some sixty miles to Bhilsa. This was a marvellous invitation, which I accepted without hesitation. He put me in the spare fireman's seat and told me to keep out of the way.

On the Indian railways there were always two firemen on the main line trains. The heat, and the effort needed to keep the engines going, made that necessary. The drivers were British or Anglo Indian, and belonged to a very close community of long tradition and service on the lines. They were distinguished by wearing suits and topis. The firemen wore dungarees, and turbans – or simply sweatrags – round their heads. But the floor of the footplate was so clean that you could have eaten a meal off it, and the controls shone like only well polished brass and steel could. So did the big connecting rods, and the boiler bands. The locomotives on the mail trains in India may have been painted mostly a drab black, unlike their many-hued cousins in England, but they were kept in immaculate condition.

Nowadays, when a small car can easily eat up mile after mile along the crowded motorways at speeds in the eighties, we have lost our sensation of speed. A giant broad gauge steam engine, running effortlessly along in the sixties across the Indian countryside, gave one an extraordinary feeling of speed. For the sheer sense of movement and power it was unbeatable.

It was a fascinating trip, but all too soon it was time to get off at Bhilsa and rejoin my compartment, so that I could get the coal dust out of my clothes and the smuts out of my eyes. The platform at Bhilsa was alive with large monkeys that, in a pack, were quite terrifying. There seemed to be hundreds of them, clustering round the compartments for scraps of food. As I tried to rejoin my compartment I accidentally trod on the tail (or foot) of a baby monkey, which set up a loud shrieking wail. Immediately its family and friends rushed to the spot to deal with the miscreant – me – and it was with great difficulty that I beat them to the door and slammed it shut, closing every window and aperture that I could find to keep the horde away. It was a most cowardly performance, but they were rather large and very angry monkeys, and were determined to get me.

Early next morning I, Nawab Khan and my baggage descended at Manmad, and changed to the local line for the fifty miles or so to Ahmednagar, this time in a very ordinary train that stopped at every station and crawled along in a haze of black smoke. In due course we arrived, secured two tongas for myself and my baggage, and reported to the Machine Gun School.

Ahmednagar was an important garrison, and one way and another I was to spend quite a bit of time there. The centrepiece was the Mahratta Fort: huge, and seemingly impregnable. But years before, in 1803, a certain Arthur Wellesley (better known as the Duke of Wellington) had taken one look at it and its large garrison and captured it from the Mahrattas before breakfast, adding to his already considerable military reputation. There was the Machine Gun School, the Tank School, a British battalion, an Indian battalion, and a huge remount depot.[3] But I was destined for the machine gun school, where I found myself joining a course of some fifty officers of various ranks, British and Indian, from a number of regiments. The course was to last two months, with an extra three weeks on the rangefinder. Our ranks ranged in age from quite senior majors to contemporaries of mine at Sandhurst, and our first priority was to satisfy our instructors that we could 'pass in', which involved a gruelling series of practical and written tests that took up the whole of the first day. One senior officer of the Indian Army failed, and to his disgrace was returned to his regiment.

We started at 7 am each day, before breakfast, with endless gun drills. The Army loved them in those days: you could have given the soldiery a broomstick and they would invent a particular way of using it, and write a users' pamphlet (with diagrams) to teach everyone the correct handling procedure. With all this practice we became rather good at gun drill, and it certainly gave us an appetite for breakfast and toned up our systems. As we got better we were introduced to our mules, and to the special saddle designed for the Vickers MMG.

The mules disliked early morning drills as much as we did; with the mules they now entailed yet more exercise, and more scope for our sergeant instructors, who delighted in inventing ever-more fiendish ways of making life difficult for us. One particular ploy was to mix us up by changing our places in the team. When the mules were partly loaded, the instructor would yell: 'Fall out ONE!' This meant that No. 1, who had perhaps half loaded the heavy tripod on his side of the team mule, had to leave it hanging in the air and take the place of No. 4. Meanwhile No. 2, who had the gun on the opposite side of the tripod, had to leave that, rush round to the other side of the mule, and try to secure the tripod in place, while No. 3 (who had now miraculously become No. 2) took over the gun! You can imagine the disorder.

What the wretched mule thought about all this I never worked out, but mules are wonderful animals, and have a sense of humour all of their own. At this sort of game they needed it.

We were introduced to the art of indirect firing, using directors, slide rules, range tables and clinometers, and such was the magic attached to all this that we had a genuine gunner officer to teach us – boots, spurs and all. We learnt about distant aiming points, parallel lines, angles of sight, angles of deflection, and predictions. We were issued with range tables stuffed with figures that we thought we had left behind at school. For the older students it was a daunting, shattering experience, and some found it all very difficult to grasp. One of the more difficult tasks was that of 'predicted shoots' from the map. Quite complicated mathematics was required. For this we needed maps at 1/25,000 scale, and there were none such available in India. So we used maps from the UK, of the Netheravon Area at the edge of Salisbury Plain.

The class did not do well on its first attempt, and the Commandant – Mickey Rodwell of the West Yorkshires – was ill pleased. He treated us all to a general 'rocket' and then, as he handed back our papers individually, added a few personal touches to liven up the proceedings still further. Eventually he came to the oldest member of the course, a senior Major in the Gurkhas.

'I would have thought,' said Mickey, 'that even if you know little about machine gunnery, you could at least read a map properly. Your answer is quite ridiculous. The position you have chosen for your guns is quite absurd: they could not possibly hit the target from where you have sited them – an elementary and extremely stupid mistake!'

'But Sir . . .' spluttered the Major.

'There's no question of "buts", Major, I know this piece of country like the back of my hand. You, being Indian Army, cannot argue with me: I know the ground well, I tell you!'

'So do I, Colonel; as a matter of fact the gun position is in my father's back garden!'

It was quite rewarding to see a senior officer punctured like a toy balloon, but we were too young and junior to dare laugh as the rest of the papers were thrown back at their authors without further comment.

Halfway through the course we were allowed away for a long weekend, and Alastair Ramsay, Philip Searight and myself chose Bombay, and the Taj Mahal Hotel. It wasn't so much the food as the joy of a proper bathroom with hot and cold running water, and a WC instead of the infernal thunderbox with attendant sweeper lurking outside the door, that were the real comforts.

And then there was the business of tickets on the way home.

As we were on leave, we used Form E rather than Form D. This meant that you still got your ticket at half fare, but you had to pay for it yourself. Unfortunately there was a traffic jam, and we only just caught the train in time, but without exchanging our Form Es for tickets. The platform inspector was not worried; he assured us that we could do this when we changed trains at Poona, two hours later. But it was not to be.

The ticket office clerk at Poona was adamant: 'Sahib, exchange of Form is impossible. Form is clearly made out for Bombay Victoria Terminus.'

'But, Babuji, we have the money and we wish to pay – it is against the law to travel without tickets!'

'Then Sahib, Tikut Inspector will arrest you, and penalties will be very severe, perhaps very big fine, maybe prison!'

'Babuji, that is why we are trying to pay you the money!'

'But I cannot accept it; Regulations are very strict. Perhaps when you get to Ahmednagar, Stationmaster can arrange matters.'

So some three hours later we arrived at the Ahmednagar Stationmaster's office, lit by a smoking hurricane lamp. He was sitting at his table filling out countless forms as we explained our problem.

He smiled, and was most helpful: 'Matter is very simple. Two Sahibs drive to camp; one Sahib returns to Bombay, and pays for the tickets.'

'But Stationmaster, the last train for Bombay has left. There is no other till tomorrow morning; our Adjutant Sahib will be very angry!'

The mention of the Adjutant and his wrath worked wonders with the Stationmaster, who saw the solution instantly: 'If the Adjutant Sahib writes me a letter on official paper, with the money and the forms, everything will surely be settled. There will be no need for anyone to go back to Bombay.'

And so it proved. Cosmo Neville, the Adjutant, dealt with us as we would have expected: we were bloody young fools and wasting his time; he would see to it that a few assorted and very boring duties came our way, and the less he saw of us the better – but he did use his best official paper, and it worked!

The last part of the course at Ahmednagar comprised three weeks on the infantry rangefinder, together with yet more mathematics. A bit of astronomy was thrown in for good measure because, to get the rangefinder to work, you had to set its lenses parallel and focus them on a far distant object: what better than a planet or the moon? So there were nights that found us shivering outside, fiddling with minute focusing screws. After the machine gun part of the course it was all rather tedious.

At last the course ended. We had earned our qualification letters (MG) after our names in the Indian Army List, and what is more we had had no accidents on the range. Some of these, when they did occur, were not so much accidents as deliberate 'geriatricide' by the local inhabitants, who had hit on the brilliant idea of tying ancient relatives to known hedges and trees. When after an exercise they were found to be extinct, the British Raj would compensate them in cash! So every morning there was a detailed inspection by the range duty officer on horseback, to see that all was clear. But six years later I got caught out, with disastrous results!

Some time in November we left for Secunderabad, the biggest – after Poona – of all the garrisons in Southern India. We were stationed in Meadows Barracks, originally laid out some time after the Mutiny as a fort of the type so popular with military engineers such as Vauban in the seventeenth century. The accommodation was in blocks, each holding a platoon with its weapons. Officers and married quarters were about half a mile outside the fort, and we relied on bicycles to get to and from our duties. We had a lovely two-storied Officers' Mess, with garden and tennis courts.

The Garrison was a large one: two British battalions – ourselves and the West Yorkshires at Trimulgherry – the 14/20 Hussars, two gunner batteries at Bolarum, a Royal Horse Artillery battery (also at Bolarum), an Indian cavalry regiment and two Indian infantry battalions nearer Secunderabad, a mule transport company, two Brigade headquarters – one for the cavalry and another for the infantry – and a district headquarters with a real live general, who would suddenly appear with his gilded staff on horseback, plus his escort of Lancers, descend on you, and ask you and the Jocks awkward questions about what you were doing.

On one occasion during a machine gun shoot, our safety officer noticed this distinguished bunch riding in the middle of the target area just as we were about to open fire with a whole platoon of four guns. We sent an emissary to politely tell them to 'Get the hell out of there', but we were gently rebuked by the great man himself, who could not understand why we had changed the exercise and the range; in past years he had always watched from that point.

I never had much luck with generals and their staffs. Six years later I shot my own General's ADC. It was not very serious really – a spent ricochet that landed between two fingers of his right hand – and when he brandished it, and said calmly to John Grover, our Divisional Commander, 'General, I've been shot!', John Grover's only reply was: 'So I see, Sonny, so I see!'[4]

Training continued at its leisurely pace until the end of November, when there was a change of command that was to alter all our lives.

Johnny Hay-Young had finished his three-year term and Hector Greenfield took over. Both were contemporaries of my father, and were familiar faces, but the new second-in-command – Ian Stewart of Achnacone – became the mainspring of everything we did for the next four and a half years. It was as if some sort of atomic explosion had hit us.

He brought with him a very different concept of military life. Soldiering was now a serious business: we all had to roll up our sleeves and get down to the serious business of war, which in his opinion we knew nothing about, and which as a battalion were not fit to take part in.

We had just come down from eight months on active service in Waziristan, where we thought we had done pretty well, and as a result were reasonably hard and tough. We could shoot well enough (our musketry results showed that at least); and we had good teams in boxing, athletics and (especially) soccer. For goodness sake, who was this man, and what on earth did he want?

Ian came from a very old Argyllshire family, the Stewarts of Appin, with a long history. The Appin Regiment, with the Stewarts leading them, had fought for Bonnie Prince Charlie in 1745, and the family had bred generations of tough hill farmers and soldiers. His eldest brother had a most distinguished career in the Gordon Highlanders, but sadly was killed in a motor accident in Ireland in 1921, and Ian found himself heir to his estate – Achnacone.

He had been commissioned in the 93rd in January 1914, and very badly wounded at Le Cateau that year, so much so that he somehow wangled his way into the embryo Tank Corps. There, as Staff Captain of the 1st Tank Brigade, he, with his Brigadier and Brigade Major, led the very first tank attack ever – on foot! When I once suggested that was a rather dangerous way of going about things, he replied: 'It was not dangerous at all. The Germans had all run away, and we were quite blind inside the tanks of those days, where we would have been useless.' His Brigadier then was one Hugh Elles, who rose to high rank and influence in the Tank Corps. Despite Ian's low medical category, which had technically made him unfit for infantry, he collected a Military Cross and Bar and an OBE. And then it was time to return to the Regiment.

At the end of the war he had passed brilliantly into the Staff College, and was selected to go there. He refused, because – as for so many others of his age – World War I had left him with a distrust of staff officers, whom in general he despised. (He was not alone in this; my father would have agreed with him.) His refusal shook the Military Secretary's department of those days, and they sent a doctor down to interview him and persuade him of the error of his ways, but without success. (Ian admitted to me years later that he thought part of the fuss was caused by the fact that his refusal was written on pink, scented stationery from a Brighton hotel, where he was staying with a girlfriend.)

The Staff's loss was our gain, regimentally, but none of us appreciated it at the time. The first douche of cold and very realistic water came at the initial officers' training day that he organised. We were told in a very cold, clear voice that we ran an inefficient battalion, which might have looked smart and was good at games, but our command structure was weak –

almost non-existent – and we were unfit for modern war. He was going to change all that, but there was very little time to get it right. He was going to concentrate on what he called 'leadership', not just for officers, but for everyone who had any responsibility whatsoever, right down to the rank of Lance Corporal. We would learn – or else!

There were all sorts of other changes going on in the British and Indian Armies of those days. The Argylls had been nominated in 1936 as a machine gun battalion, together with other regiments that included the Manchesters, the Cheshires, the Northumberland Fusiliers and the Middlesex. The organisation was to be four companies, each of four platoons, and each of those with four Vickers guns: a considerable amount of firepower. By the end of 1937 the War Office had changed their minds, and we amongst others were reconverted to infantry, but we were to lose our mules and be completely mechanised. This was a completely new ball game, and so Angus Rose and I were sent back to the Tank School at Ahmednagar to be trained on aged Albion lorries, Carden Lloyd carriers and Mark 2 light tanks. While we were there we got the Mark 6, which at least kept the rain out, and a lovely reminder of the past – a Rolls Royce armoured car called 'Wedding Bells', which had served in Sinai with Lawrence of Arabia (she is now in the Tank Museum at Bovington). By the time our ten-week course had finished we were capable of taking almost anything to pieces, reassembling it, and making sure it could go. More than that, we were able to teach others to do the same, and also to drive.

The battalion was a hive of activity when we rejoined it in Trimulgherry. There were courses and cadres for just about every department, and though the hot weather was approaching, Ian Stewart had laid down that there would be not 'hot weather routine' as in previous years, which had meant a prolonged siesta indoors between the hours of 10 am and 4 pm. He reasoned – quite rightly – that, in war, no one knocked off fighting because it was too hot, too cold or too wet, and we had better get used to working in all those conditions. Staff officers and doctors shook their heads and prophesied increased rates of sickness, sunstroke and all sorts of woes, but they were proved wrong: our health improved against that of other units who chose the easy life.

We had received some eight old Albion 30 cwt lorries, six brand-new 500 cc Norton motor cycles, two Ford staff cars, and twelve brand-new Chevrolet 15 cwt trucks. With them came a small squad of Tank Corps instructors, headed by Bobbie Rumsey, who were to teach us how to handle them. Quite a few of the Jocks had driven in civvy street, but I found myself acting as driving instructor to a lot who had previously been our mule leaders, and with the old Albion crash gearboxes the experience was electrifying. Thank heavens there was little traffic on the Deccan roads. The errant bullock cart posed problems not seen in the UK, particularly at night when the driver was asleep and the bullock was in charge – and our headlights were acetylene lamps. On one occasion my pupil and I landed up in the back of such a cart, while the Albion landed in a nearby ditch. No one was hurt, luckily, and I escaped censure at the subsequent Court of Inquiry. My experiences have left me with the highest respect for driving instructors in the UK, who have to take nervous pupils out in modern traffic.

In addition to all the technicalities of mechanisation and weapons training, Ian had turned his attention to his young officers, with lectures, TEWTs,[5] field days and – worst of all – essays. We had to submit one essay a month: it could be on a subject of our own choosing, but had to be related to a military or strategic background. I managed to gain some credits by submitting one dealing with the Russian influence on the border country north of Afghanistan and Persia. This was after one of my excursions into Kashmir and Ladakh in 1938: Gilgit was not far off, and beyond Gilgit lay numerous mysterious places where the British, Russian and Chinese empires met each other.

A battalion in India in those days ran on far fewer officers than its equivalent at home. Probably a quarter of us were either on local leave (two months), or on privilege leave, which was available after two years' service or more, and which one could take anywhere in the world. Many went back home, but the more adventurous tried places such as Australia and South Africa. The younger ones like us, who had not served as long, found ourselves left in command or at least second in command of companies and other organisations that we would never have been given charge of at home. Better than that, units in India were kept at a higher establishment of men, and a platoon actually looked like a platoon, with about thirty men.

There was another advantage. Because many officers were away on leave or on courses, much of their duties fell on senior and junior NCOs. For example, sergeants frequently commanded platoons, and with good effect. This was something that Ian Stewart seized on: the whole question of leadership. It did not matter what rank anyone held; with rank went the responsibility to lead others, and so far, except for courses at outside Army schools, little had been done to train people to command and lead, and even those courses dealt more with the technicalities of weapons than with their use in battle.

So Ian started a series of cadres for the young NCOs. Young as they were, they were trained to think as platoon commanders – two ranks above the tapes they wore on their arms. He employed outside lecturers from the Cavalry, Artillery and Engineers, and we spent days and exercises with them. They began to realise that they were part of a much bigger team than just the 93rd Highlanders. After six weeks or so, when they had been trained up, they were sent back to their companies to spread what St Paul would have called the 'Good News'. But by 1938/39

40

the expanding British Army in the UK was in great need of experienced NCOs and instructors, and almost as fast as we trained them they disappeared back to the UK, and we had to start again with fresh replacements.

From time to time a company would be sent out on a sort of holiday excursion, perhaps 100 miles from the battalion, to an area that might not have seen a British soldier since the days of the Mutiny. This was arranged with the local district commissioner, and with the forest and police officers in charge of that particular circle.[6] We would take our own tentage, and a supply of 'dry' rations. We had permission to shoot our own wild game, but in very strictly controlled numbers, which had to be logged and reported. In effect, we were to live off the country. Local police were attached as guides and interpreters. We had other tasks: to help local villages repairing tracks, wells and houses and – where necessary – the bunds (the retaining walls of the 'tanks' or *jheels* that held the local water supply during the long, dry summers). The commander of the party was probably no more than a very young captain or, like myself, a mere second lieutenant. On the party's return he had to submit a detailed report on the whole performance, complete with corrected maps, if any, and an assessment of all the tasks completed.

These trips were an excellent exercise in public relations. They gave the Jocks a breath of fresh air, and introduced them to Indian village life, which was a far cry from the cramped and sordid establishments round cantonments that they were used to. They also gave the Jocks something useful to do, which they took pride in achieving, and taught them something about wild life and how to live off the country. They gave the young officers and NCOs a real taste of responsibility, and gave all of us a chance to get away from the deadening routine of parades, blanco and boring, repetitive duties to really get to know each other.

The local villagers, whose neighbours we were for a short time, realised that the *Ghora Pultans*[7] were friends, who for all our civilised ways had no idea how to repair a water wheel with wood and hand tools, or grade an irrigation channel without the help of a spirit level. And when, later in the year, we would chance by their villages to shoot wildfowl, snipe or sandgrouse, we were welcomed as old friends. The young of the villages would flock to join the guns as beaters or cartridge carriers, and when the sport was over there would be invitations to mugs of that sweet, gooey tea that might have tasted odd (even disgusting) at first, but after a long hot day was delicious. Sometimes in the late evenings there would be gatherings round the village fire, with impromptu concerts of bagpipes, zithars, saranais and madals, and if some illicit 'toddy' – that innocuous looking but vicious drink from the coconut palm – was passed round, well, who cared? But woe betide the Jock who had one too many; he was sent home in disgrace on the next truck back.

Another astonishing idea of Ian Stewart's left me feeling that I never wanted to hear the word 'concert' again. He sent for me one day, and announced that his cadre of junior NCOs would form a choir and entertain the whole battalion – families and all – and that I was to organise it.

'Me, Sir?' I replied. 'But I don't know anything about choirs!'

'Well, you'll soon learn. You have a fortnight to train them. Get hold of the Bandmaster and the Pipe Major, they'll help; and we'll have the Band and Pipes join in too. And I want decent Scots songs, none of this modern jazz muck. Here's a list: one or two have Gaelic choruses, but they are easy. You haven't much time – get going! And of course you will sing yourself!'

I might as well have been struck by shell shock. The whole thing was impossible, and what was worse, all the rehearsals had to be done in the cadre's spare time, when they should have been cleaning their kit or refreshing themselves in the Wazir Ali's canteen. And what if they refused to sing? Did the Army Act cover such an order? Section 40 covered almost anything under the general title of 'Conduct to the Prejudice', and I could almost visualise the appropriate paragraph: 'You may say what you please, Sir, but I'll keep my trap shut!'

I rushed off and sought the counsel of my two brother officer instructors, Peter Farquhar and Michael Blackwood. They were as appalled as I was, but we were caught like rats in a trap. Luckily the Bandmaster (Mr Beat – what an appropriate name) and the Pipe Major Eric Moss were perfectly confident of putting the show on. In trepidation we assembled the boys and announced the plan. I'll never understand the Jocks. They were all for it. They bust their guts rehearsing, and the whole one-night stand was an outstanding success. It also gave me a love for Highland songs and airs, and I can still remember enough to sing some in Gaelic. This stood me in good stead many years later at ceilidhs at remote parties in Argyllshire.

In 1938 I was due two months' leave, and I went up to Kashmir to shoot. It is some fifteen years since I either sold or gave my guns away, and it would give me no pleasure to shoot anything now. Back then I would sit up trees at night, waiting for panther; I climbed up mountains after barasingh, ibex, markhor and snow leopard, and red and black bear; and I took great pride in my entries in the regimental game book, now lost for ever in the ashes of Singapore. It was a different way of life then, and different standards applied.

You worked hard for your trophies. There was no question of standing outside coverts in pleasant countryside, waiting for unsuspecting game to be driven past you, or driving up trifling little mountains in a sort of modern tracked vehicle, crawling over the moors for an hour or two, and returning to a comfortable shooting lodge for a warm bath, a fire, and a dinner with glass and silver on the table. In Kashmir you walked, many, many miles – indeed hundreds. You slept in a tent, or sometimes – not often – in the open. You alternately froze in the snow or sweated in the valleys, and you lived on what you shot, augmented by rice, *dhal* and wild fruit. You were on your own, looked after by your *shikari* and his team. You engaged your own porters, ponies or yaks, and your only communication with the civilised world was by mail runner, or by telegraph from the occasional, isolated post office. At the end of it all you had been to places few others knew of, or had ever seen, and you had achieved something – though it is hard to say what. Sadly, the countryside I knew so well is now the no man's land between the Indian and Pakistani Armies, with the Chinese not so far off; for a short time, until they were well and truly slung out of Afghanistan, the Russians were also just over the horizon.

I went up north by the Grand Trunk Express, which travelled in a more or less straight line from Secunderabad to Delhi. There, for a few rupees, you could hire a rest room in the station, which had a bathroom, and where you left your bearer and luggage. Bobbie Rumsey had arranged for me to have lunch with the light tank company that had its mess in the Red Fort, and that evening I caught the Frontier Mail to Lahore, where I changed to the local train for Sialkot. There friends of mine in the 3rd Carabineers took charge, and I found my way to Jammu, where I caught the Indian bus for Srinagar, which went over the Banihal Pass.

Jack Masters has described the Indian bus in his *Bugles and a Tiger* better that I could ever do, but for sheer terror it beat my previous journey in a taxi hands down. Imagine the chassis (circa 1935) of a Chevrolet 3 ton truck. Erect on it a wooden body, Indian built, and garishly decorated with assorted animals and Hindu deities of the more terrifying kind. Pile passengers inside, and put all their baggage on the roof, roped down in a suspect series of lashes and knots. Add a Sikh driver and his *chokra*, or youth, whose job was a sort of assistant conductor, and set off, swaying like a fully rigged ship in a brisk Force 6 and a choppy sea. For good measure take one first class passenger (me) in the front seat.

The one bit of equipment that those buses possessed was the most efficient bulb horn, with a voice like a ship's siren. It never stopped; the driver's right hand was continuously on it pumping away, while his left hand vaguely controlled the steering, the gear lever and the brake. Hills were freewheeled down with gay abandon, or crawled up with grinding gears and steaming radiator. Eventually we stopped for the night at a small town, and I took refuge in an excellent dhak bungalow, ready for a very early start the next morning for the Banihal, the southern pass into Kashmir, which was usually open for only about five months in the year. This was June, and the pass had been open for just one month; there was snow on the sides of the road, and I wondered how our bald and overloaded tyres would cope with the icy surface.

I need not have worried; we made it to civilisation and the Nedous Hotel, where I was now in the hands of Habib Shah, a firm of merchants who in past years had managed both my father's and my grandfather's trips into the mountains. They had already engaged two *shikaris*, Kamala and Azman Lone, from a little village called Ajass about twenty miles from Srinagar, had obtained my licence to shoot in a vast valley on the boundaries of Kashmir and Ladakh (shooting was very strictly controlled by the Kashmiri government), and had arranged for ponies for the first stage of my journey, complete with camp kit. There was the question of supplies: my father had suggested that five rupees a day (about 50p in today's currency) would be about right, and in fact it was more than ample.

Habib Shah acted in very much the same way as a travel agent: all arrangements were made through them. They had a big store just by the Third Bridge on the Jhelum River in the middle of Srinagar, and I spend much time making arrangements with them and resisting being sold the most beautiful rugs and pashmina wool materials that they stocked, with of course traditional Kashmiri carved-wood boxes, but I still have kept examples of all these round me today. A great source of pride were their letters of recommendation from British officers of so many regiments from many years, all written on the regimental notepaper with their many and varied crests.

Some four days later all was ready, and I found myself at Woyil Bridge at the head of my caravan of ten ponies, loaded up with tents and stores, and with my staff of two *shikaris*, one cook and one young man – a sort of 'trainee *shikari*' – known as the 'tiffin coolie'. The mark of his trade was a blanket round his shoulders, which carried a leather box in which was the midday meal, a thermos, some chapattis and some fruit. The blanket served a dual purpose: it acted as the carrying harness for the tiffin box, and was also for the Sahib to sit on while he ate his tiffin.

When all was counted and ready, my caravan set off up the Sind Valley, which must be one of the most beautiful routes in the world. In those days a small tonga could get up it; nowadays it is a motorised highway to supply the Indian Army garrisons facing the Pakistanis. The order of march was myself, Kamala (head *shikari*) and the tiffin coolie. The main convoy was led by Azman, who would be responsible for selecting the night's campsite, and for making sure that all would be ready for us in the evening. Unhampered by the animals or (in later stages) the porters, we could move faster, and could range the foothills seeking mountain hare or *chikhor*[8] for the pot.

After three days we had covered some sixty miles and reached

Sonnamarg, a valley rather like those in Switzerland, with some of the loveliest wild alpine flowers I have ever seen. This was the foot of the Zoji-La, the pass into Ladakh and eventually Baltistan, about 11,000 feet high and still covered with snow. My normal marching boots would not be much use in those conditions, so my *shikaris* produced coils of what looked like thatch and wove a sort of sandal that fitted over the felt boots Habib Shah had sold me. These had split toes, so that one strand of the boots was firmly anchored into position. Inside these felt boots were inner linings of *chaplis*,[9] also with split toes. It was very serviceable and very comfortable. As the coir or thatch sandals wore out they were thrown away and new ones put on, but in snow conditions they lasted well.

The path up the Zoji was steep, but it presented no problem for someone young and fit like myself. At the top we came to a snow-filled valley with a north wind howling down it. It took four hours to make it from the top to the rest house at Matayan. This was a grim, deserted place, which the *shikaris* disliked intensely, and so did I. The place could well have been haunted; I have never spent a more uncomfortable night. All rest houses have visitors' books to be signed for revenue purposes; while I was looking through the book I found my father's signature, dated May 1914! Years later I asked him about Matayan, and he agreed it was a horrible place, but he didn't know why.

Three days later beyond Dras we reached the *nullah*, or beat, allotted to me. I dismissed the porters for a time and got down to serious stalking. This meant spending days high up on the hills, but sadly it was not very productive: an ibex and two red bear – plus a snow leopard, which I missed. (I wouldn't shoot *any* of them nowadays!) So we came back over the Deosai and changed ground, where I managed to bag a very good *markhor*.[10]

And the cost of all this? Ridiculously little at today's prices (and in any case there is now an undeclared war on, and no one can go there), but for someone aged just 22, on his own, miles from anywhere, and being looked after by men who could not speak a word of English, it was quite an experience.

And then it was back to Secunderabad and the eagle eye of Ian Stewart. At least I had gained a point or two in his estimation by going off in the wilds on my own, rather than wasting my life and money in the fleshpots of Bombay. (For some reason that sort of leave was known as 'poodlefaking'!) I had just 30 rupees in my pocket when I arrived back; luckily my father – who thoroughly approved of the trip – filled up my bank account a bit.

In the winter months there was the most marvellous wildfowling to be had on the Deccan Plateau: teal, mallard and shoveller were there in thousands, with pintail and a lovely bird almost the size of a goose, called

45

a spotbill. They would migrate south, and base themselves on the many jheels and tanks that surrounded the countryside villages. In the *padi* fields there were snipe and quail, and, in the spring, sandgrouse.

We shot on Saturdays and Sundays. Saturday was normally a whole holiday, and we would start at 3 am to be in position on our first jheel before light. There were usually some three or four cars carrying the guns and our servants, and bedding rolls. The plan was to approach as near as we could to the jheel by car without headlights along a country track, and then very quietly surround it on foot. We usually had from six to eight guns, but eight were sometimes too many. We would wade in and take cover under the trees that formed part of the flooded area, and wait for dawn. As the light grew, if the wildfowl were in, you could see their shapes on the still water, and hear the murmuring of their talk. We had to be patient: to disturb them too early would lose the best chance of a shot. When he judged it right, the leader of the party would let a shot off, and this would start the most thrilling sound as hundreds of wildfowl rushed into the air. They took off in all directions and at all heights, and safety could have been a real problem. It was very important to know exactly where the guns on your right and left were hiding; we had gone into position in the dark, and until the shooting started, had no real idea where they might be. But in all my time we never had an accident to guns or beaters.

Once the sun got up the game dispersed to other haunts, and we would pick up the spoils and walk back to where our servants had prepared a much-needed breakfast. Then we would pack up, drive to another area, and walk up the padi fields for snipe and quail until perhaps 3 pm, when it was time to select another jheel that we hoped wildfowl would come into for the night. We had to be in position, well hidden under trees, and very patient. From far off we could hear the flocks coming in, and it was important to let the first flights land without disturbing them; then you could have a go at the rest. It quite different from the early morning flight, when after a short period the whole lot would take off into the distance. In the late afternoon the skeins would keep coming back; they seemed reluctant to leave their chosen night abode, and we always got the best shooting then.

When all was picked up we would return to our cars, where a large camp fire was blazing and supper was being prepared. It would be an early night – we had to be in position elsewhere early the next morning – and we slept under the stars in our bedding rolls, as we were well off the beaten track of rest houses and dakh bungalows. It was cold weather, and I don't remember any mosquitoes or other pests; the skies always seemed to be clear, as the monsoon had long passed.

Sunday would be a repeat of Saturday, except that we had to be back in barracks ready for what Monday would bring in the way of duties, parades and the like. But we would have brought back perhaps 250 head of game. Some we gave away to our friends, but the bulk was put into cold storage for future use. At the time we took it all for granted; it was part of our way of life. I don't think we ever realised how lucky we were, and how privileged to be part of that life.

By common agreement regiments tended to keep out of each other's ways and areas, but on one occasion we nearly came to blows when we found our gunner friends poaching on what we thought was our territory. And then there was the dreadful occasion of the Viceroy's visit. He had come to stay with his 'Faithful Ally' the Nizam of Hyderabad, and the 93rd were selected to find the guard of honour. There was to be a viceregal shoot, to which officers of the guard were invited. Some weeks before we had seen strange notices put up round our favourite jheels, large printed ones, which read:

RESERVED FOR THE NIZAM

Regrettably this was considered nonsense, and the offending notices were torn out of the ground and destroyed. On the day of the viceregal shoot, the 'cortège' approached one of these favourite jheels. Our friends the villagers lined up ready to retrieve the bag, while various distinguished officers tried to hide their faces lest they be recognised as having shot the hell out of the place the previous weekend. But all went well: the place was teeming with game, the great man got some sixty to his own gun, and the locals never gave us away. As luck would have it I was not chosen for the guard, and had not been out shooting that particular day – which was just as well, as the then Viceroy was a great friend of my family's and a very distant cousin. Years later I told him about it, and he thought it very funny.

We were garrisoned in Hyderabad, the biggest native state in the whole of India – a country rather larger than the whole of France. It was also perhaps the richest state, and was ruled over by His Exalted Highness the Nizam, reputedly one of the wealthiest men in the world. He had a large court, and his sons had married some astonishingly beautiful women. Because it was an Indian state, relations between the British and the Indians were different from those in 'British India', and there was much more scope for social intermingling. For example, Indians were allowed as full members of the Srinagar Club, and mixed with the rest of us on equal terms at receptions and dinner parties. It was a taste of what was to come – sadly perhaps too late.

There was a powerful British personage in the shape of the British Resident, who was a very senior member of the Indian Civil Service, and was behind the Nizam and his Cabinet to see that all was in order. Once a year all the troops had to take part in a great demonstration of British power and might called the Proclamation Parade. The idea was to demonstrate our duty and devotion to the King Emperor, but it took place on the first day of January every year, and so for us Scots, coming as it did the day after Hogmanay, it was the next best thing to murder.

For centuries Scotland has celebrated Hogmanay, and in the 93rd we went to it with gusto. The Officers' Mess prepared a huge silver punch bowl of Atholl Brose, combined with strange other ingredients mixed to make it really explosive. At 11.30 pm, headed by a piper, all the officers set forth with this lethal draught to the Sergeants' Mess, and then the party started. Similar scenes were taking place in the barrack blocks and canteens. Toasts were drunk, songs were sung, everlasting friendships were sworn, and if by 4 am you had reached your bed and undressed, you were very lucky indeed. But in India, for the dreadful parade, we were roused out at about 6 am, dressed in all our glory, and marched to the Maidan, an enormous cleared parade/polo ground and exercise area, where a whole Division of British and Indian soldiers were put through a military ballet of vast proportions. For English regiments of the Line, gunners and cavalry, and the Indian Army, this was just another bloody parade dreamed up by the staff, but for a Highland regiment it was nothing less than torture after the night before.

It was about three miles from the barracks to the Maidan, and we paraded at 9 am to march down. The Colonel and Adjutant horsed behind the pipes and drums (we had twenty-two pipers that day), and the exhaust from the drones of their mixed potations of the night before, combined with the smell of stale pipe bag stock,[11] must have nearly gassed them. At least the march down got some fresh air into our lungs. Just before we debouched onto the Maidan the staff had set up a sort of rest area, with hot tea and latrines. A vomitorium might have been a better description, but eventually – refreshed and sobered up – we marched to our positions on the Maidan. There, in one line, was a sight none of us would ever see again. From the far right in company/squadron frontage were lined up:

- one battery, Royal Horse Artillery
- two batteries, Field Artillery (horsed)
- one British cavalry regiment (horsed)
- one Indian cavalry regiment (horsed)
- 1st Battalion the West Yorkshire Regiment
- 2nd Battalion Argyll and Sutherland Highlanders
- 4/19th Battalion the Hyderabad Regiment (Indian Army)
- mule transport company, Indian Army
- two regiments Nizam's State Cavalry
- one battalion Nizam's State Infantry

We produced four guards, each of eighty-five officers and men, and other infantry battalions did the same. It was quite some parade.

There was a great deal of ceremony. Various dignitaries arrived, and were greeted with salutes appropriate to their rank and station: the Nizam and his Court, resplendent in silks and jewels; the Resident in a very smart grey Edwardian frock coat. At the crucial moment the Union Jack on a lone pole by the main saluting base, representing the King Emperor, was broken out at the mast head, which represented the Imperial Presence. We gave a Royal Salute; a *feu de joie* rippled down the long line; and the gunners, not to be outdone, let off their pieces.

Then it was time for three cheers for the King Emperor, followed by the march past, and this gave us plenty of scope for traditional individualism, the backbone of the British Army ceremonial. The normal command, preparatory to 'Three Cheers' is 'Remove Head-dresses', whereupon the British soldier or sailor removes his beret, cap or other headgear with his left hand (the Royal Navy add a peculiar twiddle to the movement). In a Highland Regiment the traditional order is 'Doff your Bonnets', whereupon you swap your rifle from your right hand to your left and remove your glengarry from your head with the other. This has to do with the design of the old feather bonnet, which had to be grasped by its wooden cage behind its tails!

After all this came the march past: guns and cavalry first, then the West Yorkshires, and then ourselves. This led to contention. The West Yorkshire Regiment's march past was a French Revolutionary Tune called 'Ça Ira', which they had adopted in Peninsular War days. It was a catchy enough tune, but with a typical French drum beating to accompany it, and they marched past at the regulation speed of 120 paces to the minute. By contrast, a Highland regiment marches past to the Pipes at 112 paces. We didn't manage to sort this potential conflict out, and everyone marched past at 120, to the disgust of our Pipe Major, and the confusion of one of our captains, Frank Elliot. Heading the leading company, he was well out of step as we approached the great men on the saluting base. One of our sergeants behind him tried his best, and shouted at Frank as we approached: 'Sir, Captain Elliot, Sir, you are out of step!'

'I can't be out of step,' Frank shouted back. 'Fuck it, I'm leading the Battalion – get them to change!'

On which note our part in the parade ended, and we marched back to barracks to a gargantuan dinner (the word 'lunch' didn't do it justice). And we had still to do the rounds of our platoons and companies and swallow endless tots, drams, sensations[12] and other measures of strong drink.

That was New Year's Day 1939: a marathon of entertainment. It was thirty years before I was to endure something very similar in Korea. I didn't really know where Korea was back then, and I am not sure I even knew where I was myself that evening, but the faithful Nawab Khan saw me safely into bed.

We did not know it then, but we were to have just eight months more of peacetime soldiering in India. Training continued as hard as ever. I was selected to be the signals officer, and spent long, sweaty afternoons wrestling with the Morse Code, lamps, flags, the heliograph, and the other tools of the signaller's trade. Just as I was beginning to become proficient enough to pass into the Signal School, which was then at Poona, we were put on short notice to move, but we did not know where. We were part of the 12th Indian Infantry brigade of the 4th Indian Division, and the original idea had been to send us to the Middle East, where that great division made such a name for itself. Instead Delhi found it easier to send us to Singapore, so we packed up all our kit, got our families organised, and awaited orders. At the beginning of August they came: we were to move to Madras and embark for Malaysia on the SS *Egra* of the British India Line.

Very early on the morning of 2 August 1939 we assembled for the last time in marching order, with weapons, kilt, full pack and all the trimmings. We had said goodbye to our Indian staff and servants – they could not come with us – and we set off for Secunderabad Station. The road took us straight down the middle of the 2nd West Yorkshire's Barracks. As it was early morning, and dark, we did not wish to disturb them, so we marched in silence. But they had other ideas: they were all out of their beds, lining the road and cheering us past.

Just twice in my life I have found myself with my Regiment being cheered on leaving a place, and on both occasions quite spontaneously. It was in some ways a final parting of friends: the 93rd Highlanders and the 14th of Foot[13] were never to serve together or meet again. But in World War II both of us carved a small niche for ourselves in battles that were to come, we in Malaya and Singapore, and they in the long, bitter fighting in Burma, from the very start of it in 1941 to the last battles in 1945.

The 14th of Foot have long since disappeared from the British Army. They were a run-of-the-mill English county regiment, but they have left behind a great name and a great tradition. Once a year I go to their old depot in York, now called Imphal Barracks, and I can still remember that early morning in India, with our friends, most still in their pyjamas, standing outside their barrack rooms and cheering us past. Perhaps it was as well that none of us knew what lay ahead.

It took us a day to reach Madras, where we embarked on SS *Egra*: some 5,000 tons, and partially converted for troop carrying. After four days we reached Singapore, and sailed into Keppel Harbour under the guns of Pulau Brani and Blakang Mati.

NOTES

1 *Khud* is Urdu for a trench or steep defile.
2 When my father left the Army, the Morgan Grenville family, who were City bankers, wanted someone to take their son on a shooting trip round the world, and my father got the job! He subsequently managed their estate in Kenya.
3 Remount depots bred, trained and supplied horses and mules for the Army.
4 See Chapter 7, p. 181.
5 A TEWT is a Tactical Exercise Without Troops. This entailed training leaders in appreciating situations and giving out orders and instructions on the ground or off a map.
6 'Circle' was the term used for an administrative area, part of a province.
7 *Ghora Pultans* were white soldiers in British battalions.
8 A *chikhor* is a mountain bird, very similar to the red-legged partridge but bigger and very difficult to shoot – it skims down hillsides like red grouse.
9 *Chaplis* were a form of loose-fitting Indian shoe.
10 A *markhor* is a large mountain goat with long, curling horns.
11 A mixture of sugar and honey put into the bag of the bagpipes to keep the leather airtight. When it got stale it smelt!
12 'Sensation' is a Highland expression for a small tot of whisky.
13 The West Yorkshire Regiment, now sadly defunct.

CHAPTER 5
Malaya

So this was Singapore, the great Far Eastern fortress and naval base that we all knew about – or thought we did. The entrance to Keppel Harbour was impressive: the big coast gun batteries on Blakang Mati and Pulau – Siloso, Silingsing and Connaught – with their 6 inch and 9.2s; the concrete pillboxes and searchlight emplacements guarding the beaches; and all the shipping in the Roads awaiting either discharge or their pilots. I had sailed into Aden and Karachi, but had seen nothing like this before. We were soon to find out that it was all something of an illusion.

Today, what was then known as Blakang Mati, a small fortress in its own right, is a tourist attraction, with hotels, museums, golf courses, and a miniature railway that takes you round the island. It is now called Sentoso, and contains an excellent museum of its past history and of the whole story of Singapore island, from the days when Stamford Raffles realised its potential and founded one of the great trading cities of the East. It is extremely well laid out, but to me it is nostalgic and sad. I took a small part in what was perhaps the greatest strategic defeat we have ever suffered, and there are too many memories.

But in August 1939 that was all in the future, and we had no premonition of what was to come. We disembarked from the *Egra* and marched behind the band of the 2nd Loyals down the Pasir Panjang Road to our new home, Gillman Barracks. By one of the quirks of the British Army the Loyal North Lancashire Regiment had long been old friends, and we were to share their modern barracks for some three months until Malayan Command built us a home at Tyersall Park.

The barracks were a revelation after our Indian quarters: modern, well designed three-storied blocks, with huge windows open to the sea breezes, and excellent facilities. Two battalions fitted comfortably into what had been designed for just one. The same was true of the officers' and sergeants' messes, which we shared. There was hot and cold running water, proper lavatories, excellent playing fields, and all the attractions of Singapore within twenty minutes or so in a taxi or bus.

This was civilisation as we had not seen it for years, but first we had to get ourselves organised. There were stores and vehicles to be collected.

We had left our antiquated Vickers Berthier light machine guns behind in India, and we were issued for the first time with the Bren, which we had to learn to use, as very few of us had seen it before. We were short of officers, and I found myself with three hats perched precariously on my head: second in command of a rifle company, transport officer, and carrier platoon commander. We had no Bren carriers, but soon ten of them arrived at the ordnance depot at Alexandria. I was told to collect them, but I was the only person who had ever driven one, at Ahmednagar; they had a strange steering system all of their own, and getting them up the twisty hill to our quarters at Gillman was going to be quite a test. I had to ask for a whole day to teach ten of my better drivers in the depot at Alexandria how to manoeuvre them. We were lent some Morris 15 cwt trucks by the Loyals, and earned their extreme displeasure by painting out the Lancashire rose on the front mudguard and substituting our Argyll badge. By 3 September, when war broke out, we were in a state of partial organisation, but we still had no real role in the defensive scheme for Singapore.

By the end of September 12 Brigade was allotted a role as the Command Reserve, with special duties in Johore. It was possible that the Japanese (for they were undoubtedly the enemy) could mount a seaborne invasion on a twenty-five-mile stretch of the Malayan east coast between Mersing and Endau, from which ran an excellent road straight to Johore Bahru, which overlooked the naval base, and came completely round the back of the coast defences. From Endau the river ran to the Linggi tin mines, which were Japanese owned. Off that port were always big Japanese ore carriers, and they would have known that coast well. Our first priority was to establish a defensive line along the river at Kota Tinggi, roughly half way to Mersing, and this is where the problems started. No one had any idea how we were to fight in the countryside of Malaya. There was talk of 'impenetrable' jungle, 'unfordable rivers' and the like, but in fact the countryside in which we were to operate was almost entirely cultivated plantations of rubber and palm, with well developed roads and estate tracks. The average field of fire was perhaps 200 yards if you were lucky.

The British Army had not fought in any similar terrain, and there was no pamphlet of advice on how to operate in it. There *was* a pamphlet that had been written during the First World War, about fighting in scrub country against the formidable German General von Lettow Vorbeck, which advised the construction of *zarebas* (thorn fences) to protect one's position, but there were no thorns to be had in the Malayan jungle! We had to find out for ourselves, the hard way.

Despite the fact that building concrete pillboxes along a river line was not going to be of great help to anyone, the Staffs at Singapore had gone 'concrete minded'. After all it was the fashion – there was the Maginot Line in Europe, and similar defences in other parts of the world – so concrete it had to be! The possibility that the enemy might simply outflank such a line and cut off its supplies had never entered anyone's head.

Here was the heart of the problem. Ever since the 1920s, when the Committee of Imperial Defence had accepted the idea of a Singapore base, there had been constant inter-service argument about how it could be defended. The three services could not agree amongst themselves. Staff exercises had been held, and many papers had been written, but no one had laid down any policy for training. There was no common doctrine, and – worse still – there was little intelligence about our potential enemy, the Japanese. This was odd, as we had been close allies right up to December 1921. Then, in accordance with the Four Power Treaty, we had cast aside that alliance 'like a pair of used sandals', as a senior Japanese statesman put it.[1] Now it was eighteen years later, and they were very clearly preparing for war.

Many distinguished historians have written about this period. All I can add here is a worm's-eye view of the difficulties of serving in a new theatre, where the higher command was torn by internal squabbling about what was to happen, and about who was responsible for doing what.

We were lucky in that, as the so-called Strategic Reserve Brigade, we had a free hand in how we went about things. We had a lively and extremely competent Brigadier in Archie Paris, late of the Oxfordshire and Buckinghamshire Light Infantry, and just about this time Hector Greenfield, our Commanding Officer, handed over to Ian Stewart. Between Ian and Archie training and tasks gradually got sorted out.

Initially our task was to stop a potential enemy thrust from Mersing and Endau directly to Johore Bahru. We could not defend the whole beach line (some twenty-five miles), and therefore we would be faced with a delaying action down the main road. How best to do this? The answer lay in defending in depth, down the line of the road, and from this came our doctrine that stood us in such good stead when the battle started: 'Fight for the road – from the road.'

We needed the road for all supplies and communications. The enemy knew this well, and therefore he would try and outflank any position we held and roadblock us from behind. We would then have to turn about to clear the block, which would be a costly business. But if we could hold the road in depth, the outflankers would find themselves trapped, and have to fight their way out of it.

All this was in the future; in the meantime we went up to Mersing for a month. Small parties were organised to reconnoitre and map every bit of the area. We had good one-inch maps, but no one had ever really got down to using them. They were all 'roadbound', and looked at the thick undergrowth and plantations on either side as 'impenetrable jungle'. We soon found out that much of it was neither jungle nor impenetrable, and we got quite used to moving in it. But we had no wireless, nor any jungle rations, and therefore our range of movement was very limited. There was no possibility of casualty evacuation or air supply: in the early 1940s these did not exist.

By November a brand new camp had been built for us at Tyersall Park, an extension of the Botanical Gardens. It held ourselves, 12 Brigade Headquarters, our engineers (Madras Sappers and Miners), and the 4th/19th Hyderabads. (One of our Indian battalions had been sent to Penang as garrison troops there, but where the 5th/2nd Punjabis had been I cannot now remember.)

We usually kept one company at Mersing for a month at a time, carrying on the good work of finding out all about the area, and I suppose acting as some sort of deterrent to any attempt at a surreptitious landing of hostile forces. We loved Mersing, away from the Staff and Head-quarters, with plenty to occupy ourselves, and the most marvellous fishing and bathing. Away over the sea were the Tioman Islands, but we were not allowed to go there. It was not until 1998 that I finally got to Rawa, a most enchanting place in the group, which has been developed as a holiday centre but even now is hardly known. Mersing, by contrast, now boasts a multitude of rich houses, and even air-conditioned restaurants; Kota Tinggi has grown beyond all belief.

When we were not training, life in Singapore was very lively, par-ticularly at weekends. In those days we could afford to eat at Raffles, and there was the Tanglin Club, the swimming club, the sailing club and the flying club. I taught myself to fly ridiculously cheaply there – the cost was subsidised by the government. We had many friends in the Royal Navy and the Royal Air Force, and embarked on expeditions and training with them. I found myself stuck on the bottom in HMS *Regent*, one of the 4th Submarine Flotilla, sent out after dockyard repairs on a proving cruise to see if she still leaked. None of the dockyard team would make the trip, so the captain, Harry Browne, took out three unsuspecting pongoes to shame them. He did not tell us why he had so kindly invited us as his guests, but I am sure we would have gone anyway.

By the middle of 1940 things were beginning to hot up: more equipment was beginning to filter through, and reinforcements were arriving from the UK. Many were young Territorial officers; others were straight from Sandhurst or the new OCTUs. They provided a lot of new and much younger blood in the battalion, and soon became the backbone of leadership – the very thing that Ian required. At last we were beginning to assemble a full complement of young, fit and very competent platoon commanders and NCOs. We also had applicants from the police and from business houses, but their employers were reluctant to let them go, as at that time Malaya was still one of the biggest producers of rubber, and of tin and other minerals, in the Far East.

Suddenly there came a bonus.

One hot afternoon I was sent for by Battalion Headquarters. I was to take eight of my drivers to the Alexandria Ordnance Depot at once and draw four Lanchester armoured cars, which had been allocated to us. It was rather like the business of the Bren carriers all over again. I had only seen a Lanchester once at Sandhurst, when a newly mechanised cavalry regiment from Aldershot had brought some over for a demonstration. They were shining bright and spotless, with their tow ropes burnished bright and their paintwork looking like glass. Their crews were in cavalry kit; I am sure their commander still wore his spurs! All I could remember about the Lanchesters was that their turret was the same as that in the Mark VI light tank, which I had seen at Ahmednagar, and that they had a pre-selector gearbox. My problem was to get the things from Alexandria to Tyersall without damage to them or to anything else that we might meet on the way.

When I saw them standing forlornly on the tarmac in the Ordnance Depot at Alexandria, I did not realise that I was taking over what was to prove a bit of history for the 93rd. By anyone's standards the Lanchesters were way past their sell-by date. They were designed for the Middle East, and from their log books all had served there; they well old, cumbersome and crotchety, but they packed considerable firepower (a .5 and .303 MMG in the turret and another .303 in the hull), and they had a tolerably thick coating of armour for their day. But they had been some two months in passage, and were reluctant to start until one of our fitters showed me the trick.

On top of each of their six cylinders was a brass fitting that looked like an eggcup, with a handle below. You filled the eggcup up with petrol and turned the handle to release the dose into the cylinder; you then shut the handle off. When you had primed all six cylinders you pressed the starter, and with a series of enormous explosions and black smoke she started, before settling down to a quiet but powerful rumble. You only had to do this occasionally – after a long period of inactivity – but it was quite a performance. When we had got the lot going and had signed for the enormous amount of stores for each car, and once I was satisfied that the drivers could handle the epicyclic gear box and power steering, we set forth for Tyersall, with me driving the lead car. Somehow we made it, without a scratch or incident of any kind.

What were we going to do with them? Ian Stewart knew exactly, and after a week spent getting used to them, we started training with the rifle companies. Ian's doctrine of 'fighting for the road' depended on making sure that any enemy attempts to infiltrate and cut the road behind our positions were sharply seen off. Apart from our Bren carriers, we really had nothing suitable for this, and even they were not heavily armed or mobile enough to do the job. But the Lanchester *was* suitable; the infiltrating enemy would need some sort of anti-tank weapon to deal with it, something that in those days they could not bring through the jungle. And so the Lanchesters became the mobile forts that we needed for this plan. In action against the Japanese they succeeded time and time again: they even knocked out Japanese tanks! Ian Stewart, in his history of the campaign, wrote about them:[2]

> Their work [the Lanchesters] during the campaign under Sergeant Darroch, Corporal King, Corporal Wilson and Sergeant Nuttall, to name only the most senior leaders, was truly magnificent and as vital to the Battalion tactics as had been expected. All at last fell in battle to Jap anti tank guns, but not till the Jap dead were counted not in tens but in hundreds. One only, battle scarred, survived the long retreat to Singapore island itself, 500 miles up to the Thai frontier and 500 back again, to meet a gallant end in the last dark days engaging a Jap tank in the dark on the road to Bukit Timah – a British David to Jap Goliath. They bore the names of the Castles of Scotland on their turrets, and Stirling Castle, the home of the Regiment, need feel no shame at the achievements of its namesake.

More than that, the immediate awards to the armoured car and carrier platoon included two DCMs, four MMs and three Mentions in Despatches, a remarkable achievement for just one platoon in eight weeks of battle!

There was training on Singapore Island itself, the occupation of reserve positions known as 'switch lines'. One such was the Kranji River, reputed to be a complete barrier to infantry. It was situated on the north-west corner of Singapore, behind Tengah Airfield, and from the map appeared to be an excellent obstacle for a delaying position, should any enemy be so foolish as to attempt a landing from the Johore side (if they could get down there in the first place). Ian Stewart took one look at it and decided it was a worthless obstacle of little use. But Malaya Command did not agree; none of them had even dipped their big toes in it. So one day we staged a battalion exercise, and got the whole lot across the horrid muddy affair. There is a great picture of Ian, Angus Macdonald, his Adjutant and Sandy Munnoch, the RSM, plodding their way through the gunge at the end of the crossing.

As Assistant Adjutant I occasionally had to attend what we now call 'wash ups' after exercises, and there was one that dealt in great detail with maintenance and supply: how many weeks' rations and how many rounds of ammunition should be kept, and where should they be stored?

The whole object was the ability to hold out for months until the great British Fleet came to our rescue. During one of these discussions Ian rose from his seat and pithily declared the whole affair a total waste of time and paper: in his opinion we would be totally defeated in weeks rather than months. No one had any ideas or plans as to how we were to fight the Japanese, as we had never considered what their tactics might be. We knew very little about them, and regarded them as a sort of third class enemy, who could not see at night, had no modern ideas of war, and were a peasant army little better than the Chinese of those days, whom they were fighting. Ian had seen the Japanese at close hand in Shanghai, and knew different.

The Staff Brigadier, who was the director of that particular exercise, immediately ordered Ian to shut up and sit down, adding for good measure that everyone regarded his ideas as dangerous fanaticism, and totally irrelevant! Six months later, when the shooting had started, they realised how right he was and begged him to get them out of the mess, but it was too late.

In November 1941, some three weeks before the Japanese attacked, there was a major briefing for commands and staff run by Sir Robert Brooke Popham, the overall Commander in Chief of Malaya. Sir Robert, a distinguished airman, assured us that our aircraft were superior to anything that the Japanese had, that our weapons and training were better, and that we had little to fear. He was wrong on just about every count, and it came as a nasty surprise to find that out. The Japanese Air Force had been overflying our defences for some time, and although we knew it was going on, we had no effective means of stopping such reconnaissance. At that time their aircraft in theatre were years ahead of ours in design and performance. The aircraft recognition handbook contained outline drawings of what we came to know as the 'Zero', but that was all: no figures for range, speed, armament or anything else.

By this time there was a considerable volume of troops on the mainland: the 9th and 11th Indian Divisions, and the 8th Australian Division. We had had little contact with the Indians, who were way up in the north of Malaya, defending Kota Baharu and the complex of airfields north of Penang, but the Australians had taken over our role in Johore, and we saw quite a bit of them. This was to our mutual advantage. They were commanded by a tough, youngish general called Gordon Bennett. He was not perhaps everyone's cup of tea: abrasive and perhaps too self-opinionated for the more conservative of our leaders, but a good soldier none the less.

There was nothing wrong with Bennett's soldiers, who fought magnificently, in some very trying circumstances. In March 1941 I had the good fortune to meet some of them at very close quarters. I and a small advance party from the 93rd were sent to Kuala Lumpur to prepare a base for the 8th Division Signal Regiment. We had about ten days in which to do so. We were given a huge school in the suburbs and told to get on with it. This meant drawing stores of all sorts – beds, tables, blankets, mosquito nets, fire buckets, KFS (knives, forks and spoons), plates, cooking gear and everything an incoming unit required – getting them all laid out in the various rooms, and seeing that sufficient communications were available. In due course the regiment arrived by train from Singapore, and I was struck by their physique and size: they seemed twice as large as my Jocks, and looked very tough indeed. I had managed to borrow some cooks from the battalion, and so they arrived to a really nice, hot stew, beloved of the British soldier, but I was not too sure how the Diggers would appreciate it. I need not have worried; they wolfed it down.

I stayed with them for a day or two to show them the ropes and then went back to Tyersall, followed by a very kind letter of thanks from Jim Thyer, their Commanding officer, a Regular Officer of the Australian Staff Corps, later to become GSO1 of the 8th Division.

Apart from all the training, there was a lot of unofficial inter-service friendship and fun. We were adopted by 34 Squadron RAF, then stationed at Kallang, later Tengah, who took us up in their Blenheim 1s and scared the pants off us. We saw a lot of the 4th Submarine Flotilla, based on their depot ship HMS *Medway*, until they left for the Mediterranean, where I believe most of them sank: I know a lot of my particular friends were lost with them. But our greatest friend was a 'D' Class cruiser HMS *Durban*, which always seemed to be developing mechanical defects. When she did her officers and men seemed to migrate to Tyersall, where we put them up, and introduced them to the strange ways of the Army. (They used to take us afloat and get their revenge when their engines and boilers were working.) We had great liaison between officers, WOs and sergeants, Jocks and the sailors; everyone seemed to know everyone else. It was all quite unofficial,[3] but it worked marvellously.

On one occasion I and a whole lot of others were taken to sea for a full calibre (six inch) practice shoot. *Durban* had just come out of an extensive rewiring and refit from the dockyard, and everything had to be tested. In due course the target appeared, towed by its tug, the fire gongs sounded, and everyone looked anxiously at the target. There were only five shell splashes instead of the six that there should have been – but perhaps the target had obstructed the view. Another salvo was let off, and there was another cluster of five splashes, interrupted by a yell from a safety lookout: the sixth shell had landed exactly 180 degrees off course. Someone in the dockyard had made a dreadful misconnection! The gun, in its gunshield, was pointing to starboard, following its director bearing, when it should have been pointing to port. There was considerable consternation, as the errant six inch 'brick' could so easily have ricocheted on to Singapore Island, not all that far distant, with disastrous results.

The wretched gunnery officer, who became a distinguished Vice Admiral in later life, was sent for and torn to ribbons by the captain, who ordered him to submit his reasons in writing for the shocking affair. He repaired to the wardroom to compose a suitable missive, aided and abetted by various chums, including us visitors. This did not help him one bit; in any case he was hardly to blame, as the errant gun was mounted on the centre line of the ship just aft of the second funnel, which hid it from the control top. Anyway, it was the dockyard's job to check the electrical firing control circuits. But 'reasons in writing' is an old service ploy, as it is well known that you cannot explain the inexplicable in writing to your superior's satisfaction!

The inexorable training went on, and gradually we were joined by many younger and fresher arrivals: David Boyle from Sandhurst; Bobby Kennaird and Ian Lapsley from the 7th; Michael Bardwell from the 8th; Bal Hendry, Kenny McLeod, Ian Primrose and Gordon Shiach from businesses or direct from schools and OCTUs; and Ernest Gordon, a professional yachthand, whose father had been lighthouse keeper at Toward on the Clyde. The 93rd were getting younger and tougher, with a much more varied collection of leaders. This was just the material Ian Stewart would have wished for, but time was beginning to run out.

In some ways time had already run out for me. Malaya Command had decided to start up its own OCTU at Changi. At last the big businesses were prepared to release some of their young staff, and there were plenty of youthful potential leaders in the Australian 8th Division, so it was planned to take over a small part of the Changi complex and run three-month courses to train young officers. Victor Denne of the Gordons was to be the Commandant, and I was sent as one of his instructors, but Ian Stewart promised that I would be recalled the instant any balloon went up. The remainder of the staff came from various units of the Malayan garrison, but we did not deal with the Indian Army at all; their officers came direct from India to their units. The make-up of the forty-odd cadets was 60% Australian and 40% British. The course was taken directly from that used at the OCTUs in the UK, but with special emphasis on the requirements of fighting in Malaya. At last the Command and Staff were beginning to realise that there was a need for some sort of doctrine. It was mostly founded on what 12th Brigade had tried out since their original arrival in Malaya, and that was where I came in – as a sort of minor prophet to spread the Good Word.

The first course was a great success, and we prepared for a second to start in October 1941, with two additional Australian instructors commissioned from it: Harry Illig and Jim Quinlan. The latter became a particular friend. We played in the OCTU rugby team together, I as hooker and Jim as right prop. A number of our Australians had played rugby league, and were very tough and very fit indeed: we could see off most unit sides relatively easily. Sadly, Jim did not survive the war. He was killed with the 2/19th at the battle of Parit Sulong in January 1942.

Towards the end of the course the whole OCTU would move up to Mersing, where we took over a section of the beach and came under command of the Australian Brigade, whose task was to defend the area. We were also able to train the cadets in the elements of working in the jungle and rubber country, and the beginning of December 1941 found us there with myself in command. I think we went up on 1 December 1941, and I reported to Brigadier Taylor, commanding 22nd Brigade AIF. He gave us a beach sector that we were to man, if and when required; in the meantime we were to get on with our training in the area between Mersing and Endau. On Saturday 6 December we took on 22 Brigade in a rugby match on the Mersing padang. We won, but there were few celebrations, as we were ordered to what was known then as second degree readiness. Apparently a Japanese task force had been sighted off the coast of Indo China, heading suspiciously for either Malaya or Siam – no one quite knew where – and it was rumoured that an RAF Hudson reconnaissance aircraft had been shot at. So there were no post-match celebrations: we went back to our camp, started packing up, and prepared to man our beach defences. These were just slit trenches, with no wire, no mines, and no guns in our very small sector. We left sentries at section posts, and ordered the rest to sleep.

About 1 am there was the ominous sound of a motorcycle coming down our drive. How many times later in war was I to hear something very similar; it was always a bearer of bad news. The message the dispatch rider bore was simple, and quite short:

Japanese landings Khota Bahru – man your positions.

Into our trenches we went, watching over a moonlit sea and wondering whether anything was coming our way. In the distance we could see the Tioman Islands silhouetted against scudding clouds, but no hostile ships were to be seen. There was no sound of gunfire – just the wind, the rolling surf and the breaking waves. It was a strange night. War had reached us. So far there was no sign of it, but from now on events were to move very quickly indeed.

Just after dawn we all stood to. Tea came round, and with it another motor cyclist with another message. We were to pack up completely and move to a reserve position behind brigade headquarters, which was situated on the road running south from Mersing to Jemaluang. I was to report to the Brigadier. Leaving the boys[4] to get on with this I went to 22 Brigade Headquarters, where Brigadier Taylor told me that as soon as transport had been found we were to move back to Singapore, where our cadets would be immediately commissioned and sent to join their units. He expected that the move would take place next day; in the meantime we were under his command as a small mobile reserve.

We sorted ourselves out in a rubber estate that I knew well from my days with the 93rd when we had the area. Someone had a wireless working, and first we listened to a very bloodthirsty broadcast from Singapore, full of what we were going to do to the Japanese. Then came the staggering news about Pearl Harbor, and the appalling losses there. I think it was then that we realised just what we were in for.

The next morning our transport arrived. We said goodbye to 22 Brigade, and arrived back at Changi in early afternoon. Orders for the dispersal of our cadets (now officers) were already there, and as soon as they had sorted out their kit they were off.

Then it was my turn, remembering Ian Stewart's promise: one evening I was ordered to report to the RTO at Singapore Railway Station, where I was put on a train and ordered to Kuala Lumpur, where I would receive further orders. No one seemed to know where the 93rd was; in fact it was way up north, just about to go into action at Baling behind the remnants of the defeated 11th Indian Division. In the meantime I was accosted by yet another staff officer, issued with a brand new Chevrolet station wagon and a fistful of petrol vouchers, and told to drive north as fast as I could and report to Lieutenant General Sir Lewis Heath, Commander III Corps, who would be at Ipoh.

At least this was pointing in the right direction, but what a way to go to war! The farther north I drove the more uneasy I began to feel. There was beginning to be the smell of defeat around. It started with meeting European families, their cars loaded with their most valued possessions as they made their way south, regaling me with stories of invincible Japanese with nothing to stop them, coming straight down the road. There were convoys of Royal Air Force trucks also withdrawing, but to where, and why? Their shocking losses, and the abandonment of their northern bases, were not general knowledge at that time. And all of them – passengers and drivers – were looking anxiously at the sky, as if anticipating Japanese dive bombers to appear any minute. It was the first time I had ever experienced the paralysing smell of defeat. I was to get used to it in the coming weeks.

Once I was within the orbit of III Corps, all that changed. The failure of the Jitra and Gurun lines might have been disasters, but there was no reason why all that should go on, and this was where I was to play a part.

General Sir Lewis Heath, known to all by his nickname 'Piggy', was a big man in every way. He had served with the Indian Army, was highly decorated, and had lost an arm in battle. He was invariably charming, and seemed to have all the time in the world to listen to those under him – a real leader in every sense of the word. Oddly enough he had been at

Wellington and Sandhurst with my father, as he told me when I was ushered in to see him at his Headquarters in one of the many schools at Taiping.

I was not to rejoin the 93rd as I thought; that could wait. In the meantime he had a job for me. After Jitra and Gurun, the withdrawal from Penang, and the complete destruction of the Royal Air Force in the north, the task of III Corps had changed. Its job was now to delay the Japanese, in order to gain as much time as possible while reinforcements of men and aircraft were built up. To achieve this he needed a series of good delaying positions, which could be prepared before the troops could withdraw and occupy them. His Chief of Staff would select the positions; I would be responsible for their detailed reconnaissance, and where possible would arrange with local owners, the police, and anyone else who could lend a hand to get labour to dig the slit trenches, put up the wire and prepare them. I was to start the next day, and would come under the orders of his Chief of Staff.

For someone so very junior as myself, this was quite some job, but at least I had had two years of being driven though all sorts and types of Malayan country by Ian Stewart, which was more than could be said by the majority of people. So, on the morrow I took off, armed with maps and instructions. For the next three weeks I busied myself trying to make sense out of what was rapidly becoming an insoluble problem, as the Japanese Air Force had effectively terrified the local population. There was no civilian labour to be had, and although some positions (the very effective one at Kampar for example) were partially prepared, so much more might have been done had the process been started early enough. At least I was being of some use, but it was a very undistinguished role compared with what was happening to the 93rd and 12 Brigade, who had been in continuous action since the battle of Titi-Karangan on 17 December.

There followed engagement after engagement, in which the Japanese found that they had met an opponent that could completely outfight and outmanoeuvre them. Perhaps one of the most outstanding was the action of 'C' Company under Bobby Kennaird, which held up a whole Japanese regiment for forty-eight hours down the Grik road. Colonel Masanobu Tsuji, General Yamashita's chief planner and senior staff officer, has described how he had to visit that particular regimental commander to restore his badly shaken morale!

Disaster struck the 93rd and 12 Brigade on 7 January 1941 at Slim River – one of the positions that I had previously looked at for III Corps. The Japanese attacked straight down the road with some thirty to forty tanks, and through various misunderstandings and oversights there were no obstacles or guns in place to stop them. Various demolitions failed, one being overrun by tanks in the seconds before it could be blown. Eventually, after a penetration of some sixteen miles, the tanks were finally stopped, but 12 Brigade had virtually ceased to exist, being split up in isolated packets in the plantations on either side of the main road, where they were picked off by the Japanese infantry following the tanks.

On 9 January I happened by chance to be back at Kuala Lumpur, reporting to III Corps, when in walked Brigadier Archie Paris, but wearing the badges of a major general, as he had been put in command of 11th Indian Division in place of General Murray Lyon. As soon as he saw me, he said to 'Piggy' Heath: 'I want David Wilson back now, to command the remnants of his battalion.' The news of Slim River had not reached me; I had no idea what he was talking about. What was all this about 'remnants'? I found out when I arrived at a place called Batu, a few miles north of Kuala Lumpur. There were perhaps a hundred or so men, two armoured cars and most of the transport, Captain 'Tam' Slessor, and two other officers! The rest had vanished. A few, including Michael Bardwell, managed to get boats to Sumatra and rejoin in Singapore, but the rest had little chance.

Remnants or not, we still had a job to do. 12 Brigade was to hold a rearguard line north of Seremban for forty-eight hours, and we were given the job of the Mantin Pass, just north of the town. It was a marvellous ambush position: hills guarding a steep, winding road, plenty of cover, and relatively easy to dig really good positions and completely conceal them. If only the Japanese had walked into that particular trap – but they were busy elsewhere and never came.

Our only visitor was a decrepit-looking Indian on a bicycle, who turned out to be an Indian officer of the 4th/19th Hyderabads, who had stolen a Japanese officer's cycle when he was on other duties elsewhere (looting in fact), and kept on riding south, completely ignored by the Japanese soldiery whom he passed. He had much information to tell Brigade HQ, and won a well deserved Military Cross for that and other deeds.

We were due to leave our positions at 2000 hours on the 13th, but a demolition went off prematurely, cutting the road behind us, so we had to linger on for another two hours, with the prospect of the Japanese follow-up catching us in position. Luckily our Madras Sappers managed to get a temporary wooden structure over the gap, and just before midnight we were told to withdraw.

I found myself the last of 12 Brigade, with one armoured car commanded by Harry Nuttall, and a platoon in the trucks. In my hand I had a message form designating me as the Rearguard Commander, with the authority to blow four bridges en route: they were listed, with their grid references. I felt very important!

We came to the first bridge on the list. It was a large, steel-girdered affair over the main road at the south end of Seremban. It was quite deserted. There should have been an engineer officer with a demolition party, but there was not a soul in sight. The bridge was wired up for demolition, and

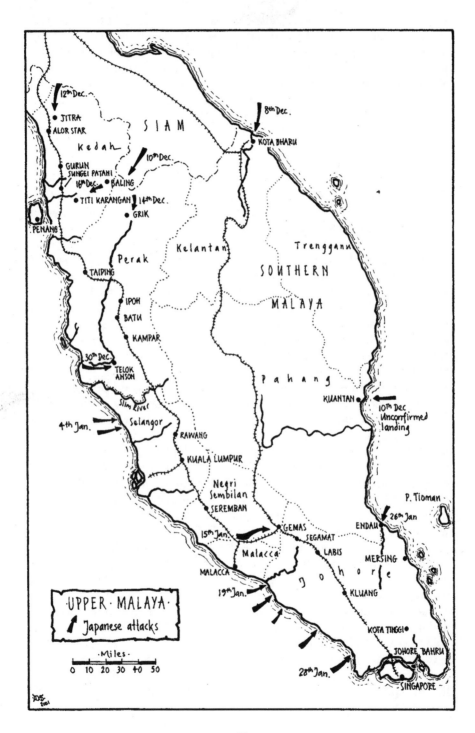

12th Dec.
JITRA
ALOR STAR
Kedah
SIAM
8th Dec.
KOTA BHARU
GURUN
SUNGEI PATANI
16th Dec. BALING
10th Dec.
TITI KARANGAN 14th Dec.
GRIK
PENANG
Perak
Kelantan
Trengganu
TAIPING
SOUTHERN
IPOH
BATU
MALAYA
KAMPAR
30th Dec.
TELOK
AHSON
Pahang
KUANTAN
10th Dec
Unconfirmed
landing
Slim River
4th Jan.
Selangor
RAWANG
KUALA LUMPUR
P. Tioman
Negri
Sembilan
26th Jan
ENDAU
SEREMBAN
15th Jan.
GEMAS
SEGAMAT
Malacca
LABIS
MERSING
MALACCA
Johore
19th Jan.
KLUANG
UPPER · MALAYA ·
Japanese attacks
KOTA TINGGI
JOHORE BAHRU
·Miles·
28th Jan.
SINGAPORE
0 10 20 30 40 50

we could trace where the exploder wires ended, but again there was no exploder, nor any secondary means. What were we to do? Forget it and leave it for the Japanese? The thought of Ian Stewart's contempt and wrath terrified me; we would have to improvise – and improvise we did, although the thought of it still makes me shiver!

Any major demolition in those days had, somewhere, a junction box of guncotton slabs from which ran the lengths of FID (fuse instantaneous detonating – nowadays Cordtex), but to set the junction box off you had somehow to produce a proper explosion with a detonator and a guncotton primer, which we did not have. What we did have were lots of No. 36 grenades, which could produce the same effect. If we could lash one of these to the junction box, tie the lever down with some thin thread, take out the safety pin, get back to the armoured car, and shoot at the girder on which all this was mounted, the thread would break, the grenade handle would fly off, the grenade would explode, and so would the junction box, setting off all the bridge charges. This was a great idea, but it was essential to use the right strength of thread: if it was too weak the whole thing would explode in our faces, and that would be the end of us. But we did it; Harry and I crept off that bridge as if we were playing 'Grandmother's Footsteps', got back to the car, backed it a couple of hundred yards away, and let fly with the Vickers gun in the turret. It worked. There was an enormous explosion, and bits of the bridge clattered down, round and on the car. We thought we had done well.

About five miles down the road we came to the second bridge on the list. Here everything was in order: Sapper demolition party, exploder, just as the book laid down. Here also was Ian Stewart. He was furious with rage. What, he asked, did I think I was up to? It was not my business to indulge in shoot-ups with the enemy; why had I not sent him back a message to say what was going on? In vain did Harry Nuttall and I try to explain what had really happened; he was in no mood to listen. Unwittingly we had caused him very grave concern indeed. He had thought he had lost his rearguard, and was just about to blow the bridge we were at for fear of its being overrun. Then we really would have been in the soup, and without any paddles! We had not thought that our actions could be so misinterpreted. Next day, when Ian had calmed down, he apologised profusely, and congratulated us on a job well done. We had used our initiative, and that was what fighting was all about.

The remainder of the withdrawal took place without further incident, and at Gemas we passed into the Australian 8th Division sector, and were able to breathe a little more easily again.

It was a handful of very tired and very unkempt Jocks that got over the causeway and back into Tyersall late that morning. We might have looked like tramps, but we were still soldiers, and there was much to come in the next few weeks.

NOTES

1   Viscount Ishii, Foreign Minister, quoted in *Old Friends, New Enemies* by Arthur Marder, p. 6.
2   Regimental History 2A&SH Malaya – Brigadier I. MacA. Stewart.
3   We organised all this ourselves; I don't recall any instructions or directives direct from Malaya Command on inter-service exercises or liaison.
4   AIF and British Army cadets training with the OCTU.

CHAPTER 6
Singapore

There was much to do when we got back to Tyersall. Just about every officer and man who had been extra-regimentally employed on the various administrative units and staffs wanted to come back to reform the battalion, but many were in key jobs and could not be spared. However, one way and another we amassed some 200, including those who had been more or less slightly wounded and were released, or had deserted, from their hospitals. Sadly Bal Hendry and Bobbie Kennaird had been evacuated, and Ernest Gordon had been impounded by the Docks Labour Unit, who made good use of his knowledge of ships and cranes. Michael Bardwell had somehow managed to get back from Sumatra, which was a bonus. Michael Blackwood had rejoined at the Mantin Pass.

We had about a fortnight to reorganise ourselves, and re-equip with weapons and vehicles. By 30 January we could field some 250 men, two 3 inch mortars, four Bren carriers and six armoured cars, including the one surviving Lanchester, 'Stirling Castle'. Where did all this appear from? A mixture of blackmail, form filling, and – on occasions – sheer piracy. Woe betide any unit that left one of its vehicles abandoned on the roadside; within a very few hours it was spirited back to our transport lines, repaired, and repainted with our unit tactical signs. There was a distressing incident when one body of our roving but keen 'recoverers' were caught red-handed at their somewhat dubious trade.

By this time the Japanese had complete air superiority, and were running a constant stream of high-level bombing runs over the island. Their method of attack was simple but spectacular. They flew at considerable height, in perfect 'V' formations of twenty-seven medium bombers in each wave. Our fighters, Brewster Buffalos, were unable to reach them effectively (they had top-cover Zeros waiting for them anyway). There were far too few Hurricanes available, and they could not benefit from our nearly non-existent early warning system.

When the warning sirens sounded, you got outside, looked skyward, and soon spotted the bombers. If they looked as though they were going to fly directly over you, you got into your slit trenches and awaited the moment when, if you were the target, they all released their complete bomb loads at a signal from their leader. Initially it was a most unpleasant experience; you felt completely unprotected, and with all this mass of bombs descending on you, the chances of one coming straight into your personal slit trench seemed high. However, having survived the first two or three attacks, we realised that, noisy and very unpleasant though it was, we were comparatively safe. The problem was dealing with the huts, stores and vehicles that took considerable damage above ground. As Tyersall was a wood and atap[1] hutted camp, it was very prone to fire. We averaged some three or four raids a day. These were not necessarily all directly at us, but when you *were* the centre of the bombsights, you knew it!

Just as frightening was the hail of splinters from the 3.7 anti-aircraft guns, of which there were many on the island. They were pretty effective, even at the height at which the Japanese bombers flew, and did good work, but, on the principle of 'what goes up must come down', we found ourselves subjected to a hail of large, red-hot shards of steel. Isaac Newton only had apples to deal with. These splinters meant business and, when you were lying prone in your slit trench, it was difficult to choose which part of your anatomy to cover with your steel helmet.

Some time at the end of January we were joined by 200 Royal Marines, the survivors of the Marine detachments of the *Prince of Wales* and the *Repulse*, under their Captains, Claude Aylwin and Bobby Lang. With them we were able to form two new rifle companies, but better than that they brought specialists with them. Drivers, machine gunners, mortarmen, signallers, cooks – you name the tradesman or specialist you required, they had them. They were real professionals in every sense of the world. I do not know who thought of the nickname 'Plymouth Argylls' for the combined battalion, but it is a proud title, which both our Regiments cherish.

While all this reorganisation was taking place, there was some bloody and confused fighting going on in Johore, with the 8th Division giving a pretty good account of themselves. But again and again the Japanese were able to turn the flank of their positions, and the reinforcements that we sent up to help them were ill-trained and not acclimatised, and – as usual – communications were hopeless.

There was a disastrous battle at Bakri/Parit Sulong, where 45 Indian Infantry Brigade were virtually destroyed, and the 2/19th Battalion AIF fought one of the most gallant actions in Malaya trying to rescue them. Jim Quinlan – a great friend – was killed with the 2/19th, and two others achieved very different kinds of fame as a result of that battle.

Lieutenant General Nishimura commanded the Imperial Guards Division that had joined the Malayan invasion force from Indo China, and had come into action on the west coast rather late in the day. General

Yamashita, the Commander in Chief, disliked Nishimura and the Guards, whom he thought were 'political soldiers', and never really trusted him or his men, but Nishimura was out to make his name, and he was to do it in the only way the Japanese knew: brutality.

When the battle at Bakri was finally over, and the wounded were collected in a school building, Nishimura personally ordered them all to be killed. Unfortunately for him there were survivors, who years later in 1946 were able to identify him. Somehow he had survived a war crimes investigation in Singapore, and was being repatriated to Japan, but the ship he was on had to stop at Hong Kong for fuel. The Australians hauled him off, took him to either Manaus or Morotai in the Pacific, where they held sway, tried him, and hanged him. It was a death he richly deserved.

Of Charles Anderson, commanding the 2/19th, there is much to be said in a very few lines. He had won a Military Cross with the British Army in the First World War, and settled in Kenya, but moved to New South Wales in the early 1930s, and joined the Australian militia forces. For his leadership in that dreadful battle he was immediately awarded the Victoria Cross. He went on to become a senator in the Australian parliament in Canberra, and it was in Canberra, at his house, that I met him for the last time. I had last seen him at a conference with Ian Stewart in Mersing, some fifty years before.

By 26 January the decision had been taken to withdraw completely from the mainland. The problem was how? Some 30,000 men and vehicles had to cross a narrow causeway in the face of complete Japanese air superiority. Then there was the question of command and control. Three separate Divisions were involved – 9th and 11 Indian, and 8th Australian – all under III Corps.

At about this date Ian Stewart was summoned to be drawn into the plan's final stages. Visitors to our Regimental Museum at Stirling will see a large picture called 'Sans Peur', which shows the very last moments of the withdrawal. As one of the few survivors, I was very much involved with all the discussions and planning with the artist Peter Archer, and it was not all easy going. To start with Ian Stewart was against the whole idea; he felt it was very wrong to have such a record of defeat painted. It took some argument to change his point of view, but once changed he threw his whole weight behind it, and I have a mass of correspondence from him on many matters of detail of the whole operation.

The 93rd's task was to hold the inner bridgehead: that is, the ground immediately overlooking the north end of the causeway. This would be protected by two outer lines: the nearest, held by three battalions of III Corps, and the outer, mostly composed of the Australians from 8th Division. We, the 93rd, were commanded by Angus Rose, who had returned from leading a successful raid up the east coast. We had just two companies with four armoured cars. Ian and his personal staff were acting as a sort of liaison link between us (the main body of the rearguard) and the naval detachment with small boats led by 'Jock' Hayes, who at the last resort would take us off if the causeway had to be blown before we could cross it.

That was the final plan, and that is how it worked out. But during the course of a lot of correspondence I received a letter from Ian dated May 1981, describing some of the planning that had gone on, and criticising it bitterly. I quote direct from this letter:

> Luckily this was a battle that never happened.
>
> Of course what ought to have been done was to have put Archie Paris and 12 Brigade in the job [of commanding the whole rearguard] i.e. someone with a proper staff.
>
> If things had gone wrong with 20,000 troops pouring back on to a blocked causeway, I was supposed to handle the job! And what a mess it would have been.
>
> At one time I was nominated to command the whole set up including the Outer Bridgehead, over four battalions, without any Staff at all. Luckily the Australians objected and their Brigadier took over. Still, it was a nice personal compliment to me, but a damned silly one! But I did at least get a Naval Liaison Officer and an Artillery one as well, but only by asking for them. Our artillery Defensive Fire would have been from three Field Regiments (some 72 guns) firing from the Island.

On 30 January, when our small force moved up into position, we knew nothing of these finer points of planning. We knew we had been given a vital job, and for the first time, if things went badly wrong, we would be Horatius holding the bridge at all costs.[2] In a small way it was to be the equivalent of the Rifle Brigade's epic defence of Calais in 1940. Strangely, we rather looked forward to the task. All the uncertainty of previous weeks had gone. There was no more cautious looking over our shoulders to see how we could get out; we just got stuck in and dug ourselves into position as best we could. We did not have long to wait. The Japanese mounted some extremely accurate high-level attacks on us, but we were well below ground by then, and they had little effect. There were one or two duds; our bomb disposal experts assured us that the bombs were British made, captured with the northern airfields – a clear case of 'getting one's own back'!

We had another twenty-four hours to wait: the withdrawal was to take place on the night of 31 January/1 February. It was beautiful weather. There was a full moon, and Angus Rose, Michael Blackwood and I, with one or two others, sat outside our command post with some whisky that had appeared from somewhere, looking over the view to the island and talking of better days. If we had any doubts about what was to happen tomorrow, I don't remember discussing them. We could have been three tourists admiring the view. But behind us came the occasional rumble of artillery fire from somewhere up the Kota Tinggi road; someone was in contact with the rearguard and pressing hard on them. Would they be able to disengage by tomorrow? We would have to wait to find out.

The next day followed much the same pattern of air attacks, but there was a noticeable increase in the transport going south over the causeway. Had the Japanese noticed anything? They gave no sign. There was no deviation from their normal activity; much of their air effort was directed at the naval base and targets on Singapore Island. We got our expected share, no more. But it was noticeable that wherever Michael Blackwood went, bombs were sure to fall. His visits to our command post were not welcomed. His Marmon Harrington armoured car was beginning to look like a mobile pepperpot, and he himself had collected a nasty-looking but harmless slash across his forehead.

We carried on improving and camouflaging our positions until evening came, dark fell, and the real business of the withdrawal began. Transport vehicles, stores vehicles and guns – all started their trip over. There were no lights. The moon was brilliant: it was almost as bright as day, and ideal for the Japanese air forces to attack, but they never came. We shall never know why; they had been caught completely by surprise. A lucky hit on the north end of the causeway, where the Navy had packed it with depth charges for demolition purposes, could have sent the whole thing up, and then where would we have been? By 7.30 the next morning the order was given for the three battalions of the inner bridgehead to withdraw, and when they were through, we left, played over by our two pipers, Stewart and MacLean. In the words of Ian Stewart, written to me years later: 'Lars Porsena missed his cue and Horatius had to take his bow alone!'

I took battalion headquarters and our signal party over just before the last two platoons of our rearguard, leaving Ian Stewart, Tam Slessor, Drummer Hardy (Ian's personal escort) and CSM Bing as the final lot to withdraw, covered by Harry Nuttall in 'Stirling Castle' with Michael Blackwood in his car, about 200 yards behind. With them was Lieutenant 'Jock' Hayes (our Naval Liaison Officer) and his signaller. When they were well down the causeway the signal was given, and the depth charge demolition was blown. It was an enormous explosion, but in fact was of limited use. The causeway was solidly built: tons of masonry and rocks went skyward, mostly to fall backwards into the crater. The gap was at the far end; we could not cover it properly by fire from the island, and the Japanese engineers were easily able to repair it ten days later and get their tanks and guns across.

Of all the operations that the 93rd took part in, the causeway rearguard was perhaps the one that most caught the imagination of the public. As Eric Linklater wrote:

> The remnant Highlanders, with steady bearing and their heads high, marched from a lost campaign into a doomed island.
>
> The broad Causeway was blown behind them. Malaya was lost, but no one would have guessed it from the tunes the pipers played. The future was darker than a winter storm, but the 93rd marched against it to a vaunting triumphal music. The motto of that Battalion is 'Sans Peur'.[3]

But Eric Linklater was not actually there. Two naval officers who *were* present described the scene in more matter of fact terms. The first, Geoffrey Brooke, had been one of the ship's company in *Prince of Wales*, and was in charge of the boats, ready to help in the evacuation of the rearguard should that have been necessary. (He was to escape successfully across Sumatra and reach Ceylon in a Malay *prahu*,[4] the *Sedeharna Johannis* – an epic voyage indeed.) This is what he wrote, years later:

> Australians, marching to the pipes, were nearly through, and the men of the inner bridgehead [a semi circle of strongpoints and carefully sited machine guns, last to retire] awaited the word. They were Argyll and Sutherland Highlanders, a shadow of the battalion which had gone into action five weeks before. The honour of covering the retreat was their due.
>
> The Bren beside me folded with a snap, as its owner ran off grinning to form up. The Commanding Officer came down the steep grass bank from Headquarters bungalow. The curtain was going to fall in style. Hayes, who was with him, waved to me, crossing his arms above his head in the seaman's sign which means 'Secure – all finished'.
>
> I stayed for a last look before going down to the boat and away. They came swinging past behind the bagpipes, mostly small men, I noticed. Hard, dour and as tough as leather, they marched with a long supple stride, and there was an arrogant confidence about them.[5]

The 'Hayes' that Geoffrey Brooke mentions was then Lieutenant Commander J.O.C Hayes, later Vice Admiral, and Naval C.-in-C. Scotland. Later in 1942 he broadcast on the BBC an account of his experiences in the Causeway operation, in which he ended as follows:

> . . . we could not imagine that without air superiority an army could retreat unmolested across one exposed ribbon of road, in full

moonlight and later in broad daylight. It was as well for many of us that it did. But throughout I felt that, if there were to be sticky moments, then there were none with whom I would more gladly have shared them than with those tough, courageous, and business-like officers and men of the Argyll and Sutherland Highlanders. The country does well to honour them.[6]

And that is what the picture 'Sans Peur' is all about. Many years later Ian Stewart accepted it and liked it. There was a great unveiling occasion in the Officers' Mess at Redford Barracks in Edinburgh, where he personally gave the audience a small taste of what he had been like some forty years before. For many it was quite an experience.

We had just about one week to integrate the Royal Marines and the remains of the battalion into an operational unit. We ourselves knew Singapore Island well, but they did not, and much time was spent showing them the various areas where we were likely to be called to operate, so that we could get into action very quickly to stop any possible Japanese breakthrough. Maps were in short supply; most of 18th Division had now landed, and as they were completely new to the place they quite rightly had the lion's share of the available maps. What were then rubber plantations and smallholdings are now built-up areas with municipal offices and multi-storey flats, and quite unrecognisable, but in 1941 much of the area west of the Bukit Timah road was completely undeveloped, and this was where we were to go into action.

The Japanese had not been idle. They had moved their troops down to the water's edge on the shores opposite the island, cleared the local civilian population out, moved their artillery forward, and started registering suitable targets. As the week went on, so the gunfire grew, but it really started in the late afternoon of Sunday 7 February. By 9 o'clock that evening there was a very considerable barrage coming down, particularly in the sector held by the Australian 8th Division, which was protecting Tengah airfield from a mass of flooded mangrove swamps. I was duty officer, and sat in the Adjutant's office (mine) until midnight, when I was relieved and went to bed. At 3 am I was woken up by one of our signallers with a message. It was from 12 Brigade, and read something like this:

Japanese landings 22 Aust Brigade Area including Pasir Labar Coast Battery. Brigade at notice to move from 0600. Ack

My kit was all together; I woke various others up and told them to get on with rousing the Jocks and getting some sort of breakfast going. Soon the battalion was in a state of organised activity. By 0600 we were ready to go – but where? No one knew – Brigade did not – and the strange thing was

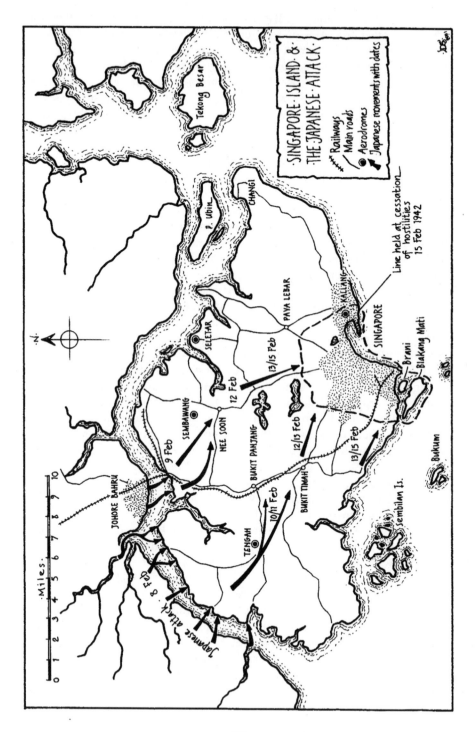

SINGAPORE·ISLAND·&·
THE·JAPANESE·ATTACK·

Railways
Main roads
Aerodromes
Japanese movements with dates

Tekong Besar

P. Ubin

CHANGI

Line held at cessation
of hostilities
15 Feb 1942

KALLANG

PAYA LEBAR

SINGAPORE

SELETAR

13/15 Feb

Brani

Blakang Mati

12 Feb

SEMBAWANG

NEE SOON

BUKIT PANJANG

12/15 Feb

13/15 Feb

Bukum

9 Feb

Sembilan Is.

JOHORE BAHRU

BUKIT TIMAH

10/11 Feb

TENGAH

Japanese attack 8 Feb

Miles.

10 9 8 7 6 5 4 3 2 1 0

N

75

that all the gunfire had ceased; it was most uncanny. And so it went on for another three hours. At 9 am we were sitting in what was left of the Mess, listening to the BBC from London, which announced the landings on Singapore Island, but added that they were being heavily counter-attacked. This was nonsense, because the only people who could have done the counter-attacking were 12 Brigade, and they were sitting some ten miles from the battle, waiting for orders. Clearly something was terribly wrong.

An hour later we did get some orders. We were to move with all speed to the Tengah area to a forward assembly position, where we would await further orders. By midday we were there. It was a fairly unhealthy spot, with desultory shelling by Japanese artillery, and a lot of attention from high-level and dive-bombers. Still there were no definite orders as to why we were there, or what we were to do about it. We were on our own – no one knew where the rest of the brigade was – and our only means of communication was by a single telephone line to Brigade, which seemed to get cut every time the Army 97 dive-bombers[7] had a go at us. Over to the west we could hear rifle and machine gun fire, plus the odd cough and thump of mortars, and shells were flying about in all directions.

It was now getting dark, so Ian Stewart gave orders for night defensive positions in our area, which we took up, blocking the Tengah Road, and there we stayed, acting as a sort of longstop to assorted Australian stragglers who had got separated from their units in the muddled battle that had taken place. They were glad to find some friends they could join up with. We were able to fill them up with tea and stew, for which they were very grateful. Most of them stayed with us for the night and augmented our depleted numbers in our position. It was a dark and depressing night. The oil tanks at Kranji had been set on fire, and their lurid smoke mingled with the steady rain that had set in. Not only were we soaked, but the oil-blackened water made us look like something out of an old-time minstrel show!

Shortly before dawn we were given orders to take up positions on what was known as the Jurong Switch line on the right of 22nd Australian Brigade, who had withdrawn completely from their original beach positions and their subsequent battle inland. Tengah airfield was abandoned completely. There was supposed to be an artillery fire plan, but we had no communications with the gunners. The only means of communication we had was our solitary telephone line back to Brigade, with a solitary telephone at our end of it. This was situated in a culvert on the Tengah road, and I, as Adjutant, manned it with two signal orderlies and the Orderly Room Sergeant. Ian Stewart disdained culverts, and strolled about on the Tengah road, impervious to the constant sniping and dive-bombing that was taking place. During one such attack I emerged from the culvert with my tommy-gun and let fly at one of the machines that were coming very close indeed. For my pains I received a volley of oaths from Ian. He reminded me forcibly that I was the Adjutant, and it was my job to see that what communications there were worked. I was to stick under the culvert with the telephone until he told me otherwise. Shooting at aeroplanes with my ridiculous tommy-gun was not my job; it was a waste of time and ammunition, and he doubted whether I could hit the things anyway! I was banished back to the culvert.

Soon I was released, and given a job to do. Somewhere the 2/29th Battalion AIF should have joined up with us on our left flank, but there was no sign of them. What was worse, a large body of Japanese had infiltrated onto a low ridge on our left flank, where they were making a thorough nuisance of themselves. Ian ordered Claude Aylwin's company of Royal Marines to clear the ridge, and try to establish contact with the 2/29th. I and our intelligence sergeant were to go along with him and, should the 2/29th be found, brief them as to their orders. We formed up and, supported by our mortars, went for the ridge under desultory but quite accurate fire. One or two were hit, including Claude Aylwin in the left forearm, which he instinctively covered with the map that he was carrying in his right hand to staunch the blood. This appalled my intelligence sergeant, who seized the map from him, saying:

'For Gawd's sake Sir, no' the bluidy map, it's the only one we have for your Company!'

Claude could have bled to death for all he cared; the map was far more important.

Our attack was successful. We ejected the Japanese from their ridge, and found the 2/29th, at half strength but most ably led by their second in command, a major who had been quite seriously hit in the leg by a mortar shell. They were a good lot; despite all that had happened in the previous twenty-four hours they fought well. We were glad to have them around. So far so good: some sort of defensive line was getting into place.

At 11 am things changed. During the night the Japanese had landed in the Causeway sector and were making for the Mandai road. There was little to stop them from advancing straight down the Bukit Timah road to Singapore. Bukit Panjang village had been lost, and it was vital to get some sort of block on the Bukit Timah road. Later on our friends the 2/29th were withdrawn by their Division, but no one told us. We found ourselves left high and dry with nowhere to go. On Brigadier Paris' orders we were withdrawn to a blocking position on the Bukit Timah road just to the south of Bukit Panjang village. By 7 pm we were digging in for the night. We had achieved very little in the previous twenty-four hours. No one seemed to know what to do.

At about 9 pm there was an outburst of firing up the road, and shortly afterwards Brigadier Paris and what was left of 12 Brigade Staff arrived.

They had been in position about two miles north of us up the road. According to the Brigadier a Japanese medium tank had suddenly appeared at his headquarters, fired a few shots, and equally suddenly disappeared into the dark – but where had it come from? There were supposed to be two Australian battalions holding the road further up. Either it had driven straight through them, or they did not exist. We now knew that the latter was the case; we were quite defenceless against tanks.

Angus Macdonald, the Brigade Major, was sent in his baby Fiat car down to Bukit Timah to rouse up any guns he could find, get them into position to defend the road, and get some sort of message to whoever was holding the sector to prepare for a possible tank attack in the dark. We had perhaps a dozen anti-tank mines, no more. I was given the job of laying them across the road, but we had barely enough to cover that, and one of our armoured cars was somewhere in front of where the block was going; somehow we had to get that back. It is not easy to unpack, assemble and arm mines in the dark, but we did it, and I went forward to contact the armoured car – it happened to be 'Stirling Castle' with Harry Nuttall in charge. Very slowly and quietly he reversed her safely through the mines. But I heard movement coming down the road, and very stupidly moved a few yards forward to see whether perhaps it was what we now call 'friendly forces'. Something was coming slowly towards me in the shadows, and too late I realised that it was far from friendly; it was a Jap Medium Tank. I turned and ran for my life, pursued by a stream of bullets, closed the gap in the minefield and reported back. This was going to be another Slim River affair.

They were on us: Japanese medium tanks, with infantry in support on either side of them. Our anti-tank rifles were little use, and 'Stirling Castle' was overwhelmed by their weight of fire. One of our mines went off, disabling one tank, but the remainder – some fifty of them – motored slowly on, firing indiscriminately to either side of the road. They had split our defensive block clean in half. There were confused mêlées of Japs and Jocks in the ditches; fighting was taking place at point blank range, but the Japs had got the road, and that was what mattered.

In the meantime Angus Macdonald had driven post haste in his tiny machine almost into Bukit Timah itself, where he found an anti-tank gun section at the side of the road, with the crew asleep. He managed to wake them up and get them into position to repel the advance. Had he not been able to do so, and had we not been able to inflict this small delay, that tank column could have driven right into Singapore; there was nothing to stop it.

Dawn found us in a disorganised state round the dairy farm, out of touch with just about everyone. There was our Brigadier (Archie Paris), a few of his staff, one Lieutenant Colonel (Ian Stewart), and perhaps 100 mixed Argylls and Marines. The rest were on the far side of the Bukit

Timah road, but that was now completely in the hands of the Japanese, and we had no contact with them, nor was any possible. Somewhere to the rear of us was the start of the battle for Bukit Timah hill, which was to last almost up to the surrender.

There was a plan that had foreseen this sort of situation, when companies might be cut off without orders. It allowed detached companies to do what they could to attack Japanese rear echelons and disorganise their advance. After twenty-four hours such units were to rendezvous back at Tyersall. A and D Companies (the ones that were cut off) proceeded to carry these instructions out, and with some success they finally joined up in the battle for Bukit Timah hill. The remainder of us under Brigadier Paris made our way across the race course to Tyersall, which was now being used as an extra hospital for casualties. We had hardly got there when it was very heavily attacked from the air and, being of wood and atap, caught fire, so we spent much of the afternoon getting the wounded out of the burning huts and trying to extinguish the flames. This was not made any easier when we discovered that the fire mains lacked water. By mid-afternoon much of the camp was in ashes, but most of the wounded had been saved.

Now occurred an astonishing incident. We were suddenly ordered to stop everything and 'get fell in' for a job. We may have numbered perhaps fifty, not more, including a few Marines (the rest had been sent elsewhere). We were drawn up in what had been the battalion offices, and which were still standing. Ian Stewart had some orders to give us, which are best described in his own words:

A small party of two officers and some fifty other ranks of the Argylls, and a few Royal Marines, was collected and organised into platoons and sections, leaving the rest to be brought on later. The men were black and greasy with oil since two nights before from the flaming [oil] tanks at Kranji, and this had been overlaid with sweat and smoke when they worked on the burning huts in the tropical heat. I have rarely seen men more tired in body, but they were not tired in spirit, for these were the hardcore men of the Argyll morale. The dross had already been purged from the Regiment by the fierce fire of war. A great commander has said that success in battle is the major factor in creating morale. These men had never known anything but the bleak atmosphere of defeat, yet they would go on unflinching to the end. Of that there was no doubt whatsoever. I spoke to them. I had made them two promises in the confident days before the war – that I would never take them into battle with an insufficient fire plan; and that in adversity I would never say to them 'Go on', only 'Come on'. Now, I told them, I was going to break my promise, the first, but the second remained; I did not order them, I asked, would they come into this last battle with me? There was no response, no audible one, only they quietly and determinedly got to their feet, and stood waiting, all of them, and the march back to the fighting line began. There is more to the morale of a great regiment than just victory.[8]

So we marched out of Tyersall for the last time, down the Reformatory Road. We had covered about a mile when we were stopped and told to return to camp. Apparently Major General Keith Simmonds, the local area commander, had decided that no more was to be asked of the regiment, and so we were put into the local defence of Tyersall. Amidst the smouldering embers of what had been our home, we sorted ourselves out.

About 9.00 that evening a staff car arrived with a message for me. I was to get in the car at once, as I was required at Fort Canning immediately. The message was signed by Ian Stewart. I had no idea what this was all about, so I told Tam Slessor and Michael Blackwood where I was off to, got into the car, and was driven through the darkened city to the Fort, the GHQ of the British forces, a huge underground complex that I had never visited before. I descended a long flight of steps, was shown through various guarded gates, and eventually found Angus Rose, who somewhat abruptly accused me of 'taking my time'. It transpired that he, Ian Stewart, CSM Bing and I were to go to Keppel Harbour and there board a ship that would take us to Java! There was a plan, which we knew nothing about, to send key personnel out before it was too late, and we were one of the first parties so selected.

The same staff car drove us down and deposited us on the dockside. There were a few others around, mostly military police; no one knew much about us, or what ship we were to travel in, and in any case there was no ship in sight. From time to time the big 9.2s and 6 inch guns on Blakang Mati would fire inland over our heads at some target or another. It was all rather depressing – not least because I had had to leave most of my possessions behind, no doubt to go up in smoke with all the rest of the battalion stores when the camp was set alight by bombing.

Eventually, out of the smoke emerged the silhouette of a ship, a cruiser, and we recognised her as our old friend HMS *Durban*. She secured to the dockside, and we were hurriedly sent aboard. Some kind friend lent me his bunk, and I managed to get most of the filth off before I climbed in, but I did have time to stand on the quarterdeck as we left Singapore, which was blacked out, but with fires burning all over the place. The small Dutch island of Bukum, an oil storage tank area, was ablaze, and from time to time the flashes of the big coast guns lit up the horizon. It was a very dramatic backdrop.

Early next morning I was awakened by a very loud bang and a very bouncy bugle call – the Royal Navy's Action Stations. My host told me to get dressed as soon as possible and report to the wardroom, where I would find myself detailed for a job. We were under attack from the air. I found myself detailed with a stretcher bearer party. The wardroom had turned itself into a dressing station, with a damage control team also in place. They gave us a running commentary on what was going on outside. We were heading for the Banka Straits escorting a small convoy, and the Japanese had found us.

Throughout that morning and most of the afternoon a great many Jap bombers had a go at us, again using the formation of twenty-seven planes, dropping from high level. It was bad enough being bombed on land, but it was much worse being bombed at sea with nothing to do except wait for the next one to come down the funnel, particularly when one was virtually a passenger. The tension was relieved by the teamwork and discipline of the Navy, which was very different from the apparent disorganisation of a battle on land. Everyone seemed to know exactly what to do, and they did it with the minimum of shouting and fuss. After one particular attack had hit the ship a young rating came into the door of the wardroom and reported to the Damage Control Officer:

'Fire in the ammunition lift to X Gun, Sir.'

'Well, put it out.'

'Aye aye, Sir.'

And that was all: no panic, a good clear report, and a concise order immediately carried out.

During one of these attacks there were a series of vicious explosions, and the nasty, acrid smell of something burning. I felt a tremendous bang on the back of my head, and something hot and sticky trickling down my neck. I wasn't knocked out, but for a brief moment I really thought I had had it. There had been a very near miss, and pieces of bomb had come though the side of the ship. A Royal Air Force officer in the same stretcher party as me had been seriously hit by a very large chunk, which missed me by inches. The ship's doctor slapped a bandage round my head, injected me with some sort of painkiller, and sent me back to my job.

The whole affair was over by mid afternoon. They never attacked us again, and the next evening we made it into Batavia. *Durban* had been badly knocked about, A and B Guns were inoperable, all fire control circuits had been knocked out, and where there had been a triple set of torpedo tubes, there was now a large hole. If the torpedoes had gone up, the ship would have been blown in two. The ships in the convoy had been damaged, and one – the *Empire Star* – sunk (you will see her name on the Merchant Navy memorial by the Tower of London: the whole crew, starting with the Captain).

HMS *Durban* never fought again; she was too badly knocked about. She went to the USA to be patched up, but ended her life as a 'Mulberry' blockship off Arromanches in 1944. Visitors to the museum there can see her position marked on the Mulberry model and map, but she has a very special place in my memory. It was a privilege to have seen her and her crew in action.

The Dutch could not have been kinder to us. Bedraggled and filthy though we were, we were taken to the Harmonie Club and given an enormous supper, and the band played the 'Wilhelmus' and 'God Save the King'. Somehow I don't think we deserved it. A month later Java had fallen too. We had been billeted in great comfort in the Hotel des Indes for about three days, when we were ordered to board a Royal Navy armed escort vessel, HMS *Pangkhor*, bound for Ceylon. We just managed to get through the Sunda Straits before the Japanese finally closed them off. In the meantime a Dutch Army doctor had removed odd bits and pieces from my head, but I was still the proud possessor of a bandage round it that made me look rather more heroic than I actually felt.

We got to Ceylon and were ordered to Delhi. What the Army was going to do with us, we had no idea.

For better or worse I was on my own now, for the very first time since August 1936, when I had first received my commission. Now it was lost, with all my possessions. Some antiquary in Singapore may have it to this day.

Whether I had it with me or not, I was what the Indian Army used to call a *nimukwalla*. I had eaten the salt; though I had never sworn an oath to defend anyone in my life, I was bound to service and all that that meant. The Indian Army had a saying for that too: '*Khabi sukh aur khabi dukh, Angrezi ke naukhar*', which means 'Sometimes pleasure, sometimes pain, the Servant of the English!'

The past was firmly shut behind me like a watertight door. To this day I wonder how I happened to be on one side of it, in safety, while so many friends were shut out on the other. Many were dead, others would die in the prison camps, and some would never recover their health.

I felt very lonely. I had no idea that within six months I would be caught in the net of an even wider set of friends and comrades, and taken with them on a long, hard road to a place that none of us had ever heard of: Kohima.

NOTES
1. Atap consists of coconut palm tree branches, used to cover the roofs of Malay houses and – in our case – British barracks.
2. Publius Horatius Cocles (530–500 BC), who in 505 BC held the bridge over the Tiber against the army of Lars Porsena in Macaulay's *Lays of Ancient Rome*.
3. History of 2A&SH, p. 98.
4. A *prahu* was a type of fishing vessel in Malayan waters.

5   Geoffrey Brooke, *Alarm Starboard! A remarkable true story of the war at sea* (Cambridge: Patrick Stephens, 1982).
6   History of 2A&SH, Appendix III.
7   The Army 97 Dive Bombers were the Japanese equivalent of the German Stuka.
8   History of 2A&SH.

CHAPTER 7
The road to Kohima

At the end of February 1942 the Galle Face Hotel in Colombo was a sort of reception camp for the refugees from Malaya. Each day another boatload of familiar faces arrived, who were eagerly questioned for news of friends. Most of them had managed to get to Sumatra, and by various routes to Padang and other ports, where they were picked up by passing ships that had managed to get through the Sunda Straits before the Japanese finally blocked them.

It was there that we heard the sad news that the ship carrying Brigadier Archie Paris, Angus Macdonald, Michael Blackwood and one of our best sergeants, 'Toorie' Macdonald, had been torpedoed by a Japanese submarine, within thirty-six hours of safety. We were not to know until years later that a boat survived and drifted all the way back to Sumatra carrying one of our sergeants, Walter 'Hoot' Gibson, and one other survivor, a Malay girl. Years later he wrote a book called *The Boat*: an incredible story of survival and courage, but with dreadful scenes of death, cannibalism and murder.[1]

After three days Ian Stewart, Angus Rose and I were put on a train, crossed over to India on the ferry, and after a long journey reached Delhi, where we were debriefed, and formed into a 'jungle training team'. Initially our job was to visit formations and units describing what had happened in Malaya and Singapore, but later we were to actually stay with them and assist in their training. Our time was spent in GHQ writing our own script under the direction and supervision of Ian. When this was complete we were to be launched forth, rather like the apostles, to spread the gospel. The trouble was there wasn't any gospel to spread except one of defeat and disaster. In some ways it was the blind leading the blind, except that we had been in contact with the Japanese and knew a little about how they worked (at that time no one else had the slightest idea), but by this time the Japanese were in Burma and the small British/Indian force there were learning the hard way. But by sheer good fortune they had the battle-experienced 7th Armoured Brigade with their Stewart tanks, who had arrived from the Middle East in the nick of time; and they had two very experienced soldiers in command, Generals Alexander and Slim.

It was vital that what we had to say about Malaya tied up with what was going on in Burma, about which we had very little information in Delhi. Luckily it did. It was the same story of the Japanese forces: very mobile, and able to get behind and roadblock our own, which were based on mechanical transport and therefore were confined to roads and motorable tracks. Once again, despite the efforts of General Chennault's AVG and the Royal Air Force, the Japanese were able to wield almost complete air superiority over the battlefield, with all the advantage that gave them.

While all this work was taking place, I was transported to stay in the Viceroy's house. The Vicereine, Lady Linlithgow, was a cousin of my mother, and in the 1930s, when we were in Edinburgh, we knew the family well. They lived at Hopetoun House, and were great supporters of the local Linlithgow and Stirlingshire Hunt, which we rode with. Their youngest daughter, 'Bunty', and my sister, Prue, were of an age and pony mad (and extremely good performers, who carted off prize after prize at the local shows). At some stage of his career I think Thelwell must have seen them, as there are so many likenesses of them in his cartoons!

One day an invitation arrived for me to stay, for as long as I liked, but what on earth was I to wear? I had arrived in Delhi in the clothes I had last worn in Singapore – washed and ironed, admittedly. I had managed to obtain spare shirts and trousers in Colombo, and an excellent tailor in Connaught Circus in Delhi was making me a decent khaki bush jacket and a pair of tartan trews (though where he got the tartan from I shall never know). At the moment of invitation all my belongings went into either my haversack or a small handbag, picked up in Colombo. In addition I still had my heroic bandage round my head, but it was leaking blood and had to be dressed every day. I was hardly the figure to present myself as a guest in such distinguished and well dressed circumstances. But the family insisted, and so I appeared in the guise of a military tramp and was greeted at the front gate by a charming ADC in the Camerons and an enormous house servant, dressed in the Viceregal livery, who regarded my appearance and handbag with the utmost disdain and distaste. I must have been the filthiest and worst dressed guest ever to walk through the door.

I was shown into a sumptuous suite of rooms: sitting room, bedroom, and bathroom, with a gallery that looked out onto a beautiful garden. On the writing desk was an embossed leather folder, inside which were sheaves of crested paper. The two most important pieces of paper were the daily timetable, and the guest list and seating places for lunch and dinner, which were both properly ceremonial affairs.

My kind Cameron friend had lent me his drill jacket, and also for the evening a white mess jacket. Both fitted pretty well, and with the tartan trews that the tailor had run up in some twenty-four hours I could at least look reasonably presentable for meals. The leather folder also contained a small booklet on protocol, a plan of the house and main public rooms, and the usual mine of information that all well run establishments provide for their guests.

For the main meals the drill was always the same. The house guests would assemble in the drawing room; I was made an honorary member of the ADC's small circle, and they looked after me. About twenty minutes before the meal was due to begin, the guests would arrive, and the ADCs would assemble them in the drawing room, introduce them to each other, see that they had a drink, and eventually line them up in order of presentation. Ten minutes later their Excellencies would appear, and the guests were presented. There would be a short pause for drinks, and then lunch – or dinner – would be announced. Led by the Viceroy and Vicereine we went to our seats in order of seniority, and as we did so the staff salaamed in a curious way, with both hands in front of their eyes. I found out that they were shielding their faces from the light shining from the distinguished personages, a custom dating I believe from the Mogul Court. There were usually some twenty people, including the family, at these meals.

When all was over and toasts had been drunk, or perhaps speeches had been made, the company retired to the vast drawing room, where the Viceroy sat down in one corner and the Vicereine in another. One by one the ADCs led the guests to each, and they had a private talk. As I was a house guest, and effectively part of the family, I was excused this particular exercise, but on one occasion I was lucky enough to have something like an hour with the Viceroy in his own study. I have heard and read that people thought Lord Linlithgow was a somewhat shy and unbending character, who could not talk readily to people, but I never found that. He could not have been kinder to me, nor more understanding, and as far as I was concerned he could not have been more clued up about what was going on in the war that had landed on his doorstep, with all the political pitfalls ahead.

There were also those that said that the life led by the Viceroy of India was far more regal than anything that went on in either Windsor Castle or Buckingham Palace. As I have not been invited to stay at either I cannot comment, but in the 1940s it was part of the tradition of India, and though I have never been back there since 1944, you can see how much still continues with the great Independence Day Parade that takes place. India loves its ceremonial, and I suspect took pride in what was the Court at Delhi.

After a week of luxury it was time to get back to duty, and our first posting was to Ranchi, then under Eastern Army, where the 14th Indian Division was training for Burma. To get there we had to take the East Indian Railway, down the main line to Gomoh: a sad, unkempt place, where you changed to the branch line for Ranchi.

I had not been on the East Indian Railway since my father was stationed at Allahabad in 1923, and I was all of seven years old. It considered itself the premier line of India, and was as arrogant as Brunel's Great Western in its day. It considered that its track, stock and engines were the best in India, and woe betide anyone who dared encroach on its territory. Even in 1941, when it did not have many more years of independent existence left, it preserved a long tradition all of its own.

Angus Rose and I were lucky: we had a compartment in one of its new 'air conditioned' carriages. In the hot weather you could keep your carriages at a reasonable temperature by having a huge block of ice in a tin container in the middle of your coupe or four-berth carriage. You directed the fans on it, kept the windows shut, and travelled in reasonable comfort. But now, with the new stock, the ice was kept in special containers between the frames, and the whole carriage was ventilated by forced draught air ducts. This worked well as long as the ice lasted; once it was gone the whole affair became like a modern fan controlled oven. You could not open the windows, and you slowly stewed. Luckily this never happened to me. Our particular compartment was very comfortable, with sheets on the bed – something we had never seen before in India – no dust, and spotlessly clean.

The train engine was a delight: a standard 'mail engine' 4-6-0 HPS, built in the late 1920s by the North British Locomotive Works. If you took her cowcatcher off, removed the headlamp and steam generator on the top of the boiler, and put on a 'Caledonian' hooter in place of her whistle, you would have seen her with her cousins at Kingmoor, Carlisle or pounding up Beattock, and even as far north as Inverness. She was pure Caledonian, with a touch of Glasgow and South Western. I cadged a lift in her just after Lucknow. Could she go! In those days the East Indian track was heavier and better aligned than most, and speeds were higher; anyway, we were the Calcutta Mail, had a tight schedule, and were not prepared to waste time. I was ashamed to remember that years before, on posting to Allahabad, my father had taken me to see the engine at Benares. When I was on the footplate the driver blew the whistle; I burst into tears with childish fright, and had to be taken back to our carriage.

We were decanted at Gomoh in the early hours of the morning, and had to wait for the local for Ranchi. Gomoh had little to recommend it – a miserable, cold and dirty, so-called 'first class' waiting room, and a somnolent staff (but who could blame them at that hour?) – and it all seemed a bit abandoned. Down the line were the signals, at red to the next important station, Gaya, the end of what the East Indian knew as the 'Grand Chord' line, which led to Calcutta, and beyond that Assam, Burma and the advancing Japanese. Little by little we were creeping back into the war, but it was going to take a long time. *Delhi daur ast*, as the Indians say, meaning 'Delhi is a long way off'. No more viceregal parties, and no more corridors of command and power in the great Lutyens buildings that housed GHQ India!

At Ranchi we were attached to the 14th Indian Division, who were under orders to move to East Bengal to the Comilla–Dacca area. Their commander, Major General Lloyd, had distinguished himself in the Middle East, but was to find himself given an impossible job in the first Arakan campaign in the winter of 1942/43, which ended in disaster. Once again we were to completely underestimate the training and capabilities of the Japanese.

Apart from a few talks to headquarters and units, it was clear that my colleagues and I were getting in the way of more important things, and so we were sent back to Delhi. From there I went to Simla, Rawalpindi and Abbottabad. It was all rather a waste of time. No one wanted to know about us; they had better things to do.

Meanwhile the Japanese carrier fleet had appeared in the Bay of Bengal and scared the pants off almost everyone. The whole of the east coast of India lay wide open, particularly the Ganges delta, and in a hurry I was sent back down the East Indian Railway to Calcutta to be attached to the Staff of 26th Indian Division, newly formed, and assigned the task of defending the Sunderbands and the main base of Calcutta. They had their headquarters next door to what was then called the Eastern Army in Dum Dum. The problem was that no one had ever considered any form of enemy appearing in that part of the world. For some time there had been political trouble in East Bengal and Assam, but this was caused by Bengali terrorists (we would probably call them patriots today), who played a very active part in assassinating senior civil servants, judges and policemen. They were particularly audacious and dedicated young men, who caused us great trouble, but not on the scale of an anticipated Japanese attack.

The Ganges Delta or Sunderbands is a very complicated affair of river outlets, mostly navigable, which separates East and West Bengal. In those days it was well served by waterways and railways, but there was little in the way of roads or bridges. All communications were by rail and steamer, and this was complicated by the fact that while the main line north from Calcutta was the 5ft 6in broad gauge, the east–west connection was metre gauge, and relied on the special railway ferries to cross goods vehicles and heavy loads over. At just about this time America was thinking of flying large amounts of aid to China over the Hump,[2] which meant that the East Bengal Railway and the Bengal and Assam Railway were to become lines of great strategic importance. But no one had foreseen this, and there was little military knowledge of what might be required and how these two systems could cope, or how they could be defended, given that we had temporarily lost all control of the sea, and the Royal Air Force was hard put to it to defend the area.

So for two months I was taken off my jungle training role and put under 36th Division as a sort of railway adviser. My job was to compile a list of stations, sidings, unloading points, transfer areas from broad to metre gauge, and all the information necessary to move forces round the Delta area to meet and oppose possible Japanese landings. Of course the railways had all the information at hand, but it was not correlated to military needs. For example, it is little use having a platform where you can unload guns if there is no road for the guns to go on when they are off the train, and what do you want the guns for in that place anyway?

I had a special railway pass allowing me unlimited travel wherever I wished to go, and a list of places that had to be reported on in detail. I travelled the length and breadth of the area on the footplates of engines, in guards vans and on inspection trolleys, writing voluminous notes and reports, which went back to Calcutta, and which may still be resting in some dusty pigeonhole to this day. At the end it was all put to the test in a considerable exercise in which two Brigade groups were moved from their normal positions to their defensive areas in very reasonable order and efficiency. Everyone was very pleased except GHQ Delhi, because someone had not told them or got financial authority, and when the railways sent in the bill, GHQ almost refused to pay. As I had been the originator of the exercise I thought for one dreadful moment that someone might send me the bill, but luckily I was far too far down the list for anyone to remember.

There was a bit of 'spin off' from all this. In those days it was the custom to keep a loose-leaf notebook of useful information, and, probably improperly, I kept quite a bit about the layout and logistics of the East Bengal and Bengal and Assam railways in the one I carried. Two years later it was to be worth its weight in gold.

It was June 1942, the Burma Army had come out, and the Imphal plain was becoming a centre of military activity. I was sent there with Brigadier P.C. Marindin. He had commanded – with great distinction – our friends of Secunderabad days, the 2nd West Yorkshires, who acted as the motor battalion to 7th Armoured Brigade throughout the long Burma withdrawal. Our job was to help set up the various jungle training schools in the Imphal plain. By now there were plenty of people who had fought the Japanese; it was really just a question of giving them a hand to get hold of the right equipment and let them get on with it. This took me up to the end of July, when our paths separated. P.C. Marindin went on to command the Lushai Brigade in 1943/44, where in their area they completely outfought the Japanese, and I was posted to Poona, about as far away from any jungle as you could get. I was to be attached to the Second Division. I had never heard of them.

It was quite a journey from Imphal: first some 200 miles through the mountains, or Naga Hills, stopping for the night at Kohima with the local garrison, and then down to Dimapur. In those days the road was being totally rebuilt, and there were anxious moments when we had to get out of the truck while it inched its way along the greasy track that had been dug out of the hillside by workers mobilised from the tea plantations of Assam. Roadfalls and avalanches were plentiful, and the forest below became the graveyard of trucks and men who had vanished into the jungle, sometimes thousands of feet below in the mist. Eventually we came to Dimapur, and to the rest camp known to all as 'Penis Park' because of the many phallic emblems that decorated the place, a relic of the ancient place of Indian worship that had once stood on the site. The soggy, dripping tents did little for anyone's morale in those days; the smell of defeat was still in the air. Then there was the train to Gauhati and the ferry across to another metre gauge train, and then the main line at Parbatipur, some five hours from Calcutta and civilisation, and the long journey to Delhi, Bombay and eventually Poona. Suddenly I found myself in another world: the British Army. I had forgotten it existed. For the last five years or so I had been with the Indian Army, and in many ways had become used to its way of life. True, I had been with a British regiment, but our administration was that which suited the Indian Army, and ran very well indeed. Second Division was different.

The Division had a long history. Formed in the Peninsular War in 1809, it had fought in every campaign since, including the Boxer Rebellion in China. Initially its home was Aldershot, from where it had gone to France in 1939. There it had shed some of its regular content, which was replaced by Territorial units, of a very high standard, and it contained a marvellous mixture of the great county regiments from all over the United Kingdom. When I joined it was based on Poona, Ahmednagar and Secunderabad. It had sailed from the United Kingdom all the way round the Cape, and was I think intended for the Middle East, but events in Malaya and Burma had resulted in its diversion to India to bolster up the forces against the Japanese. What its role was at that time, no one was quite clear.

Second Division was commanded by Major General John Grover, late of the King's Shropshire Light Infantry, wounded three times in the First World War, and wearing a Military Cross with Bar as a result. He was short, lithe, very smart, very precise in his speech, and blessed with very blue, piercing eyes. At the time I joined I think he was 47 years old. A Wykhamist[3] with impeccable manners, he set the very highest standards for everyone, and if you could not come up to them, you were out looking for employment elsewhere. I don't remember ever seeing him lose his temper, but his icy reproofs in impeccable English were something to be avoided. In all my service I never came across anyone quite like him, and I am sure I speak for all of us who had the privilege to serve under him. It was typical of him that when I joined the Division, rather than being formally marched in front of him in his office, I was bidden to dinner with him and his Staff in the Divisional 'A' Mess, where it was all quite informal, and yet I realised very well that I was being examined in microscopic detail. It was lucky for me that I came up to the mark: John Grover was to continue my instruction in soldiering, and was to be the most enormous influence on my future career.

Second Division, or '2Div' as it became known, bore the sign of the Crossed Keys of York. It had been reformed after Dunkirk in the York area, and its previous commander had somehow purloined the sign. It was an interesting choice: in feudal days, when the archbishops and bishops of the times led their levies into battle, Canterbury was naturally the senior, and York the second. The 4th Brigade (the senior of the Division) had always been composed of Guards, and had been known as the 4th (Guards) Brigade. Somehow after Dunkirk we had lost our Guards, but one or two had lingered on in the Brigade Staff to give it the cachet it had once enjoyed. We were all regular units, but in 1940 had acquired the 7th Worcesters and the 1/8th Lancashire Fusiliers, 236 Field Company, Royal Engineers (from Brighton) and the 99th (Royal Buckinghamshire Yeomanry) Royal Artillery, who brought that extra touch of good-humoured panache to our very efficient gunners.

But how do you train troops to fight in the jungle when they are stationed in a part of the world where there isn't any? Someone suggested a series of JEWTs: Jungle Exercises without Trees! You have to have a pretty strong imagination to make that sort of training work. But there were new skills to learn, and the Division got down to them.

The first requirement was to find the jungle, and that did exist about 150 miles south of Poona in the Belgaum area. With the assistance of the Forest Department and the police, suitable areas were found where one Brigade group could be sent at a time. Most importantly the Division set up its own battle school near Ahmednagar – more of that later.

I was originally sent with the first contingent down to Belgaum, which was very different from the Malayan and Assam jungle I had seen, but thick enough to acclimatise men to operating in conditions of very reduced visibility and some very rough ground. We could teach them to exist in the open, rely on their maps and compasses, and learn a bit about the local fauna and flora: which to avoid, which to eat, and – most important – which *not* to eat. We learnt to cross rivers the hard way. Once, when I was in charge of a company crossing, under my personal supervision we built a whole lot of rafts – and they were well built too. We waited till dark, very quietly approached the river bank, and launched them. They sank without trace. We had been using a particular kind of wood that does not float. No one had told me; I had never come across that particular variety before. The so-called 'jungle expert' never lived that episode down.

While we were down in the Belgaum area we found ourselves involved in an interesting international incident with Goa, which bordered the area. At the beginning of the war various German merchant ships had sought safety in Goa harbour, and Portugal – being neutral – had granted them a sort of internment. But they were illegally using their ships' transmitters to send signals and orders to German submarines working in the Indian Ocean. The problem was: how to stop it? Volunteers were called for from an interesting outfit, the Calcutta Light Horse who somehow sailed a strange lighter all the way from Calcutta, past Ceylon, and up the coast to Goa. It was loaded with explosives and all the charges necessary to sink the offending ships. The challenge then was how to distract the Goanese from their harbour when the assault was to take place.

Someone suggested that 4 Brigade, with its squadron of tanks – then training in the Belgaum Forest near Londa – should put on an exercise, which would head towards the Goan frontier post on the crucial evening. So down the road we rumbled, straight for the frontier post and the main road to Goa, only to turn left and south 400 yards from the post. But it had the desired effect. The frontier guards thought their end had come, and got on their telephone, the Goanese authorities looked fearfully backwards away from the harbour, and the German ships were boarded and sunk! It was a brilliant operation; we had no idea we had anything to do with it until long after.

In true British tradition, the very expert and brave men of the Calcutta Light Horse never received any sort of decoration or campaign medal for it all. In order to preserve secrecy they had signed off their regimental rolls and were, by their own choice, common or garden civilians. They had no business and no right to be there at all! As far as the armed forces were concerned they did not exist! For reasons of security, in case the raid had gone wrong, it made sense to have sent them in with no connection to the armed forces, but to disown their services afterwards was, we all thought, a pretty 'scabby' act.

One by one the units of the Division came down to Belgaum to learn a little about living in the country. Even fifty years or so ago there were few British soldiers who had not lived outside the glow of town lights, unless they hailed from the far north of Scotland, or the Hebridean islands, and the darkness was something they had to get accustomed to. They had to learn to work in small units, sometimes at quite long distances from their commanders; they had to get used to the noises of the bush and jungle, and recognise them for what they were; and they had to learn the smell of animals and humans. These were all senses that our ancestors way back had possessed, but which we, in our more civilised society, had forgotten. We were going to be dependent on ourselves, and there was a lot to learn.

About this time I was stricken very low indeed with what the medics called BT malaria. (The BT stood for 'benign tertiary'. What the other form, malignant tertiary, is like I have no idea; the 'benign' virus was bad enough.) One afternoon I was sitting in my office *basha*, trying to read a map. I found that I could not make any sense of it, and that I could scarcely move from my chair. Henry Clewes, then the Brigade Major, who shared the *basha*, asked me if I was all right, but I simply could not answer. In great haste he sent for our doctor, who saw what it was and bundled me in an ambulance thirty miles down the road to Belgaum and the Military Hospital, where I came under the stern and strict regime of a very senior QAIMNS matron and her extremely efficient sisters. This was as well, as I was scarcely able to lift a little finger to help myself. I just lay in a bed, sweated and shivered, and wanted to die! I suppose this lasted perhaps forty-eight hours before health slowly but surely returned, but it was clear that I was not going to be of much use to anyone for at least a week or so. General John Grover had little time for convalescents hanging around, so he sent me on three weeks' leave to Kashmir, and told me to come back when I was making sense again.

All sorts of old friends took me in, amongst them General Sir Claude Auchinleck, Commander in Chief of the Indian Army, a contemporary of my father's at the Senior Officers' School in the 1920s, who was staying in one of the Maharajah's guest houses, and of course the Purbi family, whose daughter Lynette had become an artist of some talent, and wasted her time doing a pastel picture of me. I have it to this day. But with the help of Habib Shah and the Lone family (my two Kashmiri *shikaris*), I escaped from the fleshpots of Srinagar, and went off up the Sind Valley. The exercise and mountain air sorted the malaria out in very quick time. I was soon back to duty in Belgaum.

At the end of 1942 6 Brigade, with the Royal Scots and 99th Field Regiment, had been ordered to the Arakan, where the British forces had got well and truly bogged down in the Mayu Peninsula opposite a place called Donbaik. Here for the first time we had come across the amazing skill and tenacity of the Japanese, who could fortify themselves in what we called 'bunkers', which were proof against almost everything we had in the way of guns and shells in those days. Attack after attack failed against one particular stronghold, called 'Sugar Five', and to the end it held firm. The 1st Battalion, the Royal Welch Fusiliers had particularly heavy casualties in one day's assault, in which David Graves, the son of the very distinguished soldier and poet Robert Graves, was killed. (He was recommended for the Victoria Cross for his part in the action, but sadly did not get it.)

The Brigade was hit in the flank during the withdrawal at a place called Indin, where Brigade headquarters was overrun, and the Brigadier, Ronnie Cavendish, and his Brigade Major, Basil Fanshawe, were killed. I have an eyewitness account of that incident, recorded by a sergeant major of the Durham Light Infantry, who were involved in this very desperate battle. A Japanese column led by one Colonel Tanahashi had come over the Mayu range and struck the brigade on the coastal plain between the hills and the sea. But for the staunch fighting spirit of the soldiers, it could have been a disaster; as it was 6 Brigade was able to withdraw up the coastal plain and beach in reasonable order. It was able to cover the withdrawal of the remainder of 14th Indian Division back to the line where they had started out for Akyab some six months earlier.

When 6 Brigade returned to the Divisional fold in April 1943 they brought a wealth of combat experience back with them. Despite the reverses at Indin and Donbaik, they had met the Japanese and had found that they were not supermen. In countless minor actions they had outfought them, and they had learnt at first hand about their tactics, weapons and way of fighting. It was to stand the rest of the Division in very good stead: we had a good leavening of battle-experienced soldiers, and this was put to immediate use in our Battle School, which, almost on arrival, we had established in Ahmednagar, under a very remarkable character, Major Robert Scott of the Royal Norfolk Regiment.

Scott was someone born three centuries too late: he would have been at home with Drake, Hawkins and company, singeing Spaniards' beards and sacking their towns! He was a big man in every way, with a gift for leadership and for encouraging the young to reach far beyond themselves. A great reader of Shakespeare, his language came straight out of the plays. Outrageous oaths – 'By the Liver and Lights of the Virgin', 'God's Wounds', 'The Devil Damn you all to Hell': none of us had ever heard anything like it before. Add to this swashbuckling speech a very sure knowledge of ground, a mastery of all infantry weapons, and a genius for friendship, and you had him. But I don't think I could ever describe him as the man he was. He had no time for safety as laid down by the book, but he never allowed sloppy handling of weapons or anything that could put anyone in unnecessary danger. Casualties he accepted, but never stupid mistakes. He was one of those who led from the front, and expected everyone else to be there with him. You were not ordered there; it was just a party you could not miss! That was his idea of what soldiering was all about.

My time in Belgaum and Londa was nearing its end. At Belgaum itself, which was in peacetime a considerable military garrison, the Mahratta Light Infantry had their regimental centre and training depot, which supported five battalions. It was a large affair. Each year they put on a *Tamasha* on their Regimental Day, which in the evening took the form of a sort of miniature Aldershot Tattoo. At this time 4th Brigade were in their jungle camp, and were invited to attend 'en masse'. There would be the Tattoo, and afterwards supper for all.

The invitation went down like a lead balloon amongst the soldiery. It was to take place on a Saturday evening, and they would have preferred to sit around playing Housey Housey in their jungle canteens. Our

Brigadier put a stop to this nonsense. He sent for the commanding officers, and said that it was his wish that the whole brigade attend, and what is more they would enjoy themselves! So one evening a column of trucks set forth full of somewhat disgruntled warriors, dressed in their best shirts and trousers, all prepared for what they thought was going to be a rather boring evening.

We were seated in a large arena in the front of the Mahrattas' barracks, an old fort, built in the days when the Mahrattas ran that part of the world. The floodlights came on, and out of the gates of the fort came the most magnificent band, well over 100 strong, with something like forty buglers, dressed in their regimental full dress and playing for all they were worth those magnificent light infantry marches that we have brought with us down history and have handed over to our friends who have fought beside us. This was Rushmoor and Tidworth of pre-war spectacle, but in a foreign land. We were spellbound. There were the usual displays of physical training, but then there were displays of drill and musketry with the original Brown Bess muskets, using black powder, and a wonderful show of guard mounting in the 1700s, with the officers of the guard carried on parade in palanquins, smoking their hookahs, carried along-side by their personal servants, until they were quietly put to earth, their dress adjusted and their swords neatly slung by their servants, when they assumed command of their detachments.

At the end of it all, there was the usual assembly, Last Post and Lights Out, and then all the performers marched past: first the boys' company, 15 and upwards, being trained at the Depot; then the young soldiers, in the various dress and uniform in which they had taken part; and last the Old Comrades, in their spotlessly white 'mufti' ablaze with their medals and decorations, smart as paint. Then the most extraordinary thing occurred. Some 3,000 British soldiers, who had come with somewhat bad grace, expecting a totally boring evening, stood up spontaneously and cheered themselves hoarse.

The party afterwards was a great success. Thomas Atkins may not be the world's finest linguist, but he has an incredible knack of being able to communicate with people wherever in the world he finds himself, and if his knowledge of barrack Urdu was scanty, his grasp of Mahratti was absolutely nil, but no matter: everything went like a bomb. It was a memorable occasion.

It was now June 1943, and I was suddenly summoned to Headquarters at Ahmednagar. John Grover wished to see me; I had no idea why. I did not get much information from the GSO1, Henry Conder, when I arrived, but was ushered into the presence, rather wondering which misdeed of mine had at last come to light. The general's piercing blue eyes nailed me to the wall as he said:

'I want you to take over the Battle School, immediately. Robert Scott is going to command his battalion, and will give you three days to get into the job, after which the Command is yours. Any questions?'

I hope I did not sound like a gibbering idiot, and made the right sort of reply, but if anyone had hit me hard in the solar plexus it would have had the same effect. Of all the jobs, the Battle School was quite something. It had a staff of some very distinguished instructors, Glen Byam Shaw and Jack Hawkins to name but two, a whole demonstration company of infantry (Royal Norfolks), a detachment of Engineers, and a battery of 99th Field Regiment and a squadron of tanks on call for exercises and demonstrations. It ran three-week courses for officers and NCOs, not just from 2 Div but from 36 Div and other formations as well, and from time to time had to put on demonstrations when John Grover had his Divisional Study periods. And I was going to be in charge of all this. I was just 24 years old!

Taking over from Robert Scott was quite an experience. We never stopped for breath as he showed me all the various training areas and ranges. He had a useful way of pointing things out: he carried a rifle loaded with tracer wherever he went, and would fire a shot at whatever he wished to draw your attention to. It was quick and decisive, and if perchance it gave some wretched person one hell of a fright, too bad. But I never saw him actually shoot anyone – except once, and that was when we dined him out.

We had a course on at the time from 29 Brigade, including a good many of the 2nd Battalion Royal Welch Fusiliers, one of whom, John Simmonds, was a redoubtable character, who volunteered to hold a candle in his right hand while Robert Scott shot it out with his small .22 rifle, with which he was the equivalent of William Tell. But this time his marksmanship was a bit out, and the bullet went through the fleshy part of John's hand between his finger and thumb. Luckily it was not a very serious wound – a stitch and a bit of sticky plaster soon did the trick – but I was horrified: I saw my tenure of command of the Battle School ending before it had started. Suppose the General got to hear? I would be finished.

God bless the regimental system, John Grover *did* get to hear, but three weeks later in a very roundabout way. His old friend Brigadier Hughie Stockwell, then commanding 29 Brigade, was dining with him in 'A' Mess and said to him, roaring with laughter:

'You certainly run a tough Battle School here, General. Did you know that Robert shot one of my officers at a Guest Night the other evening, and nobody thought anything of it?'

So we got away with it!

The brief we worked under at the Battle School was very clear. Training with live ammunition – and we did a lot – was to be within the strictest safety limits, to give all our trainees complete confidence in themselves and their weapons. Certainly we took risks – battles are not fought under the supervision of umpires and red range flags – but there was no deliberate shooting at people to scare them. In all my time in command I had only two casualties: one was a student, and the other was my chief instructor, Colin Hunter of the Cameron Highlanders, on top of whom I nearly managed to land a 3.7 howitzer shell. Despite that, we remained lifelong friends. And I did very nearly blow the pants off General John Grover!

One of the things we had to do was teach men to use their weapons accurately, and instinctively. Firing at paper targets on ranges was no use at all, so we set up a sort of jungle lane that the student walked down, followed by his instructor carrying a loaded rifle. As the student walked down the lane he had to watch out for the sorts of thing he might well meet as the leading scout of a section: trip wires; cunningly concealed traps along the path that might contain poisoned *punjis* (sharpened bamboo stakes), but were on our range just empty holes in the ground; and behind rocks and trees, head and shoulder targets of possible enemy. The student had to avoid the trip wire and traps and shoot the targets, rather like walking up game. If the student failed to spot and shoot at one of these targets within a couple of seconds, the instructor walking behind him would fire a live round just in front of his feet, which would make him realise he would have been shot. This livened up proceedings, and added a bit of realism to the exercise.

One afternoon John Grover, on a visit to see what we were up to, decided he would like to have a go and see if his reactions as a general would pass muster. He ordered me to take him down the course. The experience of walking behind your Divisional Commander with 'one up the spout' was something that you accepted without a tremor in those days. He was a natural game shot, and did well until he missed a trip wire. There was the most enormous explosion. The trip wires were normally connected to a single detonator, which made a big enough bang. Unknown to me, my splendid Engineer Subaltern was not happy enough with its effect, and had augmented the detonator with a guncotton primer and buried the lot in the ground some ten yards off the track. It was perfectly safe, but extremely frightening when you were not expecting to be showered with earth and small stones. John Grover was delighted. 'Just the thing to sharpen them up' was his comment. 'I should have seen that trip wire; I must be getting old!'

The experiences of 6 Brigade in the Arakan were put to good use, particularly the problem of the Japanese 'bunker'. They were brilliant at constructing them, and the bunkers were cleverly concealed and mutually self-supporting: while you were physically trying to attack one, another would be shooting you up from the flank or rear. They were proof against anything but a direct hit from a 25 pounder shell, and that had somehow to go right thought the slit. It was not until we had the Lee/Grant and Sherman tanks with their 75 mm guns, firing directly at them, that we really solved the problem, but the pole charge (a charge of guncotton on a long stick, which you could push through the slit) helped as a means to destroy the garrison inside.

So we built a replica of the Arakan 'Sugar 5' in a deserted valley, and trained teams in this very special role of assault, which needed artillery and mortar fire, smoke, and just about everything we had in our armoury, including our six-pounder anti-tank guns. Occasionally unexploded mortar bombs and shells were left around, and though we did our very best to clear the area after each exercise, there were bound to be some we missed. One day some village children found some 3 inch mortar bombs. Despite all the notices we had put up, and the warnings posted in the villages, they made a neat pile of them and set them over a fire. The result was ghastly: they were blown to smithereens. And all this had to happen when XXXIII Corps were having a major exercise for commanders, based on the Battle School. Somehow we had to get the police and the Collector's staff down to the area, clear things up, and move the villagers away. Luckily the area was some twenty miles from Ahmednagar. It was touch and go whether we would have to cancel the whole afternoon, but somehow Colin Hunter and Louis Brooke-Smith, my adjutant, did it.

There was another exercise that was to accustom soldiers to how very closely and accurately our artillery could support us. We used the whole of 99th Field Regiment, some twenty-four guns in all, took a battalion at a time, and advanced about 500 yards, with shellfire landing approximately 100 yards ahead of us. It was very carefully monitored, and times and safety precautions were rigidly adhered to. Even so, you can imagine my reaction when I was told that, on one particular shoot, the Corps Commander himself, General Monty Stopford, with senior members of his staff, the GOC 36 Division, General Frank Festing, with his retinue and John Grover with his, all wished to join in! An awful lot of shells were going to whizz over our heads: what were the chances of one dropping short amongst this distinguished gathering? But we were getting pretty professional by then, and all went well.

I had some five months in command of the Battle School, during which time I learnt a very great deal, and – more than that – I got to know so many men of the Division who passed through on the various courses. I was no longer a stranger, wearing a strange badge in his bush hat: the tartan square with 'A&SH' embroidered in yellow on it. A year before I had passed some of the Lancashire Fusiliers, resting in a ditch, and heard one say to the other:

'Wot's 'ee got in 'is bluidy 'at, A and SH or summat?'

'Dunno mate,' was the reply, 'mebbe Ashton under Lyme and Stalybridge 'Arriers!'

But now most of them knew what it meant; I was part of the team.

In October there was a big seaborne exercise. 2 Div and XXXIII Corps had been chosen to be assault divisions, and a special force of landing ships and craft was based at Bombay. The whole Division was to embark and land just south of Goa. I was told I was to be attached to 4 Brigade and make myself useful; I would be away for a week. I knew nothing of 'combined operations' or landing craft, but I did know 4 Brigade, and they welcomed me as someone who could help out. The only thing I really remember about it is nearly being marooned at sea on an amphibious Jeep, whose engine just about failed on us. It was not designed for the seas of the Indian Ocean. At the end of a week we had all re-embarked, and were back at Bombay and put back on our trains for our various bases. I rejoined the Battle School, but not for long.

Sometime at the beginning of November, the Headquarters Chaprassi dismounted off his bicycle and came into my office. *'Lat Sahib Salaam dega!'*[4] was his terse but firm message. So I mounted my bicycle and pedalled my way over, wondering which misdeed had come to light, though I could not think of any horrors that had occurred. Henry Conder, the GSO1, greeted me with a smile, so I knew that it was something other than a disciplinary offence that had cause my summons.

John Grover too was all smiles, and told me to sit down (and that was unusual in itself).

'I have nominated you as Brigade Major of 6 Brigade,' he said, 'and you will start taking over tomorrow. The chap who took over from Basil Fanshawe is wanted to command his Regiment, and has to be relieved at once. You won't have much time; 6 Brigade is to do a landing exercise in three weeks time, and we have just received orders for it. I've talked to John Shapland [he was the Brigadier], and we both think you are up to the job.'

I must have looked a bit stunned by the news, which came quite out of the blue. What I was being offered was just about the best junior staff job in the Division. I think it still is today, although it is called 'Chief of Staff'. It is still the sort of job that the top of the Staff College courses get if they are lucky, but then there are fewer Brigades around. I had not been to the Staff College, I knew nothing about combined operations except for my short week's experience with 4 Brigade, and, apart from my spells as Adjutant with Ian Stewart, I knew very little about what we used to call 'staff duties': in other words, the minutiae and protocol of setting out orders so that they made sense to all arms.

'Well,' said the General, 'do you reckon you can compete? You leave tomorrow!'

I wobbled back to the Battle School on my bicycle, told Colin Hunter to take over, and started packing my kit: a bedding roll and two suitcases. But what was I to do with my pet mongoose, whom I had picked up after some exercise, a tiny bit of scraggy mortality shivering with fear and hunger? He looked like a starved grey tree rat, except for his long bushy tail, flecked with brown, which grew to the size of a lavatory brush when he felt aggrieved or insulted. The trouble was that he looked on me as a sort of foster parent, and attached himself to me like a clam to a shipwrecked hulk. By day he would follow me everywhere I went; by night he slept at the bottom of my bed. He was called 'Tiger', and he had the heart of one, so he came too!

6 Brigade were at that time at the hill station of Mahableswar, about 200 miles south of us, and it took me just a day to drive there. It was a lovely place, about 4,000 feet up, where in the summer you could eat the strawberries that the local gardeners produced in bucketfuls for the rich of Bombay. As it was the winter season we had the place to ourselves.

We were an 'assault' brigade, and so we had a bigger establishment than normal. We had to provide two Headquarters – the second a backup for the first in case anything went wrong – and that meant that we had a Deputy Commander – Jack Theobalds, of the Durham Light Infantry – an extra staff officer or two, and an enlarged signal section to man the multifarious communications that an assault landing requires. We also had a somewhat enlarged clerical staff, supervised by WO2 Hicks, and his No. 2, Sergeant Illman, both of the RASC. They ran their office with the strictest discipline, and their work under all sorts of circumstances was meticulously accurate. Neither rain, nor mud, nor the Japanese ever disturbed the efficiency and calm of HQ 6 Brigade. I felt I was under a two-way microscope, both from above and from below.

If all that was not bad enough, we had received the orders for the amphibious exercise we were to carry out in just under a month. It was a simple enough affair: we were to embark the brigade group in, I think, five ships, and land them offshore about fifteen miles from Bombay harbour. But I had never worked on a landing table before, and the drill and calculations for LCAs, LCVPs, LCILs and the rest of the Naval Force were like so much Greek to me. Then there were tides, beaches, moons and goodness knows what else that had to be thought of, and all the business of communications with strange sets, command nets, gunnery nets and ship-to-shore nets to be sorted out – and I had not even really seen a wireless until 1942 (we had none in Malaya!).

So we worked until the small hours of the morning, fitting men into ships, and then fitting them into landing craft and somehow hoping that they would all meet up on the right beach facing in the right direction. Each day we had a coordinating conference with the senior commanders and the Navy, and sure enough something had been forgotten, or something else had to be included in a different wave, on in a different landing craft, which probably involved being carried in a different ship! It was a hard way to learn, but when we loaded the ships and carried out the exercise it all worked reasonably well. At least the Admiral in charge of our assault force, Tom Troubridge, said he was pleased enough – and praise from him had to be earned the hard way.

Back to Ahmednagar we went, and suddenly the Brigadier, Jack Theobalds, and I were summoned to Delhi for a very secret conference. Admiral Louis Mountbatten had taken over in September, and things were beginning to move. We suspected that some sort of seaborne operation was being planned. We flew up in a Hudson bomber. It was a most uncomfortable ride – very bumpy, rather cold, and the RAF version of lukewarm coffee was not all that good – to be whisked off to some very classy accommodation in a hotel. Almost the first person I met there was Ian Stewart: still a Brigadier, but now on the staff of what was called South East Asia Command. We had not seen each other for eighteen months. He had refused command of a brigade in 1942, and had left India for the UK, where he had been Chief Instructor at the Barnard Castle Battle School, which by all accounts he had enlivened no end. He was in tremendous form, but our meetings were very short, as I was closeted nearly all the time with the planning team for the new operation. He did not have the magic password that was required to gain entrance to our very secret meetings.

What we were required to do was to land the whole Division on the Mayu Peninsula, almost exactly opposite Donbaik (of evil memory)[5], get over the Mayu ridge, and establish ourselves at Rathedaung and Buthidaung. In other words we were to capture from the flank, using the seaward approach instead of flogging our way down the countryside as 14th Division had done two years before.

After three days the briefing was over, and we returned via the great Indian Peninsular Railway to Bombay, which gave me a chance to get on the footplate of the big XBs and XCs, the modern Pacifics designed in the late 1930s. John Shapland, my Brigadier, thoroughly disapproved of this particular hobby of mine, although he never actually forbade me to get on board engines. To him, as a gunner, horses were OK, but railway engines were not something the polished young officers of the Royal Artillery were expected to take any interest in whatsoever.

The whole Divisional planning team set up shop in Bombay, and for some ten days we studied maps and air photos, wrote the operation orders, worked out the landing tables and the ship sheets, and produced all the mounds of appendices, proformas and annexes that planners thrive on. We were of course next door to our naval landing force staffs, and everything was tied up as tight as could be. All we needed was the date, but we were never to get it. The whole project was suddenly cancelled; our ships were needed elsewhere – for D Day in fact. There would be no landings on the Mayu Peninsula. After all the hard work and the excitement of being given a proper job to do, and one that we had trained for for so long, we went back to Ahmednagar feeling rather like deflated balloons.

There was no let-up. The Supremo (as he was to be called), Louis Mountbatten, was to spend two days with us, half a day with each Brigade and half with Divisional troops. We were given a directive as to exactly what would happen. In each unit, he would first meet the officers, then the senior NCOs and selected soldiers, and finally the whole unit, which he would address from a soapbox, informally. All three meetings were to be out of sight of each other! Now it is very easy to organise a parade – all you need is a sergeant major, some markers and an open square – but to give a soapbox party a bit of spontaneous originality takes some doing, particularly when it is all being timed to the last minute. Give me landing tables any time! But it all went marvellously.

It is the fashion today to denigrate famous men – to try and make out that they had feet of clay, and brains not worth a capful of porridge – but in the words of one pretty 'bolshie' Royal Welch Fusilier, Louis Mountbatten's visit was worth a month's leave. As I went with him round all our four units – Royal Berks, Royal Welch Fusiliers, Durham Light Infantry and Buckinghamshire Yeomanry – I realised that although his brief, and what he said, was in essence the same to all, the way he said it was quite different in each case. Each man felt that he was speaking to him personally.

I felt this too, because when I was initially introduced, he said to me: 'You were Ian Stewart's adjutant in Singapore, weren't you? You know that I asked him to come out as part of my staff here to carry on the work he did so well there.' It was only a small thing – a remark to a very junior officer – but something that made you feel ten feet tall. He knew you, you were part of his team, and you felt proud of it.

Then it was back to the scrub and jungle of Belgaum once more. We had got new tanks – Shermans – and we were to train in the jungle with them trying out new techniques. We had a small team attached from the 17th Indian Division, that great formation that had fought the Japanese from the very beginning of the Burma Campaign. We learnt from them new techniques about 'bunker busting', and how to use our mortars in strange terrain.

Suddenly in March a message arrived. It was urgent. We were to pack up as fast as we could and get back to Ahmednagar. From there we would be going to Assam – and war. We were pretty good at moving, and our columns set off down the long dusty roads we knew so well, but it was a long drive. I took turns with one of the brigade signal 8 cwt Morris Trucks, and at one stage I remember almost hallucinating. I thought we were driving down a long avenue of trees, rather like the Wellingtonias at Crowthorne, but there are no Wellingtonias in India, and I had to shake myself awake and hand over to one of my signallers. I could have gone over the khud so easily!

When we got back to Ahmednagar orders were awaiting us. The whole Division was to move to Dimapur, the great base depot which served both the Imphal sector and the American base farther north at Dinjan, the anchor of the air route over the 'Hump'. The Japanese were on the edge of the Imphal plain, and it was going to be a race as to who could get there first. We were to move in three separate parts: infantry and Guns by rail, some vehicles by the 'short' road convoy, and others round the head of the Brahmaputra. And there was I, the one officer in the Division who had been there, and knew the railways, and the river crossings and ferries, and what we were likely to meet with when we got to Dimapur, and I had it all in my staff officer's notebook, that I had kept so meticulously way back in 1942, when I was sent on my own by 26 Indian Division! It had all come into place, all the lonely hours looking at sidings, and stations and ferries, and now the facts and figures and diagrams were coming to life again. At least I was earning my pay; I was able to help the planners with some local knowledge.

Compared with combined operations, putting troops on trains is a doddle, especially when dealing with the Indian railways, who were brilliant at this sort of movement. Our problem was one of priorities and timing: who did we want out first at the other end, and with how much ammunition and food? We knew that it would be a fortnight before most of our wheeled transport would catch up with us. And just how much could we get on the 'flats' in the way of guns, towers and limbers? When you are working against the clock it is so easy to make mistakes.

For better or worse the orders were checked, double-checked and sent to units. The various parties and convoys were mustered and set forth, right across India, across the Ganges and across the Brahmaputra. Their destination was known as Dimapur, or in railway terms, Manipur Road, but their final goal was the little hill station in the Naga Hills, called Kohima.

The Second Division was moving forward to its last great fight, and I was going to be part of it.

NOTES

1   Walter Gibson, *The Boat* (London: W.H. Allen, 1952; republished 1974).
2   The Hump was well known to all airmen who had to fly the supply route to China from Assam, as the mountain range that separated the two countries. For the machines they had in those days it was a perilous flight when the weather was bad.
3   An old boy of Winchester College.
4   'The General sends his compliments!'
5   In early 1943 6 Brigade had taken part in the 1st Arakan campaign, and had suffered heavily at Donbaik.

CHAPTER 8
Kohima

By the end of March the whole of 2 Div was on the move. The road convoys had left on their long drive, 5 Brigade train parties had already left, and 6 Brigade were loading their group on to the many 'flats' and troop carriages that, right on schedule, were being marshalled at Ahmednagar Station sidings. It was time for Brigade Headquarters to leave so that we would be there, at the far end, to organise them when they arrived.

John Shapland was our Brigadier, a gunner with a Military Cross from the First World War. He had been Commander Royal Artillery of the Division for two years, and so knew almost everyone in it. He was a rotund, tough little man with a great sense of humour, and a meticulous knowledge of organisation and planning; he knew India well, and was a connoisseur of good cigars – altogether, a most delightful commander to serve under. His Deputy, Colonel Jack Theobalds, was a very different kettle of fish: Oxfordshire and Buckinghamshire Light Infantry; tall, good looking, and deceptively quiet, but a considerable leader. He was to follow with the main body and join us later.

There were four of us in the advance party: the Brigadier, myself, Paddy Burke (the Brigade signal officer) and John Hunter Browne, the DAA & QMG, who was responsible for the administrative needs of the Brigade. There was also a small body of clerks and signallers to help set up shop when we arrived, led by the redoubtable Mr Hicks, who – unknown to me – had purloined my private Remington No. 1 portable typewriter! Somehow it had got mixed up in the Brigade's baggage, but I have it to this day.

We drove down to Manmad in a small convoy some time near midnight, and caught the train to Calcutta on the first leg of the journey, which would take us two days. We went up on a line that was new to me, via Nagpur, Bilaspur and Jamshedpur, but there was no time for trips on the footplate: we were too involved in looking at the maps of our assembly areas in Assam, and trying to make sense out of what we might have to do. What was happening there? What might we be running into? Information was almost non-existent. It was as if 2 Div, one of the major performers in a huge and important drama, was suddenly called to take the stage in the middle of the performance, without having seen the programme or the script, or having met any of the cast. Indeed the producers did not originally want us to take part at all. The Japanese had not originally wished to invade India – it was never part of their strategic plan – but people and circumstances drew them into considering it. Little by little, what had started as one general's dream became their Army policy.

The General was Mutagachi Renya, the commander of their XV Army, a capable and ambitious man who had commanded the 18th Division in the Malayan campaign with distinction. It was a detachment of his Division that had made the initial landings at Khota Bahru, and he had fought with them on Singapore Island. Years before, at the Marco Polo Bridge at Shanghai in 1937, as a regimental commander he had sparked off the affair that started the 'China Incident', as the Japanese would call it.[1] He despised the British Army; his experiences in Malaya and Burma had persuaded him that they were incapable of standing up to the Japanese, and could be easily defeated any time, any place. To his surprise, in the spring of 1943 a certain Brigadier Orde Wingate and a substantial force came over the hills, through what Mutagachi's staff and intelligence had assured him was 'impenetrable' jungle, and caused his 18th Division a lot of bother. What the ridiculous and useless British could do, he and his unconquerable Japanese could do much better – but in the opposite direction.

But first he had to convince his Army Commander, Lieutenant General Kawabe, commanding the Burma Army. Then a third actor appeared on the scene, Subhas Chandra Bhose and his Indian National Army, raised from prisoners taken in Singapore, who could be the spearhead of a force that might establish itself in Bengal and possibly lead to the Japanese conquest of India. But meanwhile a successful assault on the Imphal Plain would dislodge the British from their base there; a vast amount of stores, food and ammunition would fall into Japanese hands; and the result would be a better defensive line to hold the flank in Burma. If the whole Assam front were to collapse as a result, the American airlift over the 'Hump' would cease, Bhose and his Indian National Army could take over Bengal, and the rest of India would join him.

All this had not gone unnoticed by British intelligence, and XIV Army had taken steps to counter it. Japanese planning and discussions had been going on between Mutaguchi, Burma Army Headquarters Southern Army (Singapore) and Tokyo for some months, and eventually the operation was conceived in two separate parts: 'Ha-Go', the operation in Arakan to involve the British forces there and hopefully draw off reinforcements from the Imphal area, and 'U-Go', the actual attack on Imphal.

Ha-Go had started in February 1944, and had been soundly defeated.

For the first time, air supply and tanks had turned the scale, and the Royal Air Force had shot the Japanese out of the sky. It had failed, both tactically and strategically, and when Louis Mountbatten visited us in Ahmednagar he told us all about it. U-Go, the operation against Imphal, started in the first week of March. From north to south the 31st, 15th and 33rd Divisions started crossing the Chindwin, taking the utmost precautions not to be spotted by the RAF, but they were seen and reported by our 'V' Force special patrol units. However, their strengths and directions of attack were not so easily divined – particularly that of the 31st Division, whose objective was Kohima.

While all this was going on, General John Grover commanding 2 Div was told by General Sir George Giffard, GOC 11th Army Group, that the Division would not be required in Assam because it would be difficult to maintain it alongside the Indian Army Divisions, and as any question of combined operations was on the back burner, it would be used for reinforcements to other units. Five days later Lieutenant General Stopford commanding XXXIII Corps was ordered to get himself, his Headquarters and 2 Div to Assam as quickly as possible! At the same time 150 Indian Parachute Brigade was fighting for its life at Sangshak against 58 Regiment of 31st Division, and from a map they captured in that battle it was realised that the whole of 31st Division was headed for Kohima. They had just forty miles to go, and there was nothing to stop them. At that date we were 1,500 miles away!

We were in our railway carriage heading for Calcutta, knowing nothing whatsoever about the gravity of the situation. Perhaps it was as well. If things had gone as the Japanese hoped, they would have had both the Kohima Ridge and the enormous depot at Manipur Road. After the speed of their initial success, misunderstandings of orders, jealousy and rivalry amongst their higher command and the sheer size of the country would all combine to frustrate their plans. Add to that the staunch fighting ability of the British, Indian and African soldiers of the XIVth Army, and the superlative efforts of the SEAC Air Forces, and the result was that the Japanese were to go down to the biggest land defeat in their history. But that was all in the future. And it was to depend on a map captured from a Japanese captain killed at a place in the Naga Hills called Sangshak. The map showed, in great detail, the whole Japanese plan of attack on the Imphal Plain, and there was the direct information that the whole of their 31st Division was launched at Kohima, and perhaps farther to Dimapur. Two men from 150 Indian Parachute Brigade's intelligence section made a thirty-six-mile journey in impossible country, carrying this map and a copy to IV Corps Headquarters, and there the map mysteriously vanished. To this day no one knows what happened to it – or if they do, they have conveniently forgotten.

*

If you go to the Royal Hospital at Chelsea and see the beautiful room where the pensioners dine, with the great pictures of Charles II, Nell Gwynne and the distinguished founders, look carefully at the panelled walls with the battle honours of the British Army carved and emblazoned in gold that line the room. You will look in vain for the name Sangshak. It does not appear on the list of battle honours, because no British regiment or formation took part. Certainly there were British gunners, signallers and others, but the glory of Sangshak belongs to the Indian Army: the men of the two parachute battalions and the 5th Battalion, 5th Mahratta Light Infantry, who formed 150 Indian Parachute Brigade and had been sent to the Sangshak area for advanced jungle training.

On 19 March their training started in earnest. Up the Jessami track came 58 Regiment in strength, one of the finest regiments in the Japanese Army, with six years of fighting experience in China behind it. They were never handled so roughly as they were at Sangshak by C Company 152 Indian Parachute Regiment. Their regimental diary records:

> At Point 7378 the 3rd Battalion suffered 160 casualties, with one Company and two Platoon commanders killed, another four officers wounded . . . the enemy had resisted with courage and skill.[2]

In all, though casualty figures are hard to find and may be inaccurate, 58 Regiment possibly lost some 1,000 of its original strength of 4,000 as a result of Sangshak: a battle in which it should never have taken part, but which gave time for XIV Army to reorganise the defence of Kohima and Dimapur.

Down the line, the treatment of the survivors of the battle was disgraceful. Brigadier Tim Hope Thompson was sacked for incompetence (but he redeemed himself commanding a battalion of the Dorsetshire Regiment in Normandy), and the officers and men of the parachute battalions were welcomed with reserve by their comrades, until a special Order of the Day by Bill Slim put matters right, but not until August 1944. Whatever else they had done, 150 Indian Parachute Brigade had bought time by their action. It was to be a priceless asset, and enabled all sorts of motley forces to concentrate where they were desperately needed at Kohima. And they had knocked the stuffing out of 3 Battalion 58 Regiment.

By 1 April the first of 2 Div, 5 Brigade, was beginning to arrive at Dimapur, and it was still not clear what the Japanese were up to. They had been seen approaching Kohima, but there was still a feeling that they might make for Dimapur, and part of the key to that was the Nichugard Pass about ten miles down the road. During this time Dimapur was part of 202 Area, commanded by a major general, but his command was purely administrative; he had no fighting troops. But 161 Brigade from 5th Indian

Division arrived from the Arakan, and was available. Then ensued an unfortunate *contretemps*. Headquarters XXXIII Corps had arrived on the scene, and General Stopford took over the command. His understanding was that the Japanese would bypass Kohima and make for Dimapur, and so he ordered 161 Brigade to withdraw from Kohima, leaving it to be defended by the Assam Regiment and various odd units who were in the depots there. When 5 Brigade arrived, however, 161 Brigade were ordered back, 5 Brigade took over the defence of Dimapur, and on 5 April the 4th Battalion the Royal West Kent Regiment re-entered the Kohima garrison that they should never have been ordered to leave. They were just in time.

It was bad luck perhaps that the Japanese should have encountered one of the most battle-experienced infantry battalions that we had in Burma at that time. The 4th West Kents had fought in France, at Alamein, in Iraq, and in the Arakan battle that had just ended, and though they had suffered severe casualties, they had retained their identity as a typical, tough Territorial infantry battalion. They had faced and beaten the Japanese in the Arakan, and were confident of doing the same at Kohima. Without them the siege might have had a very different ending.

While all this was going on, the Division was moving slowly but surely across India. We were in the hands of the railways now; it was up to them to get us there in time, and time was slowly running out.

What we loosely call the 'Battle of Kohima' took place over a much wider area than the village and ridge itself. Many units of many races took part, and while 2 Div did some of the hardest fighting in the weeks that followed, their task was made possible by the fantastic efforts of a lot of very brave men of all races in 'ad hoc' units, formed on the spot and told to get on with what little they had in the way of weapons, ammunition and communications. They were up against an enemy superior in just about everything you can think of – numbers, training, experience – but who lacked air superiority, and whose top leadership was suspect, and in the end was to prove disastrous.

By the first few days in April 6 Brigade was arriving, and we relieved 5 Brigade in their role of defending the railway line and Dimapur Base Area, so they in turn started up the road to relieve Kohima. By 12 April they were encountering road-blocks. One particular specimen was on a spur to the left of the road that our tanks could not reach. It was eventually dealt with by a very bold attack by the Camerons, who climbed down the steep mountainside and attacked it from the rear, led by David Graham, who was quite seriously wounded in the affair. This opened the road to Zubza, a flattish piece of ground where 24 Mountain Regiment had their guns. There was room, too, for our own artillery, which was so urgently required. It was during these operations that Father O'Callaghan, Chaplain to the 7th Worcesters was killed; he was one of the first casualties of the Division.

At last we had physical contact with 161 Brigade, who had clung on to Kohima for so long, and we were able to relieve the garrison – originally by the 1st/1st Punjabis of 161 Brigade, and then by our own Royal Berkshires. If Garrison Hill was indescribable for its filth, its horror and its smell, the sight of its defenders was almost worse. They looked like aged, bloodstained scarecrows, dropping with fatigue; the only clean thing about them was their weapons, and they smelt of blood, sweat and death. Heaven only knows how they had survived, and they still had to march some two miles or more before we could get transport to them (we had managed to get ambulances up the road for the wounded and sick). They had earned their place in history. Their battle honour reads 'Siege of Kohima'; ours of 2 Div just 'Kohima'. Our part in the battle was still to come: there was a long way to go, and so many who would fall by the wayside.[3]

Kohima was a watershed in many ways. It was a spectacular setting for a battle. Looking at it from our advance, which was more or less due south, on the right rose a mountain called Pulebadze some 7,000 feet high, from which a spur called Aradura ran down to join the main road to Imphal. Across the valley between Aradura and Naga village on the left ran Kohima Ridge, the watershed, of which the peacetime depots and Jail Hill formed part. On the left of this ridge as you looked at it was the District Commissioner's bungalow, in the shadow of what was to be called Garrison Hill, and on the left-hand side the ridge on which the little Naga village sat, dominated by point 5120, which became known as Hunter's Hill. It was a magnificent setting, and was commented on in numerous diaries kept by Japanese soldiers (they were avid recorders of places and scenes).

From Kohima it seemed that paths and tracks led to all of Nagaland: to Merema, Jessame, Kekrema, and of course the main road from Dimapur to Imphal. These tracks kept to the ridges and the hills; progress down in the valleys was very slow and very difficult – in fact well-nigh impossible.

Kohima formed a human watershed too: it marked the farthermost point of the Japanese advance toward the West. Until Kohima, every battle and engagement (except the recent affair in the Arakan) had been decisively won by the Japanese Army. No wonder they felt invincible; no one had been able to withstand their courage in attack and their tenacity in defence. This time, though, they came up against soldiers who were better trained, better armed and better led than any they had ever met before, and though they fought bitterly, to the last man and the last round, they found in the XIV Army an opponent who in the end would totally defeat them.

So much for the stage; what of the actors?

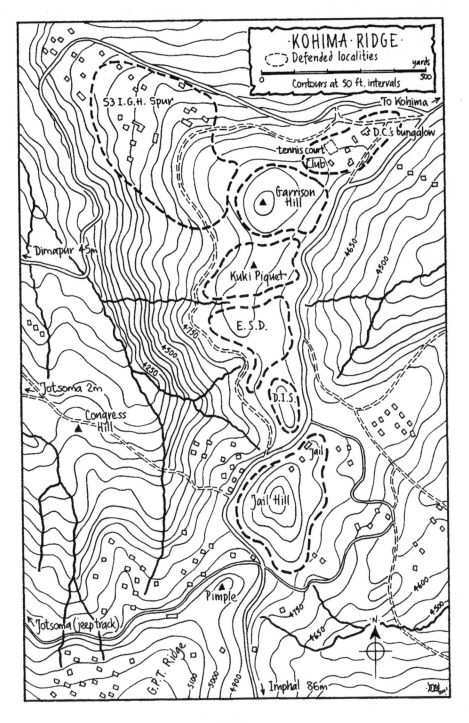

Initially 6 Brigade's task was to relieve the garrison, consolidate what was left of their final position, and prepare to retake the Ridge, at the foot of which stood a small, isolated position called Piquet Hill. This was ideal for our 3 inch mortars to occupy, to be able to support operations on Garrison Hill and the Ridge, but it was overlooked on its right flank by what we called Terrace Hill. It had to be cleared, and a company of the Durham Light Infantry with tanks did the job, killing some seventy Japanese, with the loss of one or two men and their company commander.

There was an incident at Brigade Headquarters on the second night we arrived. We were well dug in above the Jotsoma loop road, when there was a furious outburst of firing from our defence platoon on the flank. Somehow a strong Japanese fighting patrol had managed to get along the side of the Aradura mountain, and they came at us. It was a sharp engagement, but we were ready for them, and at first light next morning we went out to count the dead. Amongst them was their commander, a young lieutenant, carrying – as so many Japanese did – a silk flag, with many names and characters written on it. It was covered in blood. Someone gave it to me, and I took it home and framed it. Eventually I gave it to 2 Div Museum in York.

In 1984 a Japanese party from 58 Regiment's Old Comrades came to see 2nd Division, and of course were shown the museum. They asked me about the flag, and so I told them the story. I also asked them whether there was any clue in the flag as to who the owner might have been; he was obviously a brave and determined young man. The leader of the party, Nishida, explained that the calligraphy on the flag contained no name, just good luck greetings from friends and families – that was the normal custom – but he added his personal thanks, and that of all his friends, to the Division for keeping the flag in a place of honour as a mark of respect.

By the end of April an aerial view of the Kohima battlefield would have looked rather like a cross-section of a McDonald's burger, with bits of British and Japanese interspersed all over the place: 5 Brigade on the left in the Naga village area, then Japanese, then 6 Brigade in the middle holding Garrison Hill and Hospital Spur, but not Kuki Picket, FSD or Jail Hill, and 4 Brigade on the right on the lower slopes of Aradura. Add other Japanese areas of resistance for seasoning and you get the picture. At that time we had an advanced headquarters on Garrison Hill itself, with our main headquarters at Jotsoma. One day, during an attack by Hurri-bombers, one of our machines mistook its targets and landed an enormous egg right on top of our dugout on Garrison Hill. It exploded with a loud report, but luckily did no physical damage to anyone. John Shapland was furious, and rang up our RAF liaison officer at Divisional Headquarters to complain. He did not get much change:

1. ADRG Wilson, Christmas 1950, Korea

2. Brigadier ADRG Wilson MBE,
Liverpool 1965

3. Sylvia Marianna Wilson, London 1945

4. 2 A&SH attack on Zer, South of Mir Ali, April 1937

5. 2 A&SH Camp Site, Thal In Tochi, May 1937

6. Idak Scouts Post, May 1937

7. Tochi Scouts, Waziristan 1937

8. 2 A&SH Battalion Headquarters Signals, Sgt Gibson, April 1937

9. 2 A&SH road protection, Vickers MMG Section

10. Lunch Khajuri Scouts Post, April 1937

11. 14 Platoon, D Company, 2 A&SH entering Mir Ali, April 1937

12. 2 A&SH Hal in Shinki Defile, April 1937

13. Squeak Picket, Dosalli, May 1937

14. A&SH, Ptes Millard and Lacey

15. Gond Village, Scinde valley, Kashmir 1938

16. Srinagar, Kashmir 1938

17. Great Indian Peninsular Railway train passing

18. Great Indian Peninsular Railway 4-4-2 Atlantic Bhina

19. On the footplate

20. Kensington Palace 1936. ARGW, ADRGW, AW calling on Princess Louise, Colonel of the Regiment, on first being commissioned

21. Officers 2 A&SH, Secunderabad, 1 January 1939

22. 2 A&SH march past, The Maidan, Secunderabad, 1 January 1939

23. 2 A&SH Carrier Platoon, Tyersall Park, Singapore 1940

24. Corporal R (Bertie) King DCM and the crew of Dunstaffnage Castle (Imperial War Museum FE353)

25. Captain TBG Slessor and Blair Castle on training, Singapore Island (Imperial War Museum FE 349)

26. 1 A&SH Jerusalem 1946 – ADRGW, RSM P McPhillips, RH Lumley-Webb

27. A Company, 1 A&SH, North Korea, October 1950

28. Orly Airport, Paris 1957. C Delacour, D Esmonde Whyte, ADRGW, FM Montgomery

29. The Vatican 1958. ADRGW, The Pope, FM Montgomery

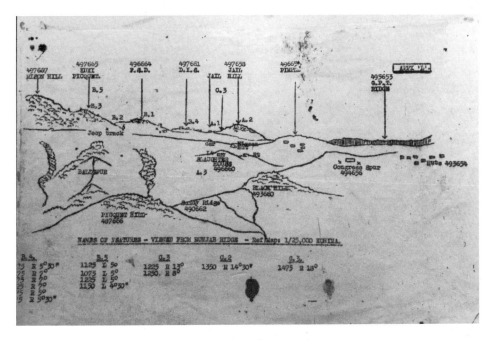

30. Kohima mortar and artillery panorama with target data

31. Potsdam. Interpreter, Colonel Pinchuk, SMW, Mrs Anne Colahan

32. DDR Brixmis tour – a snowbound breakfast stop

33. Panmunjom 1970, the EC121 conference. Standing MG James Knapp USAF

'I'm terribly sorry, Brigadier,' said the liaison officer. 'Quite disgraceful; I shall report him at once. Did you get his number?'

There was no possible answer to that one, and in any case the flying and accuracy of our air support was beyond all praise.

One early morning we heard a rather different sound, as a whole lot of strange machines dived over our gun positions at Jotsoma. They were Zeros. They had a brief go at us too; our gallant airmen were nowhere to be seen. It was the only time in the whole of the Kohima battle that the Japanese Air Force put in any sort of appearance. They did not do much damage but they interrupted a shoot supporting 5 Brigade's Lancashire Fusiliers, to their disadvantage.

Meanwhile the Royal Welch Fusiliers and the Durham Light Infantry on Garrison Hill were subjected to heavy attacks by night, and constant sniping by day. Nevertheless, even on that dreadful spot there was room for fun and relaxation. On one visit to our Advanced Headquarter Hole (I can scarcely dignify it with the title of 'Dugout') I passed Brian Bonsor, the battery commander of 99th Field, in charge of all the guns protecting the hill. He was sitting outside his own lair, next to ours, reading the latest copy of the *Tatler*, which the Royal Air Force had dropped with the mail and supplies. He waved a languid hand, and invited me to join him:

'Hullo David, how nice to see you. Do have a mug of tea; I've just got all the latest magazines today.'

They always did say that the cavalry's job was to add a bit of tone to war!

There was a great deal of heavy and confused fighting in 5 Brigade's area, with the Lancashire Fusiliers, Worcesters and Camerons away on the other side of the valley from us in the middle, trying to clear the remains of Naga Village and the dominating height 5120. No one quite knew where anyone else was; Japanese and British parties were running into each other in the dark and mist, with the British making sure but very slow progress. Early one morning Colin Hunter, commanding 'D' Company of the Camerons, was peering through his misted-up glasses at two figures in the gloom a few yards ahead. He cleared his spectacles of the misty rain and asked Tommy Cook, his Company Sergeant Major:

'I don't recognise those two – are they ours?'

The answer came quickly: both men came at Colin with their bayonet. Tommy Cook shot both, but not before Colin had received the point of a bayonet in his thigh, missing some rather more important bits by inches!

Meanwhile, John Carbonell and a party had ambushed a Japanese patrol whose officer was carrying an important pocketful of General Sato's orders to his Division.

Behind us, the Higher Commands were getting impatient. They could not understand why we were taking so long to clear the Japanese out of Kohima and get on down the road. XXIII Corps were being pressed by

XIV Army to get 2 Div to carry out further attacks, but with whom, and where? At this stage of the battle the Staff and Commanders had no idea of the difficulties. Each Japanese position had to be individually dealt with, and this was a very slow business. We were slowly strangling them with our air and artillery power, but starving or not, 31 Division was not in any mood to give in. They were too weak now to attempt the mass 'Banzai' attacks by night; the initiative had passed to us, and we had a very detailed and well organised plan of harassing fire and patrolling to dominate the area, coordinated by Division.

One day a new face arrived at the coordinating conference. It was the new deputy Commander of 5 Brigade, Colonel Michael Alston-Roberts-West – or Mike West as he preferred to be called, *tout court*. He was late of the Oxfordshire and Buckinghamshire Light Infantry, and was like a dose of jumping powder. In no time at all, the details for the night were settled. He looked at his watch, and announced that as the conference had ended sooner than expected, there was time for a little relaxation. Would anyone care to stay for a hand of poker? We should have known better; those who did stay were well and truly cleaned out. What a way to run a war!

The details of the nightly artillery and mortar strikes were in the hands of 'Watty' Scott Plumber (Brigade Major, Royal Artillery) for the guns, and me for the mortars and patrols. We had a joint dugout on Punjab Ridge, where we could see the whole battlefield, and where the wireless reception was particularly good. At dusk every evening we assembled there with our operators and lookouts and kept trace (or tried to) of where people were and what they were doing. Early one morning, just after daylight, we heard the rumble of tanks on the road below us. There was a column of six Lee/Grants going up the road towards Garrison Hill and Kohima Ridge. We knew of no tanks that should have been on the move anywhere, and we were unable to get in touch with them by any form of wireless. Something was very wrong. If the tanks kept going they would drive straight into the Japanese in Naga Village; they had perhaps two miles to go.

There was a military police post at Lancaster Gate (the name we had given to the junction between the Jotsoma road and the main road to Kohima and Imphal). The tanks were already past that point, but Watty managed to get in touch with the post to alert them. An extremely brave MP got on his motorcycle and, roaring past all six tanks, finally stopped the head of the column just short of the final corner, where the road doubled back on itself to go round the far side of Garrison Hill. He then turned the tanks round in their own length, one by one, on the main road. Up till then no one had fired a single shot. Clearly the Japanese had been waiting to ambush the tanks when they rounded the corner. When they saw them turning round they opened everything up, but to no avail: six tanks trundled back to safety. The brave Military Policeman received a well earned Military Medal.

What had gone wrong? The explanation was simple. The tanks had unloaded the evening before at Manipur Road as reinforcements for 149 RAC, our attached tank regiment. They were filled with ammunition and their normal kit and, with just a driver and one man in the turret to help, were told to 'get up the road to Kohima – you can't miss it.' But they had no maps, their sets were not open, and in any case they would not have known who to speak to. Up the hill they went. They passed post after post, and no one stopped them to ask what they were doing; they were happily waved through.

The nearer you get to the front of a battlefield, the quieter and lonelier it gets. Soldiers in the front lines are usually minding their own business and keeping out of sight of the enemy. Unless there is a specific operation on, the guns are silent. There may be the crack of the occasional sniper's shot, or the quick burst of an automatic weapon, but in general the infantry are minding their own business, getting on with repairing trenches and positions, and sleeping if they can. So there was nothing to warn the tank crews who were new to the area that they were in any sort of danger.

After that episode we always put a physical block on whatever road or track we were operating down, manned by MPs, who would stop each party or truck, and ask them who they were, where they were going, and whether they knew exactly how to get to their destination!

History has a strange way of repeating itself. In November 1950 a ration truck from our 1st Battalion drove up the road northwards towards the Yalu River in Korea (we were perhaps thirty miles short of it at the time). It was dark, and the truck's crew happily followed the signs for 27 Brigade marked 'NOTTINGHAM', past what had been the front lines, and parked themselves with another unit in a large North Korean school playground. They were given hot mugs of what passed for tea by what they thought were rather strange-looking soldiers, after which they got out their sleeping bags and dozed off. But later they somehow realised that all was not well. They quietly got into their truck and drove back the way they had come, arriving back with us somewhat shattered. They had been spending the night with the Chinese Army, and no one was any the wiser. So much for front lines.

It was now the end of April. 5 Brigade were engulfed in Naga Village and Point 5120, 6 Brigade were locked solid on Garrison Hill and the Ridge, and 4 Brigade were trying to get to Aradura round the lower slopes of Pulebadze. They were having a very difficult time. The countryside was appalling: the hillside was so steep that they had to cut steps and build handrails to make any progress at all. To ensure secrecy any form of fire was forbidden, and the troops were living on their waterbottles, biscuits, cheese and jam. The Japanese were very active in their area, and there were constant ambushes and skirmishes that held up the advance.

Eventually on 4 May the Norfolks broke through and, after a very confused battle personally led by Robert Scott, cleared what was called GPT Ridge. The cost was high: some twenty-two officers and men killed and sixty wounded, including Robert himself, who, covered with blood, passed through 6 Brigade, where I met his stretcher party. He was not pleased at being put out of the battle.

'David,' he said 'I'm too old for this ridiculous war – there was I sorting out the Japanese with my battalion, and I am asked to speak to the general on the wireless to report how we are getting on. If he wants to know, why can't he come and see for himself?!'

What Robert did not say was that he had been almost in the front of his leading company, lobbing grenades through Japanese pillbox slits. It was not quite the place where a Divisional Commander should have been, but Robert got one of the quickest 'Immediate Awards' of the DSO, and Jack Randle, his leading Company Commander, the Victoria Cross. Sadly Jack was killed.

On 4 May a major effort was made by 6 Brigade to deal with Kuki Picket, DIS and FSD. The Royal Welch were to deal with Kuki Picket, and the Durhams in infantry carriers were to get behind the ridge and attack it from the rear. Once again the Japanese defence proved too strong. Both battalions' casualties that day were very heavy. The attack on Kuki Picket had been a disaster: the Royal Welch Fusiliers had lost two Company Commanders, three Platoon Commanders and some sixty killed. However, one tank and the remnants of a Royal Welch and a DLI company had got onto DIS, and had formed a small perimeter with its back to the near cliff edge of the ridge at that point. Somehow they had managed to reel out a telephone line to Garrison Hill. They were commanded by one Captain Ogbourne of the Royal Welch Fusiliers, assisted by 'Dickie' Sparrow of the same Regiment.

This tiny perimeter held for a week, but it had to be supplied. The tank required petrol for its auxiliary motor, which kept the wireless batteries charged. Food, ammunition and – most of all – water had to be carried up by porters at night (here the Nagas came into their own), and the sick and wounded had to be evacuated and looked after. The Japanese could have overwhelmed this little garrison, but they never made a serious attempt to do so; had they tried, the defensive fire of our guns would have made it very difficult. It was a tiny chink in the Japanese defence, but was to prove vital a week later in the decisive attack on the Ridge and Jail Hill.

On the right, 4 Brigade was still making progress along the side of Aradura, but at the cost of Willie Goschen, its Brigadier, and Jack

Theobalds who succeeded him: both were killed. 5 Brigade had lost Victor Hawkins, shot through his right hand and his scrotum (without serious damage to either).

'Let that be a lesson to you, David,' he said, waving goodbye with his bandaged flipper; 'Never scratch your balls in the face of the enemy!'

We were beginning to run out of Brigadiers; mine was the next to go!

To add to our troubles the monsoon had started, and the rain was coming down in buckets. The steep hills became mudslides, and our dugouts swimming pools. We lived in a continuous sea of squelching mud, but we still had the Ridge to clear – and Jail Hill, and Aradura. We started on 11 May. It was a perilous affair. The whole of the Royal Berks were to climb the ridge and squeeze themselves into the tiny perimeter that the remnants of the original attack on 4 May had held with its one tank. The Divisional Artillery and the mortars from Picket Hill would put down a three-sided curtain of fire round the edge of this perimeter, and when it stopped – just at first light – the Royal Berks would go in to the attack. All sorts of things could go wrong: if the artillery barrage was inaccurate, or the mortars (notorious for breaking tail fins and falling short) hit the troops in the assembly area, the casualties would be horrific. And could a whole battalion get up a hill track that only Naga porters had used? What if the Japanese rumbled what was going on, and counter-attacked while we were forming up? I was responsible for the Brigade mortars. We were being asked to fire with a precision and accuracy dependent on the highest training. Were we good enough? In the end we were; by the end of the day the Royal Berks had cleared both DIS and FSD.

By 14 May the Ridge, including the tennis court and Jail Hill, was in our hands. Terence Cuneo's picture of the Dorsets and Sergeant Waterhouse's tank shows a microcosm of the total devastation of the area. Naga Village still had to be cleared, and so did Aradura Spur. The latter was our job.

One morning John Grover sent for me. Back in my days at Singapore I had learnt to fly, and had amassed some 130 hours solo. He thought I might put this acquired skill to good use. I was to leave at once for Dimapur, where I was to report to the Air OP Squadron that was based on the landing strip there, and act as observer for a reconnaissance of Aradura. I was given a map, with the area I was to observe very clearly marked out.

I collected my jeep, told everyone where I was off to, and drove down the road to the airstrip, where the Air OP Flight knew all about the project. We would set forth at first light the next morning, when the sun would be in the right direction and altitude. I would be back on the ground by midday, and back with the Division two hours later. All this was 'weather permitting', of course: the monsoon had started, but the forecast was not too bad. It was nice to spend a night in comfort with them, on a proper camp bed in a decent tent.

Next day was fine, and we took off without any problem and flew up into the hills. I began to worry, and the farther we went the more I worried. Suppose the engine failed – where on earth would we land? What about Zeros? They had visited us once, why not again today? However, these thoughts did not last long, as we were soon over Kohima and the area I was supposed to reconnoitre. What did I see? Nothing. That is not quite true; we could see where the British were – entrenchments, vehicles, guns, gunpits, washing hung on lines to dry, soldiers moving around – but beyond there was just countryside. The only thing that we could see were tracks in the grass where there had been columns of troops or perhaps porters. These gave a clue, and I could mark them on my map, but the Japanese Army could have been back in Japan for all the trace of them I could see round Kohima. I thought I was wasting my time, although not completely: we were called to observe a counterbattery shoot, and flew back towards Naga Village. There we spotted the flash and smoke of one of 31 Division's mountain guns. If it had not fired when we were nearly over it we would never had seen it. My pilot called for a regimental target and twenty-four guns engaged, but I do not know whether this was a success, as we had to return to base; our time was up.

At Divisional Headquarters I reported to John Grover, who quizzed me in great detail on what I had seen, which was not really very much. While this was taking place Mark Maunsell, the GSO1, came in and said that 5 Brigade wanted him on the telephone. He picked it up, and I made as if to go, but he waved me back into my chair. There wasn't much in the way of conversation: mostly 'I see' – 'I see' – 'I agree' – 'Thank you for letting me know'. Then the phone went back on its hook. He sat for a minute or so, saying nothing, just looking at his map as if stunned. I might not have been in the room. Something had happened that had shaken him very badly indeed. Then he gave a sort of shake of his head, and apologised:

'That was 5 Brigade. They rang to tell me that Ian Thorburn has just been killed by a sniper.'

Ian was a Royal Scot, a Wykehamist like John Grover, a friend of mine and a contemporary, doing the same job but across the valley.

For the first time I began to realise the terrible weight that a commander carries with him. John Grover had commanded now for two years. He must have known almost everyone in 2 Div if not by name then certainly by sight, and the loss of so many was beginning to affect him, particularly his young officers like Ian Thorburn, whom he regarded as part of his team – almost his family. But what is a General to do? He has to disregard personal friendships and casualties, and order men into action and perhaps to their death without counting the cost. Years later, as a battalion and company commander, I was faced with the same problems on a much smaller scale, but that was bad enough. Thank heavens I never became a

General; I still remember the names and the faces of those who, but for me, might still be around today.

The job of 6 Brigade was to clear the Aradura Spur. The air photos did not give us many clues, as the trees were far too thick; our maps were up-to-date reprints, made from air reconnaissance, but all they showed was a spider's web of viciously steep contours. No one had been up the place before; we got some assistance from 4 Brigade, but it wasn't worth much. We were going to go up the beastly place.

While we were sorting things out, one afternoon the chaplain of the Royal Welch Fusiliers, and a delightful young captain, Johnny Rostron, who had earned a DSO in the Arakan, came to Headquarters and asked to see the Brigadier. They said it was a private matter, and I ushered them into our dugout.

After a moment or so John Shapland said:

'David, this is very serious. I want you to listen to what Padre Ken Parkhurst and Johnnie Rostron have to say.'

What they had to say was very serious indeed. All the principal people were friends of mine whom I knew and admired. They are all dead now; I am older, and – I hope – wiser, and have faced defeat and disaster many times since.

The 1st Battalion, Royal Welch Fusiliers were a magnificent battalion, but they had had severe casualties at Dunkirk, in the Arakan, and probably more than most at Kohima. They were badly in need of a rest (but then so were many other units of the Division). So much of the fighting against the Japanese took place by night, and sleep by day was not all that easy to get, what with the duties that had to be carried out, and shelling and sniping. Weeks of this had worn them down. This had had an effect on their Colonel, Garnett Braithwaite, who was so determined not to be surprised by any further Japanese night attacks that he insisted on 100 per cent 'Stand To' all night. The result was that the men were getting less and less sleep, and this was beginning to demoralise them. Both Parkhurst and Rostron strongly recommended that their Colonel should be relieved of his command. They felt that, like his men, he had reached his limit of endurance.

I could see that John Shapland was very shaken by this. Here we were at the start of a very tricky operation, and two very experienced soldiers had had the moral courage to come to him with some pretty bad news. He knew them both well, and trusted them completely, but where was he going to find a replacement commanding officer in the twenty-four hours before we started up Aradura, in which operation the Royal Welch would have an important part to play? There was some discussion; he thanked them both, swore the three of us to silence, and told us to get on with the job.

The Aradura climb started on a filthy day, with the rain bucketing down. The Royal Berkshires led, followed by the Royal Welch, with Brigade Headquarters, and finally the Durham Light Infantry. Conditions were about as bad as you can imagine as we tried to get up the hill. Sometimes we had to use both hands to make any progress at all. The Berkshires managed to get to their objective on the top of the spur, but the Royal Welch, toiling up after them, were caught in a well laid Japanese ambush, firing from above. They could barely use their weapons to fire back, and many were killed and wounded. John Shapland got a bullet in his neck – somehow it missed his spine – and we all landed back where we had started from in some disorder. John Shapland was forcibly evacuated; he was furious, because his blood had soaked his cigar case with his finest cigars in it.

With his departure I found myself in charge (I dare not use the word 'command') of 6 Brigade. We were in a mess. The Royal Berks were on their objective on the top of their ridge, but no one knew exactly where it was or where they were; the jungle was far too thick. The Royal Welch were collecting themselves on the spur below Brigade Headquarters, and the Durhams were somewhere halfway up the hill with the Burma Regiment. Communications were reasonable – at least we were in touch with each other – but it was now getting dark, and we had no idea of what the Japanese might be up to. I contacted Division and explained what was going on as best I could. They told me to hold on to all our positions for the night; I would get further orders in the morning. Luckily the Japanese left us in relative peace, and we were able to consolidate our positions.

Early next morning General John Grover talked to me on the phone. I was to go to the Royal Welch and tell their CO that he was relieved of his command; he was to leave the battalion immediately and report to Divisional Headquarters. I have never had to do a more distasteful job, particularly to someone who was a friend whom I liked and admired. He acknowledged the order, thanked me and left. His Second in Command took over the reorganisation of the battalion. Later that day Jack Stocker (late of the South Wales Borderers) arrived and took over command, which he held till the end of the campaign. Under him the battalion performed magnificently.

I was still without a Brigadier. I was told that one would arrive next day: no one knew who he would be – someone from outside the Division. In the meantime, 4 Brigade below us were having considerable trouble with the approaches at the bottom of the Aradura Spur, and were suffering serious casualties. To help them the mortars of the Royal Welch were firing in support from a position about 200 yards away from Brigade Headquarters.

There is a drill when using mortars in the jungle. Because of the mortars' high trajectory, the No. 1 of each team is responsible for ensuring that the barrel and path of the bomb are clear to shoot, and not obstructed by overhead branches. That afternoon during one particular shoot something went wrong: a bomb hit a branch some fifty feet up and exploded, with devastating effect on the crews. We all rushed down to give what help we could. Just at that moment our new Brigadier arrived, to witness a scene of disorganised carnage, with me, his so-called principal staff officer, busying myself with morphine syringes and field dressings amongst the wounded. It was not the best time for him to arrive, but the message that he was on the way had never reached us.

I need not have worried. Our new commander was a very tough, battle-experienced soldier. W.G. Smith (or Bill as he was known) was one of those many Australians who had joined the Indian Army at the end of the First World War. He had been commissioned in one of the Punjab regiments, but he had spent most of his service with irregular units such as the Tochi and South Waziristan Scouts. He had already won a DSO as a battalion commander in the Arakan, and he had a sixth sense about fighting the Japanese: he seemed to know what they were going to do before they did it. He was the ideal commander to serve under, except for two foibles: he had an ingrained dislike of Generals, and he hated any form of written orders.

I took him into our flea-ridden Command Post (it had lice as well, we found out later – the Japanese who originally built it had left behind two small, delayed-action presents for us), and briefed him on the strange situation that 6 Brigade was now in. But he knew this already, having been thoroughly briefed by Division en route to us, and immediately set about the task of getting things straight. He brought a touch of fresh air and professional expertise with him, and he had the knack of making you feel like a friend at the very first meeting.

It took three days to get the Brigade together and organised again, but great things had been going on elsewhere. Derek Horsford and his 4/1st Gurkhas in a series of brilliant night operations started the clearance of Naga Village, which was soon completely in our hands. The hills behind Kohima Ridge were cleared by 5 Brigade under Mike West. This meant that Aradura Spur was virtually outflanked, and on 30 May the Japanese withdrew their troops from it. This was the date that marked the end of the fighting at Kohima; from start to finish the battle had lasted sixty-four days. Years later John Grover told me that, in his experience, conditions were as bad as and sometimes worse than the battlefields of the Somme and Passchendaele, which he had experienced in the First World War.

Now the race was on to get through to Imphal. 2 Division with its armour was to go down the main road, and 7 Indian Division the Jessami track. The Japanese had plans for delaying all this, and one Captain Nishida was in charge of the rearguards down the Imphal road. The countryside was in his favour: the road ran alongside the steep mountains in and out of long spurs, which enclosed waterfalls and near-vertical streams, each with a small bridge or culvert, easily destroyed by a retreating enemy and equally easily covered by fire. We had some sixty miles of this to go before we reached the Imphal plain, and it was going to be a hard slog.

4 Brigade started off, with the Lancashire Fusiliers leading, and it was at almost the first of these delaying positions that their commander, Willy West, was killed. This was a small warning that, though the enemy might be short of food, ammunition and men, they were still full of fight. 5 Brigade then took over the lead, and then us. We were held up badly short of Mao Songsang at a place called Viswema, and it was here that I got involved in my first contretemps with Bill Smith. When operations were on he hated being disturbed by the wireless, and the appearance of generals anywhere near him drove him round the bend. He would vanish into the jungle! He and Robert Scott shared the same philosophy: when they were engaging the enemy they liked to be left on their own.

John Grover was very displeased when, for the third time, he visited us only to find that Bill Smith had vanished yet again. He icily remarked to me that the organisation of 6 Brigade headquarters left a lot to be desired, and that I had better put it right. I had to square up to Bill Smith on the subject. It was all very well, I said, for him to absent himself from the visits of High Command, but I didn't see why I should get the blame and face the flak that descended. To his great credit he apologised, and promised to do better, but I took the precaution of getting Sergeant Willie Mackenzie, our Brigade rear link operator, to stick to him like glue, and never let him out of his sight. That worked – up to a point. Bill Smith was a highly independent character: he hated being chained to a wireless set and operator, and was as slippery as an eel!

One day the Royal Berkshires were faced with a nasty little action at Viswema, just north of Mao Songsang, the highest part of the road. The wireless sets started crackling. The High Command was on us in a big way: Bill Slim himself, with John Grover in tow to see what was going on. We were on one spur with the Japanese on the next, and the Royal Berkshires trying to dislodge them. The mountainside was very steep, but somehow we had to get above and behind the Japanese. It was not easy, and we were well and truly held up.

Bill Slim seemed to know everyone in his army. He got hold of Leonard Tetley, commanding 99th Field Regiment (our gunners), and suggested that he called forward his battery of eight 3.7 inch mountain guns, deployed them on the ridge we were on, and shot up the Japanese over virtually open sights at about 3,000 yards range. Soon eight marvellous little guns were on the ridge, blattering happily away at the Japanese to excellent effect, but they were followed by a very angry senior officer, the Corps Commander Royal Artillery – 'Hair trigger' Stevens himself – who wished to know in no uncertain terms: 'What fucking fool ordered these guns forward without telling me?'

He had not noticed that Bill Slim was standing quietly with the rest of us. Bill quietly came up behind him, and said: 'I really am terribly sorry Brigadier, I am afraid it was me.'

With the help of the guns the Japanese positions collapsed, and the Berkshires were able to move forward. While this was going on, Bill Slim turned his attention on me. Somehow he knew that I had been with Ian Stewart in Malaya, and he started talking about how things had changed since then, particularly our position in the air, which made air supply possible: that in its turn had made us less dependent on the road, so that we could now get behind the Japanese and cut them off. Our old doctrine of 'fighting for the road from the road' was finished.

I must have been mad – or perhaps it was loyalty to all those years with Ian – for I had the temerity to reply: 'Sir, if the road does no longer matter, why are we being so pressed to open this road to Imphal?'

A wonderful grin spread across Bill Slim's face. 'Young officers should not argue with their Army commanders in the face of the enemy!' he said, and roared with laughter.

But we were still being pressed to get through to Imphal, for all sorts of strategic regions, and it was vital that we got there quickly. In fact we were through in a very few days more.

On 18 June we captured Mao Songsang, wreathed in drizzly mist, and on 19 June the Worcesters of 5 Brigade ejected the last properly organised Japanese rearguard position from Maram, ten miles or so down the road. General Myazaki's rearguard plans were now in tatters. Bravery was not enough; the Japanese 31st Division had been smashed, and columns of stragglers were all over the countryside, making for the Chindwin. Few succeeded.

6 Brigade took over for the last breakthrough. The countryside was more open now, and sometimes there were wide views and good fields of fire. Just after Maram we spied a Japanese column winding its way wearily across the other side of a valley. A battery of 25 pounders got into action on the roadside and shot them to pieces; they never had a hope. This was the pattern for the next three days. On the night of 21 June we had information that we might very well link up with IV Corps from Imphal, our leading tanks of 149 RAC and the Durham Light Infantry who were with them were warned, and sometime about 10.30 in the morning there they were, tanks of the 3rd Carabineers and an infantry battalion. The road was open. There were still occasional disorganised parties of Japanese on the flanks, but they were exterminated quite mercilessly, like rats in a trap. I don't remember taking any prisoners – but then I don't remember any of them wanting to surrender either. Even in the field hospital that we overran near Kanglatongbi, the patients had either been

killed by their friends or had killed themselves to escape the shame of being captured.

We spent about a month clearing up and making the road safe for the convoys that went pouring into Imphal with much-needed supplies, and then the whole Division was moved back up the road to the area of Milestone 82, not far from the Maram battlefield. Here we were to stay to the end of the year, reorganising on a mule-based system, and getting fit again, absorbing reinforcements to replace the many casualties we had suffered.

Some time at the end of September there was to be a presentation of decorations to the Division by Field Marshal Lord Wavell, now Viceroy, but once both Commander of 6 Brigade and Commander of the Division. We, 6 Brigade, were to provide the Guard of Honour, the very same battalions that had been part of the brigade when he had commanded it in Aldershot all those years back before the war. (The Durhams were particularly displeased; as they were the junior battalion they would be in the rear rank and have to do ordinary infantry drill!) The great day came. Archie Wavell arrived, the medal ribbons were pinned on their recipients' uniforms, and then Cameron Nicholson, our new General, suggested that perhaps the Field Marshal might like to say something to his old Division.

Archie Wavell could at times be the most taciturn of men. He was inherently shy, and it was clear that he was not prepared for grandiose speeches at this moment, but he accepted, and what he had to say astonished us all. It was like standing under a very cold shower. There were no heroics, no false praises, no great promises of victory: it was all quite short and very much to the point.

The war was won, he said. He couldn't say when, but both Germans and Japanese were heading for defeat. There was still hard fighting to come, and we would be in it. And when peace was declared and we got back home we would find a lot of things had changed – indeed we might think a lot of the things we thought we had been fighting for had gone for ever. Life would not be easy, and we would need all the training and discipline we had received in the Army to overcome the difficulties. He congratulated us on what we had achieved, but he said it was what he would have expected of his old Division – no more and no less. He wished us the best of luck.

And that was it; the great occasion was over. We went back to our tents and bashas in solemn mood. He had made us think a bit about the future. Up to then we had been living from day to day, hour to hour even. From time to time the chances of getting out of a particular place alive and with a whole skin had been all that mattered, but now there was a future to be faced, and no one knew what it held.

My own future was in the balance. John Grover, to whom I owed so much, had been replaced by Cameron Nicholson, a gunner and a very fine soldier. At the end of September he sent for me and told me that he was sending me home with a recommendation for the Staff College, chiefly on medical grounds. The malaria I had picked up in Belgaum was still coming back from time to time, though now we daily took mepachrine tablets, which suppressed the symptoms. Also, my left ear had taken the full force of the blast of some explosion – I cannot remember where or when – which had seriously damaged it and necessitated surgery. I was not considered fit for operational duties, and in any case I was now two years past my repatriation date.

So one day I packed my kit, said my farewells, and drove back down the road that it had taken us so long and cost so many lives to come up. It was almost worse than leaving Singapore. The Americans have an expression for it: it was a 'bug out'. Certainly I had been ordered out – I had papers to prove it – but was I as bad as all that? Could I not have stayed and carried on? But then suppose something had happened, if I had fallen down on the job through sickness and put people's lives at risk as a result. But the decision was out of my hands now. It was back all the way to Bombay, to a troopship and then to a home that I had not seen for eight years.

It is now more than fifty years since the battle, but the memories keep crowding back. I can still play the bagpipes (albeit not so well), and on Remembrance parades they sometimes ask me to play 'The Heroes of Kohima', which was written in 1944 by Bombardier Stewart of the 100th Anti Tank Regiment (Gordon Highlanders), then part of 2 Div. I first played it that same year at Milestone 82 with David Murray and Pipe Major Evan Macrae of the Camerons, very soon after it was first written. Its origins are very much older, maybe back to 1677, when it was called 'Bodaich na' Briogais'. Then it changed its name to 'People of the Glen', and some say it was played at Glencoe on 12 February 1692 to warn the Macdonalds of the terrible fate that awaited them. There is a tradition that the pipes of the 79th and 92nd Highlanders played the regiments out of Brussels to the battle of Quatre Bras in 1815, and therefore it may be questionable whether it is indeed an original composition! But those of us who fought there do not care for the pontifications of learned piping societies; it is our tune, and we cherish it.

For many years, I and others have wondered who composed what has become a famous and poignant epitaph:

> WHEN YOU GO HOME, TELL THEM OF US AND SAY
> FOR YOUR TOMORROW WE GAVE OUR TODAY

These words, or something very near to them, were composed in the

1914–18 war by John Maxwell Edmunds, a distinguished classical scholar and author. It was one of several epitaphs suggested by him for use in the British War Graves cemeteries in France.

It is reasonably certain that Edmunds drew inspiration from the ancient Greek historian and poet, Simonides of Ceos, who wrote the Epitaph for the memorial the Greeks raised at Thermopylae where, in 480BC, in a desperate stand to the last man, a small Spartan force under Leonidas held the pass against a vast Persian army:

> GO TELL THE SPARTANS, THOU WHO PASSETH BY
> THAT HERE, OBEDIENT TO THEIR LAWS, WE LIE

After the battle, when the Divisional Memorial was being planned, Major John Etty-Leal, then GS02 of the Division, remembered Edmund's lines, and with minor alterations suggested them to Major General John Grover as suitable for the great Memorial Stone presented by the Nagas to the Second Division.

And the Japanese, too, have their own adaptation of Simonides' words:

> GO TELL OUR PEOPLE, YOU WHO READ
> WE TOOK THEIR ORDERS AND ARE DEAD

As a member of the Burma Star Association I am called to say it at parades, meetings, dinners and on the other occasions when we who served out there meet. I wonder what those whom we left behind would think of the 'tomorrow' that they never saw. Would they be disillusioned? And does anyone know or care about them anyway? As a member of a war pensions committee, I sometimes wonder.

There remains the connection between Kohima and Thermopylae, and Leonidas and his Spartans. Both were decisive battles: not great ones in the context of the wars they were part of, but decisive none the less, and the similarity between the opening lines 'Go tell the Spartans' and 'When you go home' after so many thousands of years is striking indeed.*

Years later, in 1964, I was commanding a brigade based on Liverpool and Lancashire. One of my battalions was training near Dundee at the camp called Barry/Buddon. I had been up there for some days, and was now going back to the rest of the brigade via Liverpool. It was a complicated journey from Dundee, with a change at Perth and another at Carstairs for

---

* I am indebted to Colonel Rex King-Clark MC, late the Manchester Regiment for permission to quote from his book *The Narrative of the 2nd Battalion The Manchester Regiment – The Battle for Kohima, 1944*

Wigan, where I would be picked up. I was in uniform – kilt and all – and at Perth found myself in a first class carriage with two very nice ladies from the USA, of what I would call the 'blue rinse' age. They were charming, and delighted to share their carriage with a kilted 'general'. (Brigadiers rank as generals in the US Army – they did once in ours.) We were getting on well, when the compartment door opened and a ticket inspector came in, complete with his braided cap. He forgot all about his duties, seized my hand, shook it warmly, and sat down on the seat opposite.

'Weel Davie, hulloa, hoos yersel?' he said with a broad grin.

It was Willie Mackenzie, once Sergeant, Royal Corps of Signals, rear Link Operator 6 Infantry Brigade: the man whom I had put in charge of Brigadier Bill Smith to see that he could not escape into the jungle when generals were around. All question of ticket inspecting was forgotten, and we had a long talk about old friends and strange places. Eventually we arrived at Stirling, where he was based and he excused himself: he had to get off, his shift was over.

My American friends were nonplussed. What on earth was a common-or-garden ticket inspector doing, apparently on Christian name terms with a general, and how did we know each other so well? I tried to explain that it was during the war, at a place called Kohima – amongst others.

'Say, General,' said one, 'where in the hell is Kohima? Some battle or something?'

And something clammed me up: I just couldn't tell them. I don't think they would have understood; they lived in a different world. And in any case there was not time – I had to get out at Carstairs.

I have met the Japanese, too: the men of 31 Division and 58 Regiment who were our deadly foes and whom we exterminated like dangerous animals. I have had them in my house, and have been with them at York when they have come to pay their respects to the Divisional Memorial in the Minster grounds. It is a replica of the Naga Stone at Kohima. It is so hard to think of these men, impeccably dressed in smart suits, as the savage enemy they once were, and their emotion is quite genuine when they lay their wreaths of chrysanthemums on our Memorial.

I asked one of them why they held our Memorial in such esteem. He answered: 'Because, Brigadier, it is part of our own history too now. We have nothing in Japan to remind us of our friends and comrades who lie with yours in Burma. It is our privilege to remember them here.'

And I wonder what the young soldiers of today's Second Division, who act as escorts to these parties, think of the old men of two such different races standing in silence together before the replica of a stone sited half the world away. What could they have in common? Something written by a British seamaster who lost his ship and most of his crew in the Northwest Passage over 200 years ago might help them to understand:

We who survive, perchance will end our days
In some employment, meriting no praise –
They have outlived that fear, and their brave ends,
Will ever be an honour to their friends.

NOTES

1   In 1937 General Mutagachi was the Regimental Commander at Shanghai, whose troops fired the first shots against the Chinese troops guarding the Marco Polo Bridge. This gave the Japanese the excuse for starting what they called the China Incident, leading to war in China and Manchuria.

2   Harry Seaman, *The Battle at Sangshak: Burma, March 1944* (London: Leo Cooper, 1989).

3   What follows is not the story of the battle, but a disjointed account of my experiences over the next two months: a tale of people and the way they behaved, as seen by a small cog in a complicated chain – me! And if my memory has played me false, as it must do after so many years, then I apologise to those whom I may have ill described, or put in the wrong place, at the wrong time and in the wrong context.

CHAPTER 9
Round the world

The *Stratheden* brought me home up the Mersey on a bleak foggy day in October 1944. I had the unenviable job of Baggage Officer, and spent a great deal of time down the holds with the stevedores. They were a great bunch, but the way they hurled cases and goods about made me apprehensive for the contents. Luckily I knew that mine had nothing breakable inside!

The next morning we were put on our trains. I was due to go to London, but I had first to get to Edinburgh for documentation. This took place at Redford Barracks, which I had last seen in 1935. The documentation was very thorough and very quick: I was issued with ration cards, clothing coupons, an identity card and a warrant to London. A train left Waverley Station at 9 pm, and I was sent down in transport with my baggage, a suitcase, my bedding roll and two tin uniform cases. I just had time to ring my mother to say I was on my way (she had no idea I was in the country), before finding a seat in a very crowded train, blacked out with only dim blue lights in the compartments. It was an uncomfortable journey.

My mother had bought 28 Sydney Street, Chelsea, in 1937. I had never seen it before, but it was nice to be back with the family furniture and pictures after eight years. It had survived the bombing, though houses on either side and across the street had been knocked down, and one or two of the doors in the house were so damaged by blast that they would not shut properly. Apart from my mother, the other residents were Paula (my mother's cook/housemaid) and George the cat. My father was still serving abroad, in Abyssinia. My sister had joined the Order of the Sacred Heart, and was a novice at Stamford Hall, near Rugby, where the Order had moved with their school, normally based at Roehampton. I found it all rather strange.

I had some six weeks' leave due to me, but first I had to report to the doctors at Millbank, as my left ear was in a sad state. During the Kohima engagement blast had severely damaged it, and some sort of infection had set in. The experts looked at it and sent me to the military hospital at Shenley to have it fixed. For a very minor operation it was a most unpleasant experience. First they froze my nose by making me stand on my head while they dripped anaesthetic down it. They then blindfolded me so that I could not see what was happening, and – as far as I could feel – proceeded to gouge bits out of my skull with a chisel, using my nose as a point of entry. When they were satisfied that they had removed enough bits and pieces, they stuffed an enormous length of what felt like greasy 'four by two' (the stuff we used to use to clean rifle barrels with) up my nose and into whatever cavity they had excavated. I was then confined to bed for four days, almost unable to breathe, and forbidden to move in case I dislodged their handiwork. It was extremely boring, and most uncomfortable. Eventually they came and removed their horrid greasy dressing and I was allowed out of bed, and finally sent home. But they had not quite finished with me.

I was given a 'do it yourself' nose clearance kit, which I had to use every day for months afterwards. It consisted of a rubber tube with a bulb in the middle, which acted as a pump. One end went up my nose; the other was put in a jar, in which was a special solution (I had pills, which dissolved into the correct mixture when added to water). I had to inject this up my nose under pressure, by pressing the bulb. The liquid washed out the infected passages, and somehow ended up in the back of my throat: from there it was ejected into a nearby basin. I had to do this for over a year, to the horror of those who sometimes had to share rooms or tents with me.

It was no wonder that my mother once said to a friend who had come to see me: 'You may be a bit surprised when you see David: he looks bright green, his nerves are shot to ribbons, and he drinks like a fish!'

The 'green' bit was true enough – the result of mepachrine, which we still had to take – and she was not all that far off the mark with the rest of the description.

By the time they had removed the yards of 'four by two' out of my nose, my posting to the Staff College, Camberley, had come through. In order to keep me gainfully employed they attached me to a reserve Divisional Headquarters, which was in Broadwater Down, Tunbridge Wells, almost opposite my grandmother's house. There were four others awaiting the course, amongst whom was Marcus Linton, an enormous Horse Gunner of great distinction. Like all Horse Gunners, he had a wide circle of influential friends. He knew all the ins and outs of the Staff College, and assured me that the best part of the course was situated at Minley Manor. He had made sure he would be sent there, and advised me to get myself similarly organised. The trouble was that, coming from the Far East, I knew no one of influence who could arrange these interesting postings.

In the first week of January a gaggle of eager students gathered at Waterloo Station to travel down to Camberley. It was rather like going to school again: there were all sorts of friendly faces I had not seen for years, all destined for the same course. Most of them were contemporaries of mine from Sandhurst, plus one or two from the Far East. It was just like the old days: as we came off the platform we walked into the arms (or rather onto the list) of a Guards sergeant major, who detailed us off to the waiting troop-carrying trucks. To my surprise – and Marcus Linton's fury – I found myself bound for Minley, while he was sent to Camberley. Fate certainly moves in a mysterious way.

Minley was a special place. It was built by a rich shipping family in the 1850s, just off the A30, about five miles out of Camberley towards Hartley Wintney. It had beautiful grounds and gardens, and a really lovely cricket ground. There were some forty students there, plus directing staff under John Sleeman of the Tank Corps, who had been one of my instructors at the Tank School at Ahmednagar. The DS were a delightful bunch: all very experienced, but much of an age with the rest of us. We were divided into syndicates of eight, of mixed arms of the service. Every six weeks we were changed over, rather as in a game of musical chairs, so that in the six-month course we each worked with a whole lot of different people. For special lectures and demonstrations we were bussed down to Camberley and the Main Staff College building to join the rest of the course, but somehow we at Minley thought of ourselves as something rather special – as indeed we were. We preserved a country house rather than a military atmosphere, discipline was much more informal, and like other small detachments we developed an *esprit de corps* of our own.

There was virtually no gap between the instructors (or DS) and their students. We had all seen action in various parts of the world, at different times of the war, and there was a great deal of experience around from clandestine operations in occupied territories, the jungle, the desert, combined operations and airborne landings. This made our syndicate discussions worthwhile and fun.

There was a great deal of paperwork. Appreciations, operation orders, convoy planning, papers on political matters – they kept our noses well down to the grindstone. As fast as you completed one exercise, another appeared in your pigeon-hole, and a third was returned to you covered with comments from your DS, in red ink, on all the various mistakes and omissions that he had found. Woe betide any student whose efforts reached the Commandant or Assistant Commandant, who penned their remarks in green. Some of the exercises were deliberately set to test your reaction to pressure, in that the time allowed was kept to a minimum, so that you could be led into error by taking short cuts and compounding mistakes.

The week's last lecture usually ended on Saturday mornings at noon, and there was a rush to get the train to London, where we all seemed to meet up at the same shows and night-clubs, returning late on Sunday evening far from refreshed by the weekend's activities. The managers of the restaurants and clubs that we invaded must have been heartily sick of us, but they took it in good part.

Despite all these activities, which were supposed to further my military career, I somehow managed to get myself engaged, and a week after the end of the course married Sylvia.

I was due to be posted back to Burma to rejoin Second Division – General Cameron Nicholson, the GOC, had specifically asked for me – but in July 1945 the war was rapidly coming to its end, and the Division had been withdrawn to India to reform and retrain. Nevertheless, on 12 August I found myself on a bus travelling to Lyneham to catch an aircraft to Colombo. It was a York, with bucket seats on the side of the fuselage, sacks of mail and stores in the middle, lukewarm coffee out of a large thermos, and sandwiches out of cardboard boxes. We stopped at Malta (for fuel), Alexandria (for a night in a tent), Shaibah and Karachi (another tent), and made Colombo in four days. They sent me up to Kandy, where HMS *Wimbledon* was sited.

This was Lord Louis Mountbatten's headquarters. It was a beautiful place, surrounded by lovely gardens and equally lovely Wrens, exceedingly smart officers, and a good selection of flagstaffs flying the emblems of his multifarious command. I am not sure what its official title was, but the hardened veterans of 14th Army declared that it was a centre of 'rackets and balls' – hence the name Wimbledon. His staff were known generally as 'The Dickie Birds'. Very few had had a sniff of the jungle. And there was the natural antipathy of the ordinary soldiers towards these newcomers.

It is strange how these prejudices last down the ages: Shakespeare's brilliant characterisation of a Staff Officer in *Henry IV* speaks volumes:

> . . . neat and trimly dressed
> Fresh as a bridegroom; and his chin new reaped
> Shewed like a stubble land at harvest home
> He was perfumed like a milliner
> And twixt his finger and his thumb he held
> A pouncet box, which ever and anon
> He gave his nose and took't asway again.

I received a bit of backblast from my father when I first went to Minley, and he remarked in a letter that in his day regimental officers did not go to the Staff College in the middle of a war. He was kind enough to add that I had earned my place.

After a week doing nothing at Kandy, I was posted to Allied Forces Western Pacific as a Lieutenant Colonel, to report to their headquarters in Manila in the Philippines. What I was to do there was not specified, but I gathered it might be something to do with the occupation of Japan. To get there meant a trip first to Australia, then round the edge of the Pacific to Leyte and somehow to Manila. I got to Australia in a DC4 Skymaster, with one day at Perth, where my grandfather had been Commandant of the West Australian Militia for three years. My father had unwisely given me a few addresses, and I was taken in tow and treated to some marvellous hospitality by some very old family friends.

In Sydney I went 'out of the frying pan into the fire', as the late commander of 6 Brigade, Bill Smith, had a house there. He and his wife could not have been kinder, but their hospitality was misguided as I had a long onward flight ahead of me in a Dakota, part of the logistic force supplying the British Pacific Fleet. There were no seats – just mailbags and assorted spare parts. We also had as passengers two Royal Navy captains, whose habit it was to pace up and down their quarterdecks. They saw no reason why they should not take similar exercise in our crowded Dakota, and so up and down the plane they walked. After some twenty minutes the cockpit door opened, and a furious RAF aircraft commander burst in on us. He had been having problems getting the trim of his machine right: one minute she was nose heavy, the next tail heavy, and he could not understand why. When he realised what was happening, he admonished two very senior officers in language that they had not had directed at them for many a year. They shamefacedly sat down on their mailsacks, and did not stir from them again.

The first day took us to Townsville on the east coast of Australia, about 500 miles north of Brisbane. We had to rise early the next morning to get over New Guinea and the Owen Stanley range before it became too hot and flying conditions near impossible. We refuelled at Lae and spent the night at Manus. The third night was spent with the US Navy on Peleliu, and we reached Leyte on the evening of the fourth day. Here I left the machine, which was due to complete its journey to Hong Kong. The US Navy would take me to Manila in a Catalina. It was an incredible journey.

We had barely touched down in Manila when I was seized by an Australian brigadier, one Hugh Wrigley, like so many of his compatriots once of the Indian Army, but with the AIF during World War II. He asked me what my orders were, and I showed him what little I had. As the senior Commonwealth officer he suggested that I disregard them (he could square it with the US Army staffs) and join his very scratch organisation, which existed under the synonym of RAPWI. This stood for the Recovery of Allied Prisoners of War and Internees. He and a small staff were based on the 29th Replacement Group of the US Army, situated at a camp about twenty miles south of Manila. You did not argue with people like Hugh Wrigley, and soon my kit was in the back of his jeep and we were on our way.

*

The 29th Replacement Depot (or 'Repple Depple' in GI language) was an enormous tented camp. Offices, cookhouse, messes and stores were quonset huts[1] with concrete floors, and there were a few buildings left over from the Philippine village that had once occupied the spot. The US Engineers who built the place had also constructed a baseball field and a huge amphitheatre, where cinema shows and live entertainment were put on, usually every night. It had been intended as a base depot for all arms, and still operated as such, but a large area of the camp was allocated for the reception of prisoners of war and internees, gathered up from a very large area: China, Manchuria, Korea, Japan, Formosa, Taiwan and some of the newly conquered Pacific islands. Here they were received, fed like fighting cocks, medically inspected, kitted out and – as far as possible – prepared to be sent home. There were no problems for the Americans – they all wanted to go back to the USA – and the Canadians likewise, but the Brits . . .

During the Malayan and Burma campaigns many families were evacuated to Australia and New Zealand, some from Hong Kong went to Canada, and some families stayed in India. On arrival I found myself immersed in files from the War Office and Home Office, giving the options for reuniting families. It was harder than trying to solve the most difficult cryptic crossword. The Japanese had deliberately withheld mails from POWs, so that many did not know where their families were. This entailed a great deal of signal traffic to find out, and so instead of simply sending all the Brits back to the UK *en bloc*, we found that we were running a sort of Thomas Cook tourist and repatriation service to destinations all over the world, but with a shortage of shipping and aircraft to transport our clients.

Then there were the Dutch, all from their colonial army in the Far East. In 1945 Indonesia was a hot spot of rival governments and revolution, whose inhabitants did not want their pre-war masters back. In the meantime British Indian divisions were holding the ring in a nasty little war in Java and Sumatra. The Dutch Government wished to repatriate its POWs to Indonesia, but this policy did not endear it to the Americans, who posed every possible delay and obstruction in providing shipping for them, and the Dutch had little enough of their own to use. It was a diplomatic nightmare.

Little by little Hugh Wrigley assembled a small Commonwealth staff. Many of them had been prisoners of war themselves. There was a flight lieutenant with a Military Cross, gained for a remarkable escape from a camp. He subsequently wrote a book about it called *The Wooden Horse*, which was made into a most successful film. His name was Eric Williams, and he proved a tower of strength in the organisation.

We acted as a sort of sieve for the Commonwealth, and did a bit of intelligence gathering as well. Particularly in Japan many POWs were split up into relatively small camps, augmenting the labour force in tin

134

and coal mines, and it was important that the American occupation forces be told of their location, as communications had been severely damaged by US action in the last months of the war. We started a card index of everyone who passed through our hands. This entailed slow and detailed work, but it eventually proved very valuable for checking the whereabouts of individuals.

The most urgent problem were the sick, as they were taken straight to hospitals in the Manila area, and did not initially pass through our system. Some of them were in a very bad state: a few died, and many were quite unfit to travel. Somehow we had to find out who they were, where they were from, and what we could do for them. Many owed their lives to the expert and devoted care of the US Army Medical Corps, who did everything and more to help, and sometimes it was difficult to do one's job without appearing to be a nuisance. One lesson I learnt very quickly was that it was almost a criminal offence to address a member of the US Nurse Corps as 'Sister', as one would with our own nurses. That was a term of familiarity: you addressed her as 'Lootenant', Captain', 'Major' or sometimes even 'Colonel' – or else!

Slowly but surely the ships came. Two of our aircraft carriers – *Implacable* and *Indomitable* – took a great many off our hands, Admiral Sir Bruce Fraser came in his battleship, and Lady Louis Mountbatten spent two days visiting the sick in hospitals. She was marvellous with them, and morale was sky high after her visit.

Little by little the POWs realised that they really were on their way home: it was just a matter of waiting their turn till a ship came in heading in the right direction.

Many old friends from Malaya passed through my hands, including friends from the Australian 8th Division, and Corporal 'Bertie' King of my own regiment and my old carrier platoon. I was able to tell him of the DCM that he had won, and from somewhere we got a bit of ribbon and sewed it on his shirt. He was delighted – as were we all; we got Hugh Wrigley as our senior officer to pin it on him in a little ceremony. And then there was Christopher Man of the Middlesex: while in transit from Hong Kong to Japan in an unmarked freighter, he had been torpedoed by an American submarine in the China Sea, and had a lengthy swim before being rescued. He was one of my oldest friends! There were many others.

By mid-November our job was almost done. There were still a few sick to be evacuated, but a Canadian hospital ship, the *Letitia*, was due in to take the last of the sick off, and I and my party were ordered back with them. We had an uneventful voyage to Seattle and Vancouver, where we were put on a train for Montreal. Strange to relate, the captain of *Letitia* had carried my father and the 91st from India to the UK in 1914 as First Officer of their troopship.

Since our party included numbers of sick, we had a Royal Navy doctor and two RN nurses with us, which was very lucky. Forty-eight hours after leaving Vancouver we ran into some severe weather, and early one morning ran at near full speed into the back of a train that was ahead of us. It was south of a place called Lake Nipigon, and very cold. Visibility was very poor, the train ahead of us had had some sort of engine failure (it was steam in those days), and though the rear guard had protected his train with flares and detonators, we could not stop on the icy line.

The first thing I knew was finding myself – along with fellow passengers in the sleeping car – on the centre floor, having been ejected from my bunk while still half asleep. The car conductor came along and said there was nothing to worry about: he 'guessed the Engineer had been a bit hard on the brakes'. I was not so sure. Our car was at the rear of a long train; looking out of the window I could see only thick fog, but from way ahead I could hear the sound of escaping steam. I rooted out our naval doctor and his two nurses to come forward and check our casualties in their two cars, and went myself to the front end of the train, where I found that the leading car had been derailed. It was still upright, but was skewed across the track. The goods van ahead had taken the brunt of the collision, and was reduced to matchwood, and our own engine was lying, with its tender on its side, some twenty yards off the track in very deep snow.

We had hit the preceding train fairly and squarely on its parlour car – the rear coach – and it had telescoped into the next two cars. As it was early in the morning, except for the rear guard the parlour car was empty of passengers, but there were some very badly injured in the next three cars. This was a job for our medical team, who had two full panniers of kit with them, and for the able-bodied members of my small unit. With the help of the train staff we cleared two coaches of the front train and moved the casualties into them. Some were fatally injured and past help; we had to make a temporary mortuary in some of the compartments to isolate them from the other wounded.

One problem was that as our own engine was on its side, off the rails, we had no heat on our own train, and soon it became bitterly cold. It was some six hours before any effective help could be got to us. A new engine was coupled onto the rear of our train; it drew us backwards from the mess, and pumped some heat back into the carriages.

Along with the relief party a Canadian medical team had arrived, and they took over the care of the injured from us. They – and the train crews – were most efficient, but admitted that without our presence on the spot with our medical team the casualties could have been very much higher. Even so, the toll of dead and injured was bad enough. Some of the injuries were horrific: telescoped coaches, large wheels and steel frames can do dreadful things to the human body.

Thirty-six hours later we reached Montreal, and I was detailed to fly home by BOAC (as it was called in those days). The aircraft was a converted Liberator Bomber: it was rather noisy, and not exactly the height of luxury, but very comfortable compared with the flights on my outward trip. We were supposed to land at an airport near London, but fog intervened and I found myself at Prestwick. I just had time to ring home – to the surprise of my mother and Sylvia, who knew that I was on the way, but had no idea of the day or time – and caught a Dakota that was making for Blackbushe, the airfield opposite Minley Manor. There I cadged a lift on a coach going to London.

I had taken rather longer than Jules Verne's eighty days to get round the world, but I had met many people and seen many places that I would never have thought possible – and someone had paid me to do it!

It took about three weeks to clear up the documentation with the War Office. There were all sorts of reports to be written, and records to be handed over. As a unit we had been formed completely from scratch, and I had to invent an 'establishment' showing ranks and duties, which had to pass the scrutiny of the Admiralty and Air Ministry so that my team could be given the pay and allowances due to them. Some, like myself, had been posted from India, where we were borne on the books of GHQ Delhi; others came from the British Pacific Fleet, and still others from Australia. All this had to be ironed out, but eventually I found myself in a cellar in the bowels of the War Office, presenting my 'establishment' for approval before a stern, humourless, but very efficient civil servant, who ranked as a 'Principal' (a 'High Heid Yin'), whose word was indeed law. Luckily his assistant was a Brigadier, Gordon Maclean, from my own regiment, who had been one of my father's subalterns at Ypres long ago, so all went well.

By the end of January 1946 everything was squared up, all documents were handed over, and I was technically out of a job – but not for long. We had a new Colonel of the Regiment, Gordon MacMillan, one of our most distinguished soldiers, and working (I think) as Assistant Adjutant General in the War Office. I had served only briefly with him at Tidworth when I first joined, but I was to see a lot of him in the next fifteen years. He and his wife Marion had a house in London, and one evening Sylvia and I were bidden to attend for drinks. I suspected that the evening was not going to be entirely a social affair, and it turned out that I was right.

As our 1st Battalion had returned from Italy at the end of the war, the 91st had been posted to the 6th Air Landing Brigade, and were in Palestine. Their second in command, Sandy Bardwell, was due to take the next Staff College course, and I was to replace him. I had to be out there by mid-March. That was in just one month's time, and it would take ten days to get there. On 2 March I got my marching orders by telegram: I was to proceed by Medloc (the acronym for Mediterranean Lines of Communication), with 112 lb of baggage!

On a damp and dismal Sunday Sylvia and I said goodbye in gloomy old Victoria Station, and I set forth for Brighton and then Newhaven, where I arrived in time for supper. We embarked at midnight, wearing life-jackets in case of mines! At dawn we disembarked at Dieppe, and were taken to a tented transit camp a couple of miles from the town. We would have two nights to wait before our train left. Luckily there was an excellent officers' club in the town, where the food was of a somewhat higher standard than the camp could provide, and extremely cheap. This helped to pass the time. There was nothing else to do; I had no camp duties, and – as I was travelling as an individual – no soldiers to look after.

Two afternoons later we were assembled at the station and boarded our troop train for Toulon, where we were to catch a ship to Port Said. At that time the French railways had barely recovered from the war, and we took a very roundabout route, way down to the Pyrenees and then along the south coast. From time to time we stopped at watering points, and meals were dished out on the platform by Army Catering Corps cooks, rather in the way we used to do it on troop trains in India. Considering the damage the French railway system had suffered, the journey was efficiently organised, but six to a compartment for two nights was a bit trying for me, a non-smoker, surrounded by a permanent fog of tobacco, particularly the very acrid smell of the Gitanes that one of our party puffed away at with evident enjoyment. After forty-eight hours we arrived at our destination, and into another transit camp near Hyères. Luckily it was for only one night.

Toulon harbour was a mess. The wrecks of the scuttled French warships were still visible, awaiting clearance, and it was a sad place in 1946. Our troopship was specially converted for the run from Toulon to Port Said, and lacked any sort of comfort – after all, we were only going to be aboard for five days. The dining saloon consisted of long tables with plastic tops, and was a self-service affair. The food was good, but there was no bar: trooping had gone 'dry'! We had managed to smuggle some French refreshment on board, which we were able to consume in our cabins.

Many of the passengers were members of the Jewish Brigade, discharged after their service in Italy, and they were an interesting bunch to talk to. For the first time I realised that they did not have much time for the British. They weren't actually anti-British, but they felt that we had let them down by reneging on political promises. I had never served in the Middle East before, and was very ignorant of the history of that part of the world. Talking to those Jews, still in British uniform, was an eye opener. For the first time I realised that service in Palestine was going to be a bit tricky.

When we arrived at Port Said the ship was invaded by staff officers of all types, eager to set us on our various ways. I was called on the ship's tannoy to report to a particular cabin, and when I entered I was confronted by a young Lieutenant Colonel, immaculately dressed, with a GHQ brassard on his arm, and with several important-looking files on his desk. He invited me to take a chair, and explained he was from the Military Secretary's Department; since I was Staff College trained, he was interested in my particulars. He asked to see my posting orders, and his face screwed up with distaste.

'Palestine?' he said; 'Regimental duty? You will be wasting your time. There are a number of Grade 1 jobs available, which I can fit you into; these orders are easily changed. Now, where would you really like to go?'

I was astonished. I realised I was in the presence of what the 8th Army called 'The Gabardine Swine'. I had heard of them, but for the first time in my life I was face to face with one of the breed. I explained that I had direct orders from the Colonel of my Regiment to get post haste to the 91st, that my predecessor was at this minute waiting in the transit camp at Port Said for this same ship to take him home to Camberley, and that in no way would I have my orders changed.

I don't think for one minute that he understood. His home in the Army was bounded by the Groppis restaurant and the hotels and bars of Cairo, such as the Mena House, and the myriad offices of Grey Pillars, where all the best staff officers and generals gathered. If he had ever been a regimental soldier he had long forgotten about it. For the first time in my career I understood why my father and his contemporaries loathed and despised the Staff.

We were hustled off the ship and transferred to the other side of the canal to yet another tented camp, where I ran straight into Sandy Bardwell, whom I was relieving. We repaired to one of Port Said's excellent French restaurants for a substantial meal. Sandy was my oldest friend and contemporary in the Regiment; he had been best man at my wedding, and our families were great friends. (He was to disappear with Jean, his wife of just two days, when the *Star Tiger* vanished somewhere in the Bermuda Triangle eighteen months later.) Sandy gave me the low-down on what I was going to meet when I got to the 91st. We got back across the canal to our camp and into our sand-filled tents; next day he was on the ship, and I was on a train to Kantara, where I had to change for Palestine.

Both times I had been through the Suez Canal were at night, and I had never had a chance of seeing it by day. The railway ran right alongside the canal. On the left was the canal, and on the right the desert, with the road from Port Said to Ismailia, the occasional field and village and not much else, but it was evening, and there was the most wonderful sunset. From time to time we passed a ship, and there were others tied up alongside in the passing bays. Sitting in a comfortable train with a cold drink was certainly the way to see life.

We reached Kantara, with its swing bridge, as dusk fell, and I had to catch the chain ferry to the north bank to get on the train for Palestine. We clanked across slowly, and got to a rather aged station with little to recommend it: a flyblown waiting room, a dirty, smelly lavatory, and no bar. I had about an hour to wait until the train came in from Cairo. It was headed by an engine that was vaguely familiar. She was a Stanier 2-8-0, the cousin of Sir William Stanier's Black Five, but fitted with a cowcatcher and headlight: hence my failure to recognise her at first sight. The carriages were not much to shout about. Sand had seeped in through cracks in the window mountings, and the seats were encrusted with grains of it. But I made myself tolerably comfortable, hoping to get to Nathanya on time the next morning; we were due to arrive at 7.30 am.

We crawled across Sinai at a leisurely pace and I managed to get a mug of tea at Rehovot, before reaching Nathanya (on time) to be met by my commanding officer, 'The Squire' himself, otherwise known as Lieutenant Colonel R.H. Lumley Webb, one of the legendary characters of the regiment. I had known him since I was a boy and he a young subaltern. He was the epitome of an Edwardian gentleman: a great soldier, good at games, a great shot, and very knowledgeable about game birds. He had a tremendous sense of humour and a magnetic personality. He won his Military Cross in 1940 with Lorne Campbell in an epic march behind the German lines that saved the best part of two companies of our 8th Battalion from captivity, and had been severely wounded in North Africa with the 8th Battalion Argylls. He had no time for political intrigue, and distrusted the press: sadly that was to lead to his downfall later that year in Jerusalem. He had little time for either Jews or Arabs – but then neither had the rest of us, for that matter.

It was four years since I had last served with my regiment; a great deal had happened since then, and a great deal had changed. It was marvellous to be back, but I very soon realised that in some ways I was the odd man out. The 91st in 1946 was a mixture of three battalions. It was composed of reinforcements and drafts from all sorts of other units: mostly the 7th Battalion, who had served with the 51st Division and had ended up in Germany, having fought their way there from Normandy; the 8th Battalion, who had served in Italy after North Africa with the 1st Army; and the 91st itself. From officers to Jocks it was a mixture of all the types that made the regiment, but most of the senior NCOs were originally from the 91st. There was no one like myself who had seen their war in the Far East, and therefore I was looked on as something of an outsider.

There was another factor at work. Except for a few senior NCOs, all the rest had joined during the war. Fighting Germans and Japanese was one thing, but keeping a tottering empire together was something else. They had not joined to police the Palestine Mandate – whatever a mandate was – and they had no particular quarrel with either Arabs or Jews. The one thing everyone had was a release or group number, and when it came up they were out of the service. There was an expression – 'group happy' – which applied to those whose number and date of release were just round the corner. People like myself had no such release number – the Service was our career – but we were in the minority.

We were a young, tough and very experienced battalion, part of the 6th Air Landing Brigade, where we had replaced the 4th Devons, the other two Battalions being the Royal Ulster Rifles and the Oxfordshire and Buckinghamshire Light Infantry (of Pegasus Bridge fame). Initially we did not get on with them, having refused to wear the red beret of the airborne troops; we stuck to our Balmorals. But they accepted us, and we became great friends.

But it did take them a bit of time to accept me. Except for some of the senior NCOs no one had ever seen me before, let alone heard of me, or even of Bill Slim's 14th Army. Take the company commanders, for example. Muir Moreton had come from the 7th, the Desert, North Africa, Sicily and France; Dougie Graham Campbell from the 8th, the 1st Army, and then badly wounded and a prisoner; John Graham, my cousin, from the re-formed 93rd, John Tweedie's great battalion; and John Penman from the 6th, also a prisoner. Then there was a young captain called Colin Mitchell, also from the 8th; Angus Stroyan, our Mortar Officer, from the Black Watch; and Hector Macneal, ex 8th and heir to considerable estates in Kintyre, who did not care two hoots for anyone and became a lifelong friend. It was a very mixed bag that I had walked into.

The senior warrant officers and NCOs were much more homogeneous. Led by the Regimental Sergeant Major, Peter McPhillips, who had a DCM and Bar, and the two brothers Logie, they formed the hard core of the unit, and we had some superb material in the ranks, far above the standard of what I remembered of the pre-war regular army. The problem was that everyone was looking over the shoulders to the great day when they would be released; why were they wasting their time being shot at by Jews and Arabs, and being blackguarded by the American press as 'colonialists' repressing the 'peace loving' Jews, who were trying to escape to Palestine from the concentration camps of Europe?

The Americans had a point. One of the most distasteful duties I have ever had to perform was lining a beach and preventing illegal immigrants from Europe landing from the clapped-out, overloaded and stinking ships in which they had sailed from Italian and other ports. The Royal Navy blocked them by sea, we prevented them from landing, and they were somehow escorted to camps in Cyprus. This was not a job designed to raise our morale, but it had to be done. No wonder the Israelis do not like us. It was all very well for the US State Department to make statements requiring the British Government to take 100,000 immigrants from the concentration camps and resettle them in Palestine, when they themselves had closed the doors of the USA to immigration. And where were we to put the 100,000? Presumably into Arab properties and lands, which we ourselves would somehow have had to clear. If ever there was a political game of Pig in the Middle, we were in it, and it had been going on for years – ever since the First World War.

The Arabs, with Syria, Egypt and Jordan, outnumbered the Jews in men and weapons, but the Jews had not been idle. By 1946 they had built up illicit forces throughout their territory, with the initial object of defending their homes. But some groups, such as the Stern Gang and the Irgun Zvai Leumi, were organised with different objectives in mind. They were set on ejecting the British by force, political assassination and the destruction of bases and communications. The Haganah and Palmach were much more like our Territorial Army, based on farms and settlements; initially they were purely defensive, and did not cooperate with Stern or IZL. But they were something to be reckoned with, and all were ready to receive recruits from the influx of refugees from central Europe. Outwardly they were farmers, engineers and ordinary citizens. Their weapons, mostly small arms and explosives in 1946, were skilfully concealed in underground bunkers specially built into and around their farm buildings and settlements. It was a tricky problem. We – the soldiers – were gradually losing our best-trained men back to civilian life, while the Jews slowly, surely and very quietly were increasing their numbers and efficiency.

And in the middle of all this were the 1st Argylls: young, tough, individually well trained and experienced for battle, but not for this kind of surreptitious conflict. Every month, releases took away our experienced NCOs and men and replaced them with drafts of the young, called up to do their National Service only to find themselves in a strange land, fighting for a cause that they knew little about and wanted no part of. Such was the common lot of the Army, particularly in Palestine in those years.

In November 1945 the Jews struck, attacking the Cairo–Lydda Railway in a number of places. It was a very successful operation, and alerted everyone to the explosive situation we were involved in. A joint Anglo-American commission was set up to try to deal with the problem, the Jewish Agency was involved, and initially the situation was calmed down. At this time the Battalion was not directly involved except for a few road-blocks and searches in the Tel Aviv area. Our camp at Nathanya was a relatively peaceful spot, and it was during this period that I had arrived. We were under orders to move to Jerusalem; all I had to do was to stick around, get to know people, and find my place. There was excellent local shooting and riding to be had; the one thing that no one seemed to be thinking about was training.

When we got to Jerusalem, I sat down and wrote for the Squire what I could perhaps call a 'learned paper'. It summed up what I had seen in the four short weeks I had been with him, and it was all about training. I pointed out that release was haemorrhaging away our best men, and we were doing nothing about training others to take their place. We had no SOPs (Standing Order Procedures); if we were called out on any operation we made it up as we went along. Our signallers were being reduced in efficiency by release. Few of our leaders had been taught to operate their sets, and without efficient communications we were as good as useless. Training with live ammunition had been badly neglected. There was little dissemination of any form of intelligence: we had no real idea of whom we were supposed to be operating against, what their organisation was, how they worked, or the political direction behind them. I suggested how we could put this right, by a series of cadres and courses. The Squire was delighted, and gave me the go-ahead to get things organised.

In Jerusalem the Battalion was accommodated in two large areas. Two companies, and Headquarters, were at the Hospice de Notre Dame, a huge building overlooking the Damascus Gate of the Old City. The remainder were at the Syrian Orphanage, some two miles away in the Mea Sharim area. Of the two other battalions of the Brigade, the Ox & Bucks were at Mount Scopus to the north of the city and the Ulster Rifles were to the south. Brigade Headquarters was not far from the railway station, about half a mile from the King David Hotel, which housed GHQ Palestine.

One of our more important jobs was controlling the Old City, or rather assisting the Palestine police in this task. The Old City was a rabbit warren of narrow streets, churches, shops and tea houses. Situated at its eastern end was the Haram es Sharif (the Dome of the Rock), a most beautiful mosque and – I was told – after Mecca the second most holy place in the Islamic religion. Next door to it was the Wailing Wall. Both were accessible only by very narrow streets, and both were potentially explosive meeting places of two faiths. In the middle of the rabbit warren was the Church of the Holy Sepulchre, which was shared by three branches of the Christian faith, each determined to protect its own patch.

There was a very remarkable member of the Palestine police in charge of all this, which he ran with an iron fist. He was a tall, good looking, distinguished and very senior officer called Syed Bey Idrissi. He had numerous medals, and he was the sort of man one instinctively calls 'Sir'. We became great friends, and I once had the temerity to ask him where he got his bottom row of ribbons as I was unable to recognise any of them. He explained that he got them for fighting the British in World War I, when he served with the Turkish forces, as his family had done for generations. He came from a Circassian family, and after the war had transferred to serve under British rule. He enjoyed serving with us, he told me, but we did not understand either Arabs or Jews, and were much too soft with them. In his young days, malefactors who threw bombs and shot at people were, after arrest and trial, publicly hanged over the Damascus Gate. There was, he said, nothing so efficacious as a public hanging for concentrating criminals' minds and maintaining discipline.

'Look at what happens under your rule,' he said. 'You catch the guilty, try them, then they appeal, and months later you hang them quietly in Acre Jail, and they have become heroes!'

After all these years I think he had a point.

There were two of my young soldiers I could have gladly handed over to him. They had come out from home with a very suspect draft of young ne'er-do-wells, who should never have been accepted into the Army. In the end we got rid of the lot and sent them all back home, but these two were an interesting exception: they positively begged to be sent elsewhere!

There had been a series of shoot-ups in various towns in Palestine, and after one particular episode we had been ordered to carry arms at all times. These two managed to find out that there was a Church of Scotland canteen near the Old City, with a safe reputedly bulging with money. The padre who ran it was an ex-Gordon Highlander and had been a prisoner of the Japanese. One evening they forced their way into his office, held him up at gunpoint, and made off with the contents of his safe – which in fact was not very much. They returned to billets and bragged about it, which infuriated the Jocks in a manner I had never seen before. The two were very roughly handled, and the next day appeared before me, as acting Commanding Officer, for trial and sentence. They looked as if they had both had fifteen rounds with Joe Louis. I was told that they had missed their footing on the staircase – though that did not quite explain why one was missing three front teeth, and there were three suspicious teeth marks on CSM Rab Logie's balding skull. Never have I seen anyone so eager as those two to be clapped into a detention barracks.

Another draft turned out to be quite the opposite, though their imminent arrival caused some serious doubts. Something had gone very wrong with a parachute battalion in Malaya: to a man they had apparently refused duty, and were court-martialled *en masse*. The Battalion was disbanded, split up and sent to other units. You can imagine our misgivings when we were told that we were to received some fifty of them, and they were due to arrive within the week. Mutinous Jocks I thought I could handle, but fifty tough mutinous parachutists was a very different problem. We need not have worried: they were some of the nicest and best soldiers we ever received. Many stayed on with us as regulars, just when we needed them. Little by little, as we got to know them, we found out what had gone wrong in Malaya: it was a sad tale of misunderstandings and poor leadership.

After about three months the Battalion was in good shape. We were ready for whatever we had to do in Jerusalem, and it came to us with a bang when IZL blew up the south wing of the King David Hotel.

There had been a prelude to this. In early July the British Government had had enough of the machinations of the Jewish Agency (the embryo government of the future Israeli state), and in a massive operation every Jew of any importance was roused out of his bed before dawn and arrested. One of my clients was no less a person than Golda Meir. She responded with great politeness, offering our arresting officer and his team cups of tea all round. The whole operation was probably necessary, but bursting into people's houses at three in the morning and carting them off to the local detention barracks was a rather distasteful affair. The city was put under curfew, which meant little sleep for any of us, and there were numerous cordons and searches of suspected areas. I do not remember finding anything of great importance; I suspect all we did was infuriate a great many law-abiding people.

The Squire was at home on leave, and so for two months I was in command. At about midday on 22 July I was sitting at my desk in the Hospice when there was a loud, heavy thump. It didn't sound like a bang, but it was obviously an explosion of some sort. Simultaneously all our telephone lines went out, but we had a drill to cover this, and immediately opened all our wireless sets.

Gordon Munro, one of my company commanders, had been driving past the King David when it blew, and was able to report what had happened. He was incredibly lucky not to have been killed, and the blast wave and debris missed him. He was a very experienced soldier, and suggested I get as many men as I could spare with picks and shovels to the scene immediately, plus ambulances – there were many casualties. James Moore, our Brigade Major, was with Gordon and was able to get the more powerful Brigade Headquarters Communications on the air.

Once help was on the way I went to the King David myself to see the devastation that had been caused. The IZL had put milk churns filled with explosive in the basement beside the main structural walls of the south block, which housed Army Headquarters and the signal exchange. They had sliced the building to the ground, like a house of cards that has collapsed. Such was the force of the explosion that on the YMCA building opposite, about 100 yards away, was the outline of a man in his own blood, where he had been blown across the street. We found his body at the foot of the wall: it was almost completely flattened by the impact.

Without specialised rescue equipment there was little our soldiers could do, except deal with the less seriously wounded. If they had tried to burrow under the enormous slabs of masonry, they could have done more harm than good to those trapped underneath.

After two hours of our amateurish rescue attempts, help began to arrive from outside. The first was none other than Glubb Pasha, who was driving through Jerusalem en route to Jordan. As he was a Royal Engineer, he knew exactly what was required and where to get it from, but it was nearly twenty-four hours before all the heavy equipment that we needed could be assembled.

Jewish and world opinion was horrified at this incident. Jews and Arabs lost their lives as well as British, and no one has yet managed to establish whether a warning was ever sent out, as IZL stated. There are many conflicting stories.

Sylvia and my mother were staying in Beckenreid, Switzerland, when all this took place. They heard the news about a big explosion in Jerusalem, and about the large number of casualties. There was no way they could check with anyone whether I had been involved, as all communications had been destroyed, and it took two days to get them working again. (There were no mobile phones in those days.) This lack of knowledge was the price of being an army wife sometimes.

The King David affair led to more curfews, more cordons and searches – and more retaliation in the way of bombs and booby traps. One speciality was the 'explosive dustbin', which could be left at a crossroads where we were used to putting a standing patrol. Another was the electrically detonated mine concealed by the roadside, and the twisty, mountainous roads leading from Jerusalem were ideal for this ploy. The road to Jericho, which we had to patrol, was a favourite area, and I can never hear about the good Samaritan without remembering drives at night in my Humber, with an escort jeep, wondering what the next corner would bring.

We had an excellent Pioneer Platoon Commander, James Masson, who quite irregularly (it was well outside his normal duties) became an expert in sniffing out and dismantling bombs and booby traps of all sorts. He was joined by a Sergeant Smith of the Palestine police, an ex-Royal Marine, who had done some training in this very dangerous business, and together they did a remarkable job, and must have saved many lives.

One day there was a report from Jerusalem Railway Station that a suspicious suitcase had been left in the waiting room. Messrs Smith and Masson were soon there, and discovered that it was rather more than suspicious – there was a steel lining inside the leather. Together they removed the suitcase from the station building, carried it out into the car park, and considered what should be done. At least if it went up the station would be undamaged. Smith then did a very remarkable and courageous thing. He ordered everyone out of harm's way, saying that he would tackle it himself, and that there was no sense in anyone else getting hurt if things went wrong. He would shout out what he was doing, and one of his constables under cover in a ditch would take notes. When Jimmy Masson protested, Smith said that though he might be the senior, Jimmy had dealt with the last booby trap, and now it was his turn. Sadly,

146

something went wrong, and the suitcase blew up with tremendous force. Smith was killed instantly; all the others – and the station – were safe.

When I had the full report I decided that I would put in Smith for a George Cross. This is not an easy process. As for the Victoria Cross you need three independent witnesses to submit statements, but these we had. I submitted the dossier through Nicol Gray, the Head of the Palestine police, and a highly decorated Royal Marine commando in his day. Perhaps I am not much good at writing citations: Smith got a posthumous King's Police Medal for gallantry, in the Colonial Police Services the next highest award; Jimmy Masson received the George Medal, which was nearly unique among the Argylls. It can sometimes be easy to be brave when the blood is up and battle is on, but the cold-blooded courage of dealing alone with booby traps and high explosive is something very special. It was a privilege to have known such men.

At the end of September I was sent to the Staff College at Haifa, which had just closed, to help organise a course for officers taking the newly established examination for candidates who wished to gain admission to the course on pre-war standards. I and six others, who had been lucky enough to squeeze through without taking any such exam, were ordered to put together a fortnight's period of study to help them take the paper. We had little idea of what the course was going to be like, though the syllabus had been laid down. Although Haifa Staff College had closed its doors, many of its administrative and clerical staff remained, and a few instructors – including Bill Forbes from my own regiment – were on hand to assist. The place was a welcome change after the tension of Jerusalem, and there was almost a holiday atmosphere. After about two weeks' preparation our students arrived, and we put them through a sort of mini-practice for what they would get when they arrived at Camberley – or whichever staff college they went to.

In the middle of this, on 19 October, an event occurred in Jerusalem that was to take me away from Haifa post-haste. That night the Battalion was on a routine curfew operation, but the Jews had noticed that they had been using one particular crossroads as a 'firm base' rather too frequently, and booby-trapped it with one of their explosive dustbins, which detonated in the evening, causing a number of casualties. The world press was onto it in droves, flash cameras and all – to the fury of the Squire, who rounded the lot up and took them under escort to the Hospice de Notre Dame. There they were kept under guard, unable to communicate with anyone, until somehow news got through to Headquarters Palestine of their fate, whereupon they were immediately released. But many had missed getting the news through to their papers, and were furious at such treatment. A considerable row ensued. The Squire in particular, and the 1st Argylls, were accused of violating the freedom of the press by force of arms. The diplomatic knock-on effect of this resonated round the world.

The press were out for blood – and they got it. The Squire was immediately removed from command, and the GOC Palestine gave him twenty-four hours to pack his kit. I was ordered to leave Haifa, rejoin the Battalion and assume command on arrival. I drove down as soon as I got the message, and had just about an hour to say goodbye to the Squire before he was sent into exile. It was the most unhappy 'take-over' I have ever had. There was nothing I could say or do about it. Certainly there had been a serious error of judgement; the press presence all round the roadblock site was hampering operations and putting soldiers' lives at risk, but we had scant training in dealing with the press in those days, and the Squire's first concern as ever was his men. He had to get rid of this interfering horde of correspondents. The trouble was that he chose the wrong way. Had I not been 100 miles away in Haifa I could well have found myself in the same boat. It was a very sad day for the Regiment.

First Slim River, then Kohima, and now Jerusalem: this was the third time I had found myself pitchforked into a responsibility that I had neither expected nor wanted. I experienced the same mixture of feelings all over again: lots of people looking at you for some sort of orders, and others wondering if you are going to be up to the job. I had had a bit of practice when the Squire was away on leave for two months, but that was different. I had been just a caretaker then; now I was the boss. And there was one thing I had to do, and do very quickly.

The battalion had lost a much loved and respected commanding officer in extraordinary circumstances. They did not understand why; they were bemused and angry. It was up to me to tell them the facts. Unpleasant those facts might be, but they were going to get them from their CO rather than in the form of exaggerated 'Latrineograms'. So in turn I had them on parade in company groups, and briefly passed on the Squire's farewell message to them. He had been denied the opportunity to do so himself, such was the limited time allowed for his departure by Command.

What a way to run an Army!

About this time the Government had extended the period of service by six months, so that men who thought they would be released in November were going to have to wait until May before their number came up. There were disturbances in units in the Canal Zone, but luckily we were not affected. However, we were 'stood by' to move to Ismailia, in case our presence was required to deal with what the soldiers concerned called strikes, but which were in effect the next best thing to mutiny. It affected base and signal units only in the big depots in the Zone.

Altogether, the end of 1946 was an unhappy time to be in the Middle East.

Reorganisation was in the air, and 6 Air Landing Brigade was due to be broken up. We were to move down to the Canal Zone to join the 3rd

Division, and would be there in December. Initially we would move to a tented camp outside Moascar, a sort of suburb of Ismailia, which meant I had to travel down to the Zone by road several times to get things set up.

The road to Ismailia goes down from Jerusalem to Beersheba and then straight across the desert. It was an eight-hour drive in the big Humber station wagon that was my command car. We used to go south by day and return by night. The East Yorkshire Regiment, who were stationed at Ismailia, looked after us when we had to stay there. Headquarters 3rd Division, who we were to join, was in a camp near Ismailia, and my new General, 'Bolo' Whistler, and his family had quarters nearby.

There were the usual permanent facilities on the barren site by the Sweetwater Canal, where we had to pitch our tents, latrines, washplaces, cookhouses, storehuts and officers' and sergeants' messes, but the rest of the accommodation was in tents. These would be put up for us by a most efficient unit, formed of ex-Africa Corps POWs, who were used by the British Services as support staff. They were extremely efficient. Their transport, which was meticulously maintained, had the badge of a dachshund on a black rectangle. After pitching our camp a party of some thirty would remain under my command for camp fatigues and duties.

I think it took three visits to arrange all the details of the move. The real joy was the drive back to Jerusalem by night. After dinner we would motor down to the Ismailia chain ferry, cross the canal, and pick up the road north. This was simply a long line of tarmac through the desert, marked at intervals by 50-gallon oil drums, each painted a particular colour. (Each desert road had its own colour-coded drums, and there was a map stretching along the whole north coast of Africa showing the routes.)

Ours was probably the only car on the road, which for miles was completely straight, but sometimes, way in the distance, we could see the glow of headlights approaching. They were probably ten miles or more away; from time to time they might be obscured by gradients, but eventually we met and passed, and all was blackness again, except when the moon was out. But if there was no moon, after the hours passed I felt as though I was driving though avenues of tall trees, and then it was time to hand over before I started hallucinating!

By 2.00 in the morning we would have reached Asluj, a staging post where there was a NAAFI canteen. This opened at 6 am, and for the first time we found other vehicles, parked with their crews asleep beside them. We would get out our sleeping bags, zip ourselves into them under the stars, and crash out. Nothing moved; there was no sound except the gentle breeze and the odd metallic noises that a hot engine makes as it slowly cools down. Soon we would be sound asleep, to be woken at dawn by a mug of hot tea from the canteen. Then it was back to our Mess in Jerusalem for breakfast.

149

Of all the long drives that I have done, those across Sinai in the winter stand out most vividly in my memory – particularly sleeping under the bright desert stars, which Bernard Fergusson described so well:

The soldier stars that pace the beats of heaven.[2]

My father had sent me a book that he had used in the First World War, which described detailed methods of navigation using the stars. I carried it then, and I carried it four years later in Korea. It proved invaluable time and time again.

Our move to Egypt went off without any snags, and it was great to escape the endless grind of curfews and patrols, though there were unseen dangers for the unwary. Two young Jocks decided to go for a swim in the Sweetwater Canal, despite severe warnings that the water was heavily polluted. They were seized by our doctors, who stuck them with so many needles that they would have looked like porcupines had the needles been left in place. No one else tried swimming in the canal.

There was every form of sport that we had lacked in Jerusalem, with football and hockey matches all the time. There were some major training exercises with our new Division, including a very realistic live artillery shoot, with a whole field regiment of twenty-four guns firing over our heads. This sort of thing had been everyday stuff three years earlier at our battle school in India, but things are different when you are actually in command, and you start worrying – particularly when the exercise takes place on 3 January, after the Battalion has had its fill of celebrating Hogmanay. Luckily for us our gunners had not been involved in the celebrations, and so there was little chance of range and deflection bubbles being misplaced, with the consequent misdirection of projectiles.

In mid January Cluny Macpherson came out to take over command. He had been caught in 1940, but had survived prison life very well indeed. He was an exceptional athlete – he once ran the half mile for the Army – and as tough as they come. It was a pleasure to hand the Battalion over to him, but I had enjoyed my three months or so of independent command.

My time with the 91st was about to come to an end. Disbandments, reorganisations, and the return to active service of those who had been prisoners of war – all this meant that there were many officers, senior to me, who were eager to get back to the Regiment. When we moved back to Palestine from Egypt to a new camp, Quastina, they posted me back to the War Office, and after a hair-raising flight and landing at Lyneham (it was the middle of the March 1947 freeze-up), I once again turned up unannounced at Sydney Street; snow and frost had completely cut communications from Lyneham. There was no one at home when I arrived; I had no key, and no means of contacting either my mother or Sylvia (they had gone to the theatre that afternoon). I had to leave my kit outside the house and take refuge with our friends next door until they returned.

I did three years at the War Office. I do not think I influenced British defence policy very much, but I certainly worked hard. Life consisted in sharing a large dusty office, looking out into one of the inner courtyards through a dirty window, and reading and writing more reams of paper than I thought existed. I was a humble Grade 2 Staff Officer. I was not quite the lowest of the low: there were some Grade 3 ones as well. Six of us inhabited a large room heated by a smoky fire, and from time to time a War Office porter would enter with a trolley full of files, which he distributed to us for whatever action we thought necessary. Some of the files were venerable documents indeed. They bore on their minute sheets the signatures of past officers, some of whom had attained high rank and were now our bosses. One file that came into my tray was a museum piece: someone had left his sandwich lunch in it, and it had decayed into a nasty, unreadable mess.

Then there were the green files that meant parliamentary questions: we had to deal with these immediately. One Saturday morning one such file came my way. It concerned a rifle range at Ewshot. The local citizens had complained to their local MP, who had put down a question for the Secretary of State. I composed what I thought was a sensible answer, and went down to our senior general, Sir Richard Gale, with a draft for his signature. He looked at it, and then looked at me; we had never met before.

'Have you sent for the file?' he asked.

'File, Sir?' I questioned, almost gobbling like a turkey.

'Yes, file, of course – there is always a file for everything. You come up early on Monday morning, send for the file, read it, and bring me the answer.'

So on Monday the file arrived. It had last been seen in May 1939: a similar question, and an answer drafted and signed by a young GSO2 – R.N. Gale.

I carefully copied his reply, and sought his office.

'Ah, the file,' he said, 'let's see.' He looked at my draft reply: 'An excellent answer; I'll sign it, thank you.'

Then he took the file up and threw it at me, roaring with laughter as he said: 'Get out of here! I've done your bloody work for you, haven't I?'

Richard Nelson Gale was a great character. I served him in 1958 for six months as his military assistant at SHAPE, but he never forgot the file! He was a delight to work for. He had an extremely astute brain, which he cleverly hid behind an exterior that could make you think you were dealing with a typical British Blimp, if you did not know him. Then you would be led straight up the garden path, to find you had made a complete idiot of yourself.

My particular job was to oversee basic infantry training, which included responsibility for the organisation of the primary training centres, where the young draftees reported and were trained for twelve weeks, and the infantry training centres, where they went for another eight weeks before joining their operational units. I also had the School of Musketry at Hythe, the Infantry School at Warminster, and the Support Weapons School at Netheravon under my care. As well as the organisation of these places, I was also responsible for the whole question of what was taught there.

I reported directly to a Grade 1 (Lieutenant Colonel), who was under a Major General termed the Director of Infantry, who in turn was responsible to a Lieutenant General, the Director of Military Training. Our areas of responsibility were very clearly laid down, particularly where finance was concerned. There were strict limits on who could authorise what expenditure might take place, and under what conditions. Shortly after my arrival I fell foul of this network.

A delegation from a rich Arab state was in the UK to consider a large purchase of arms. They were about to attend the School of Infantry at Warminster, for a battle demonstration of our new Centurion tank. All was arranged except for one small point: we had no blank ammunition for the Centurion's gun. On the Saturday morning I had the mischance to be the sole duty officer of my Grade present. Peter Hunt of the Camerons, the GSO2 of the School, rang me. They were to demonstrate the tank first thing on Monday morning, but they had nothing to shoot; you could not very well impress a high-powered Arab delegation by having the tank commander stand up in his turret hatch and either wave a red flag or shout 'Bang!' to simulate his main armament firing.

But, Peter said, there was an answer: take the shell out of the normal high-explosive round, and use the cartridge (minus shell) to simulate blank ammunition. The trouble was that his ordnance officer, who would remove the shell, needed authority from the War Office to do so. That was why he was ringing me.

To me, in my ignorance of channels of procedure, this seemed to be a perfectly reasonable request, so I told Peter to go ahead, made a note to that effect in my duty officer's logbook, and sat back. I thought it was a good and proper decision, and on the following Monday the demonstration went ahead as planned. The Arabs were impressed, and in due course a large order for Centurions went on the books.

About three days later all hell broke loose over my head. My GSO1 sent for me and marched me in front of my General, who had with him a very senior principal from the finance branch – clearly a very angry man. Unwittingly I had committed a serious crime. I had vastly overstepped my authority by authorising the destruction of expensive live ammunition. I had no business to take such decisions on my (very junior) shoulders. I had breached just about every financial regulation about ammunition in the book. It was the finest and most ceremonial rocket I ever received in my service, and all because I had undermined the system! I soon realised that my job was merely to push paper around quickly and efficiently: decision making played no part in the job of a mere Grade 2 Staff Officer. Luckily, since I looked after so many training units, I was allowed to escape from time to time to visit them and get a breath of fresh air.

The great Lord Curzon, when Viceroy of India, apparently had a great love of annotating files. He wrote a celebrated minute about the stately and inevitable progression of one that landed on the Viceregal desk, ending with:

> . . . on the whole I am inclined to agree with the opinion of the gentleman whose signature resembles a trombone.

On one such visit I had to deliver a dossier of highly confidential medical documents personally to the Adjutant of the Guards depot at Caterham. In those days I had a little BSA Bantam 125 cc motorcycle, which was exceptionally useful for getting me to work. I rang the Adjutant up and told him to warn his guard that a rather scruffy figure in waterproof kit would arrive at 9.30 the next morning with the documents. He assured me that I would be expected.

The day of my visit was a typically cold, sleety March affair. Snow-encrusted from my ride I arrived at the gates of Caterham. A smart Guards sergeant stepped out, saluted, and asked: 'Major Wilson, Sir?'

I produced my identity card, which satisfied him. He turned to his guardroom, and shouted 'Drummer!' in a stentorian voice. A diminutive young soldier appeared and also saluted.

The sergeant continued: 'Double in front of this officer and take him to the Adjutant's office. Move!'

With his hobnailed boots slipping and sliding in the slush, and his bugle on its cord banging on his bottom, he led me about 100 yards to the headquarters office, where I parked my little BSA. Curious faces looked out of the windows, as if wondering who on earth this strange despatch rider could be, and why the Drummer was saluting him.

Feeling somewhat out of my depth, I was made most welcome in the Adjutant's office, where I was refreshed with coffee and biscuits, and handed over the papers. It did not take very long. As I was about to leave, I saw a curious sight. On the frozen square were squads of guardsmen being drilled by a clutch of young officers. At the edge of the square stood a mess waiter, carrying a silver salver on which were a decanter and

153

glasses. From time to time an officer would approach him, pour something from the decanter into the glass, take something else off the tray, shake it over the glass, swallow the lot, and then start drilling his squad. I asked the Adjutant what was going on. He looked at me with some surprise:

'Very simple, it's Port and Pepper. Don't you use it in your Regiment before taking a drill parade? Helps the voice no end, and it's great for giving a bit of confidence to the young when they first start.'

God bless the Guards! They set us a great standard!

On 29 February 1948 Sylvia produced a daughter. The fact that she was born on Leap Year's Day may explain a thing or two about Maggie's character and behaviour in the years since. That very same day I found a house for us in Sussex, within easy commuting distance of the War Office, and by May we were installed in it. I reckoned that, once I was in the War Office Mafia, I was likely to return there from time to time. I was quite wrong, I never did – thank heavens, I was not the Whitehall type – but it was a lovely little house; we had a lot of fun there, and made many friends. By 1970 the planners had ruined it all, but that is no part of this story.

By April 1950 I had had three years of commuting and paperwork, and I was due to get back to active soldiering. The Battalion was now in Hong Kong, and I was to join it in August. Using my inside influence, I managed to get myself on what in those days was called the 'Support Weapons Commanders Course' at Netheravon, part of the School of Infantry, at Figheldene on Salisbury Plain. It was a six-week affair: two weeks on the Vickers machine gun, two on the three-inch mortar – both of which I knew pretty well – and two on the anti-tank guns, 6 and 17 pounders, about which I knew nothing. It was great fun. We were about a dozen students, all of the same age and seniority, and we lived in a lovely manor house, which was part of the School. It was hard work, but very interesting. We finished on Friday afternoons and could go home for the weekend, and in the middle of it all there was a memorable cricket match.

The local villagers had heard that we had a few reasonable players on the course, and invited us to take them on. It was the sort of game that Siegfried Sassoon could have described so well: there was both gamesmanship and skulduggery of a high order in the play.

We could raise a couple of Free Forester caps, with the odd Straggler of Asia sweater and a Sandhurst Wanderer or two, but rumour had it that our opponents had an Air Marshal in their side, and this was an ace that we had to trump. This meant that we had to produce at least a General. We had the very man on the course: he was a major not a general, but he looked like one, could put on an act like one, and was no mean cricketer. Our Commander, Charles Archdale, who ran the school, was eager to join in the fun, and provided the 'general's' staff car, flag and plates. We had

154

to square the Air Marshal, who was a member of the opposition. (Although he was retired he could have given our deception away, and so we had to let him know that our so-called 'General' was bogus.) We weren't sure whether our cricketing skill would match that of the opposition on their own pitch, but bluff might give us a chance.

The great evening came. It was to be a twenty-over match, and our General arrived in style, ADC and all! He was just a trifle late, to give us a chance to impress the village of his importance, and of how very busy he was. He came in first wicket down for us, and demanded a runner, as – he asserted – his left leg had been badly shot up by the Japanese, and had not completely healed.

There is nothing so good as a runner to disorganise a fielding side, particularly when the so-called 'runner' is the bogus General's ADC, and is acting under his orders. When our runner was not being berated for setting off when he should not have moved, he was being panicked by his batsman (the 'General'), who tended to forget that he was supposed to stand still and let his runner do the work. As a result of all this nonsense, our second wicket partnership was doing rather well, until runner and General met in the middle of the pitch, and were well and truly run out.

We amassed a reasonable total, and then it was our turn to field. Our General took the field with a pad on his left leg 'to protect his wound', and stood at a sort of silly point position, where he glared at the batsman and used his padded leg with great skill to stop balls coming towards him. At the same time he did his best to upset the batsman by delivering a running commentary on the excellence of the bowling, with comments such as: 'Ah, nearly got you that time, you know!' It says volumes for the good manners and patience of the village team that they did not beat him up on the spot!

Then we put him on to bowl – good, old-fashioned 'donkey drops' cast high in the sky like the trajectory of a mortar bomb, to land temptingly in front of the batsman, whose one idea is to smash them over the boundary fence. But somehow it does not often happen that way. Provided your fielders are good enough to hold their catches, it is surprising how many aspiring batsmen 'hole out' time and time again.

Of course, despite all our efforts, the village won, but it was a good match, and everyone enjoyed themselves immensely. We had all subscribed so that our General could take over the local pub and pay for the opening round of drinks for everyone present. Then, pleading an urgent return to some unspecified duty, we got rid of him, his bogus ADC and his equally bogus staff car and driver, before anyone suspected the truth. The local team thought he was a splendid character, and a real sport. Little did they know – I don't believe they ever found out. And to think that some folk say that cricket is a boring game . . .

*

There was one final farewell to my job: a guest night at the headquarters of the School of Infantry at Warminster. In the three years that I had been at my desk in Whitehall I had had a great deal to do with the operation of the School, and had made a lot of friends there, who wanted to see me off in style. Others on my course were also invited, and we had the luxury of transport to take us. We had a great party, which ended up with that somewhat dangerous game, 'Billiard Fives' (a billiard ball travelling through the air at high speed if it leaves the table is an object to be avoided!).

During a series of matches I found myself partnering Brigadier Cecil Firbank, the Commandant of the School, and a noted exponent of the game. No holds were barred; it was fast and very furious. During one long, fierce rally he hit the ball very hard towards the left-hand pocket of the far cushion. It just missed going in; instead it rebounded at great speed, straight towards my face. The ball hit me just over the right eye, knocking me out (only briefly – strong refreshment soon had me on my feet again), and causing a stream of blood to spout all over the table, ruining both the cloth and several people's blue patrol jackets (we had no mess kit in those days).

Eventually the damage to billiard table and my face was cleared up, the evening ended, and we all went happily home. But next morning my face was a sight to see; it caused some comment, not least from Charles Archdale, Commandant of the Weapons Support Wing, School of Infantry. What sort of affray had I been in, and who had caused the damage? When I replied that it was none other than the Commandant of the School himself, he was horrified, and found it difficult to believe, but eventually – as I had three witnesses – he did accept my answer. But my story had gone down even less well when I got home to Sylvia.

The next couple of weeks were taken up with a round of farewells and packing: two tin uniform cases, a cabin truck, a bedding roll, my trusty *kukri* made by Mantons (the gunsmiths of Calcutta so many years back), and my battered hunting horn, which was so much more useful than the regulation whistle in times of need. There were to be arrangements to be made with Messrs Cox & Kings[3] so that Sylvia and Maggie would not starve, or be ejected by bailiffs, and then it was time to catch the train to London, and from there to Southampton for the troopship. I was off again, ostensibly to Hong Kong, but there was something brewing in the Far East, in Korea: the Royal Navy had been in action, and there were rumours of British help in the way of ground troops. But Hong Kong was a good posting, and with luck Sylvia and Maggie could follow in due course; other regimental families were already there.

The ship that awaited me was the *Empire Trooper*, a big ex-German pre-war 'Strength through Joy' liner that had been taken over by us after the war. It was very different from the old *Dorsetshire* that had sailed me out in 1937 – over twice the size and twice as fast – and now, as a Major, I expected to be ensconced in a proper, comfortable cabin! It was not to be. We were four to the room – admittedly a bigger and better-equipped room than the *Dorsetshire* could provide.

We were lucky in that we had the 1st Battalion of the Wiltshire Regiment on board, with families, band and drums, and a lot of old friends. They took over and ran the ship, but since they mistakenly thought I knew something about training, they made me the ship's training officer. This meant that I had plenty to do in allocating space and drawing up programmes of lectures, musketry, fitness and the like.

Two things of note happened during the voyage. The first was the news, which we received in mid Mediterranean, that the 1st Argylls were earmarked for immediate service in Korea, and would have left Hong Kong by the time I arrived. The second was that, during a violent storm when the ship was being bounced about just off Ceylon, I was hurled from one side of a corridor to the other, and somehow caught my right thumb in a door. This neatly sliced off the top, just above the joint. I found the top in the door jamb, but there were problems in sewing it back on – which left my right hand rather inefficient.

We spent twenty-four hours in Singapore. We had sailed into Keppel Harbour just as we did in 1939, but now there were no great guns on Blakang Mati and Pulau Brani; the batteries had been destroyed by the Japanese, and their guns removed for use elsewhere. The Tanglin Club had hardly changed, our camp at Tyersall had been rebuilt and was still in use, the names of the streets and roads were just the same, and Raffles seemed undamaged, but there were a host of missing faces. I was glad when we left the next evening.

Four or five days later we berthed at Hong Kong. I was seized by Mark Maunsell, late of Second Division and now Chief of Staff to the C.-in-C., who insisted that I stay in his home in the Peak for the five days I had before I was sent on to Korea. I had to arrange for my baggage to be put into the cold storage warehouse along with the rest of the Battalion's kit, get suitable tropical kit for Korea, sort out what was necessary to take out there, fix the local paymaster who would deal with my pay and allowances 'whilst on active service', and open an account with the Hong Kong and Shanghai Bank. There was not much time, and in the middle of all this who should I run into but Brigadier Hugh Wrigley – now Australian Trade Commissioner in Hong Kong, but once in charge of the 3rd Australian POW Reception Group in Manila. He had me to his house and filled me with some excellent advice about serving with the US Army, which he knew very well from Pacific War days.

Early one morning, I reported to the BOAC desk to check in (they were to take me and a small party to Japan). There was a very attractive girl manning the desk. She looked up at me and said: 'You are David Wilson; we last met in the Tanglin Club in January 1942!'

It was true. In those days there were two pairs of twins: the Elder girls, who were dark, and the Thompsons, who were fair. She was one of the Thompsons, had married a chap in an Indian regiment, who had been killed. You would not have thought that she had endured three years of being a prisoner of the Japanese. We chatted happily about old times, until it was time to go. I had no idea where we would end up, but then, that was the Army for you. There was a recruiting poster in the 1930s, which said in large letters:

JOIN THE ARMY AND SEE THE WORLD.

That certainly rang true in my case.

NOTES
1   The US equivalent of Nissen huts, but larger.
2   'Towards the East', in B. Fergusson, *Lowland Soldier* (London: Collins, 1945).
3   Cox & Kings were the Pall Mall branch of Lloyds Bank, Army Agents with whom I and my family had banked for many years.

CHAPTER 10
Korea

Five o'clock in the morning is a grisly hour, and it was a particularly grisly morning at Haneda Airfield, Tokyo, in September 1950. Along with two young officers – Alan Lauder and Ted Cunningham – and seven assorted Jocks I was being briefed by a Master Sergeant of the US Air Force, before embarking on a battered DC3 for Korea. He was the epitome of a Giles cartoon American: short, tough-looking and somewhat unshaven, but very businesslike. And he had reduced us, his audience, to a state of immobile serfdom by fitting us out with parachute harnesses, which were very tightly strapped up. We were all dressed for war in the kilt, and the resulting problem with the parachute harness was most uncomfortable, and very embarrassing!

'OK, you guys, here's the briefing. This flight takes off for K2 (that's what we call Taegu) in twenty minutes. Our pilot today is a desk jockey bird colonel from Tokyo Staff, getting a few hours on his logbook. He says he knows the way, but the cloud over Korea ain't so good! We sure will run into turbulence, and your vomit bags are under your seats, but they ain't all that hot, as they're made in Japan, so clench your teeth and keep the bigger bits back otherwise they'll burst! Right guys, load up.'

This was not the most cheering of starts, but not only was our pilot very skilled, he also *did* know his way, and got us to Taegu in about six hours. There we found that no one knew anything about us, or what to do with us. We hitched a lift in a three-ton truck to the centre of Taegu, where in a large school we found the Advanced Headquarters of 8th US Army and their Air Force. We arrived just in time to take part in a medal presentation parade in the courtyard, with the sound of guns not all that far off north of us at Waegwan.

When the parade was over I tried – with difficulty – to get in touch with 27 Brigade. The problem was that the US Army had adopted a coded system for their units: for example the 1st Cavalry Division, under whose command we were, was called Saber, and all its subordinate units had names beginning with S (Sandbag) for their engineers. 27 Brigade was attached to the 7th Cavalry Regiment, but being an independent unit were called Nottingham! However, I eventually managed to get through on a very bad line to Brigade headquarters, who promised to send a truck out first thing the next day. In the meantime we settled down with our hosts to watch a film!

We were awoken next morning by the whistle and crash of bombs, and a great deal of shooting. We were under attack. Four Mustangs of the 8th Air Force were carrying out a spirited assault on their own General, and as ever the wireless was acting up. There was a large radio truck in the courtyard, through which we could hear the pilots' voices as they wheeled about the sky, but their infuriated General on the ground could not get back to them. Also in the courtyard were Bofors guns, and two vehicle-mounted quadruple 50 mm anti-aircraft machine guns. One of these, expertly controlled by an over-zealous gunner, neatly sliced all the chimneys off one of the school blocks. The four gallant pilots, oblivious to all this, kept returning, convinced that they were doing a great job at Waegwan, where fighting was going on in earnest. Eventually communications did work, the General told his men to buzz off in no uncertain language, and peace was restored. It had been an interesting introduction to the Korean War.

When our truck arrived we got in, and were driven about ten miles to Brigade Headquarters, where I met our Brigade Commander, Aubrey Coad of the Wiltshires, Brigade Major Douglas Reith and GSO3 Alan Cookson (both Argylls), and other familiar faces. We were all given a welcome mug of tea, and then sped forward another few miles to Battalion. It was now about midday; we hadn't done all that badly after a shaky start.

I had last seen the 91st when I left them as Second in Command at Quastina in Palestine in 1947, and three and a half years had passed. Before that, in 1946, I had commanded them for six months. There had been many changes in the intervening years, not so much amongst the NCOs, but of the officers I had known then, only John Penman remained. Leslie Neilson, the CO, had been adjutant of the 91st when I had joined them in Tidworth fourteen years before; Kenny Muir, Second in Command, I had served with in India and on the Frontier; John Slim, adjutant, I had very briefly met socially. All the rest were new, and some were very young. They were a tough lot, and very fit (they had not wasted their time in Hong Kong and its hills), but they had a lot to learn. I suppose forty per cent of us had been in World War II; the rest were National Servicemen, who were to do us proud.

27 Brigade was holding the bend of the Naktong River where it changes its course from east to south; we were very spread out. The Argylls held the corner, with the Middlesex in support; and apart from a battery of six 105 guns from the US Army there was nothing else. No company could support each other, and this in some ways applied to platoons. 'A' Company, which I was to take over, held the bottom of what could be

described as an inverted L, covering about 500 yards of the Naktong. In front of us there was a gap of many miles before the nearest US forces (the Marines) coming up from the south. In the middle was Tom Tiddler's ground, into which a good many North Koreans had infiltrated.

Leslie Neilson, plus a small escort, led me over some five miles of paths and hills to take over 'A' Company from Miles Marston. I had never met Miles before; originally London Scottish and then an Argyll, he had served mostly with the 7th Gurkhas in Italy in World War II, coming back to the Regiment in 1947. He ran his company with Cromwellian discipline, and I don't think I've ever had a better bunch of men left in my care.

That night we decided to reorganise the company position, and withdrew slightly to the hill crest of the ridge that we had to hold. This made all sorts of sense: it was a stronger position, and we had better communications and a better view. Next morning Miles left for the UK, for the Staff College, and to marry Jill. He and I may have only served a mere twenty-four hours together, but we have been firm friends ever since.

In our area, the war had reached a sort of stalemate. The North Koreans had run out of steam in our sector. They could shell and mortar us (which they did), and they could patrol at night; they had tanks, which could not get at us because the hills were too steep, but we could see them wandering around their positions on the other side of the river, setting up the mortars and MMGs, and generally making a thorough nuisance of themselves. I got hold of my US Army Gunner Officer, Ted Marley, just out of West Point and their Artillery School, and asked him if he would kindly direct some of his 105 shells onto these pests. He explained that ammunition was short, and his orders were not to shoot at anything other than a full-scale attack by a battalion.

'Well, why not?' I said. 'Let's have one.'

There is – or was then – a difference between the British and American Armies in the way artillery fire is directed: the British forward observer 'commands' fire; the American 'requests' it.

So Ted got on his set, described the target and grid references, and proceeded to repel this imaginary assault by a non-existent battalion. A couple of dozen shells came over and landed amongst the foe, who quickly took to ground, and behaved respectably with their heads down for the rest of the day. But what shook me was Ted's final conversation on his set: 'Mission completed – target destroyed!'

'But you never hit a soul,' I said.

'That's our procedure, Major,' he replied, 'that's the way we sign off; it means we don't want a repeat of fire.'

It all seemed a bit curious. Three weeks later I was at Battalion HQ and looking through bits of news and intelligence reports. There I came on it: the date : time : grid reference, and on the right-hand side of the page a

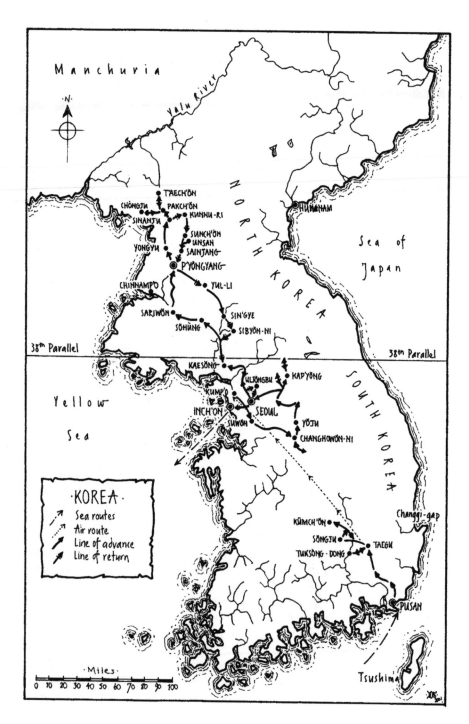

column showing the numbers of officers and what the Americans called EM (soldiers) killed in each engagement. Against our small shoot-up were figures of something like thirty officers and 650 EM killed. At the foot of the page all the engagements were added up, giving a grand total of North Koreans killed by friendly artillery fire in the week. On the evidence of such detailed statistics, the KPA had been wiped out, on paper at least. But if they had been wiped out, where on earth did these belligerent chaps who persisted in shooting at us keep coming from?

We had one minor skirmish in that area. One day in early September we had orders to withdraw completely, in order to take part in a battle elsewhere. The position was to be abandoned after dark. Then it started to rain. Lugging weapons, particularly Vickers machine guns and their tripods, up slippery slopes is not easy, and it was about 2.00 in the morning before we had made our way the five or six miles back to Battalion Headquarters. There we were received with horror. Shortly after we had moved – according to plan – the operation had been counter-manded by 7th Cavalry; we were to stay where we were. But by then the main battalion wireless had been packed up, and they were powerless to tell us to stand fast. There was no way we could move back that same night, and so a fresh platoon under James Stirling was sent to reoccupy our abandoned position so that the North Koreans would not realise we had gone.

James carried out his orders to the full: any North Korean who showed his face was well and truly shot up, and there was no doubt that the belligerent British were still around. But when I and 'A' Company got back that evening we had no real idea what had gone on during the day, or the fact that James and his merry men had stuck their fingers into an angry beehive. That night infuriated North Koreans jumped our Vickers position, which was slightly isolated, caused a few casualties, and took off.

Next day we took stock. We reckoned they would try it on again, and made suitable preparations. We moved the MMGs, set up a dummy post in their place, well booby trapped, and sent out a standing patrol with a telephone line, under Sergeant Robertson, to watch what was the KPA's only line of approach. It worked like a dream. An hour before dawn, Robertson and his men saw about thirty North Koreans making their way up the hill. He reported this quietly on the phone. I stood everyone to. They knew their orders: no shooting until daylight – bombs, but nothing else. We waited.

There was an outburst of firing, and shrieks and yells round the dummy post as the booby traps went off. Then the North Koreans panicked: they must have realised their operation had been blown, but which way should they go? Dawn was breaking, and they had no way out; they were halfway up a hill, and surrounded. There were not all that many, but we made them pay for what they had done to Neil Buchanan and his men in the same area a fortnight earlier, when they had been similarly caught on a patrol that should never have taken place. C Company 1 A&SH had sent out the patrol in daylight, without any means of support from ground, air or artillery. They ran into a string North Korean position, and were all killed – we found their bodies later. It was all so unnecessary: we knew perfectly well where the KPA were, but it was the result of confusing orders from Brigade, and an inexperienced company commander on the spot.

Up to now it had been an odd war for 27 Brigade. There were just the two battalions of us. We were holding an important sector, but the real fighting was going on elsewhere; we were shortly to join in. And General MacArthur's Inchon landing force was on its way.

Meanwhile there was a change of plan. The US Army were finding Waegwan a more difficult nut to crack than they had anticipated, and decided to try to outflank it round to the east, via a small town called Songju. They withdrew both the Middlesex and Argylls from their position on the Naktong, and moved us farther north to cross the Naktong again. The actual crossing points had been gained by the 5th Infantry attached to 24th Division. This time the operation went like a dream; we met up with our transport, US Army trucks that we suspected had been used for clearing some battlefield, because they smelt horribly of dead bodies. By 4.00 on the afternoon of 21 September our two battalions had arrived at the river crossing assembly area, the far bank being held by the Americans.

It was an odd sort of assembly area: a bottleneck really, which the KPA could readily exploit. Our means of crossing was a small 'kapok' bridge,[1] carrying just one man in single file. It would have been perfectly adequate, except that the North Koreans had a sniping artillery piece accurately ranged on it, and occasionally a shell would land far too close for comfort, with the odd soldier being killed or wounded. It was a most unpleasant way of running the gauntlet, but we got across with very few casualties.

Meanwhile the mechanised ferry that was to have taken the tanks and guns across had broken down, and by evening only three jeeps and two tracked carriers had got across. Brigade Headquarters and their Signals vehicles had to be left on the far bank, and this was to have a serious effect on the battle, which was led off by the Middlesex with an attack on Plum Pudding Hill led by Major Willoughby. This was a most successful operation compared with what was to happen on the Argylls' side of the valley.

My first objective, Point 148, was easily captured with the help of three American tanks, who could support us from the road. There was a small party of KPA on it, but they did not stand and fight. I was told to dig in and act as support for the next day's operation by B and C Companies.

This was the capture of Point 282, which commanded the road to Songju. From our position at the bottom we did not realise that 282 was itself commanded by a far larger feature, Song San (Point 348), some 2,000 yards away. Anyone sitting on 282 was wide open to Song San.

B and C Companies set off on their assault on 282 at 4.00 am on 23 September, and by 5.00 am had achieved complete surprise, driving off a small party of KPA, who were having breakfast. They now realised that they were overlooked by 348, but there was little they could do about it except dig in, but this was not easy – the ground was rocky and hard.

As the morning wore on, things started to deteriorate. First, Jock Edington of B Company realised that the KPA were beginning to infiltrate round his position from 348, and then both American artillery observers were withdrawn, on the orders of their Divisional Commander, for duty elsewhere. The tank guns could not help, because of the lie of the land, and our battalion mortars were out of range. Despite Leslie Neilson's protests to Brigade, and Aubrey Coad's protest to 24 Division, B and C Companies were now sitting ducks, on a hill with no supporting fire.

Murphy's Law began to come into operation. The KPA started to infiltrate round my left flank, which was guarding the rear of 282. We were well dug in, and our mortars and machine gun could hold them off, but it meant that I could send no one up the hill to help B and C Companies. Then three USAF Mustangs appeared, in an air strike intended to help B and C Companies. They were flying around uncertainly, even though the companies on the hill had put out their red and yellow recognition panels in the correct code of the day. To our horror the Mustangs commenced their dives on those very panels, and released their load of napalm and bombs directly on B and C Companies. The napalm, in particular, wreaked terrible havoc. They had a go at my company too, but we had had all night to dig in, and as a result suffered only one casualty.

The disorganisation caused by this misguided attack was terrible, coming as it did just when the KPA were massing to put in their own counter-attack. Then suddenly, through the haze of smouldering napalm, burning brush and the smoke of small arms fire, I saw a line of men – perhaps fifteen or twenty – led by Kenny Muir, our Second in Command. They were going back up the hill to give time to get the wounded down. This was the age-old drill that had applied on the Northwest Frontier for so many years: you never left your wounded behind. How much they achieved will never be known, but for magnificently brave conduct it is something that none of us will forget. Kenny Muir, mortally wounded, died on 282; he was awarded an immediate Victoria Cross.

And the airstrike? All who took part are dead now, and the whys and wherefores are best forgotten. One thing we do know: the pilots could clearly see the recognition strips, and refused to attack them, but someone told them that they had been overrun by the KPA. Once Murphy's Law takes over, the worst will always happen, no matter what. At least in those days we did not have hordes of counsellors and the press around, with their satellite links and their instant communications throughout the world – and threats of lawsuits and damages for casualties from what we now call 'friendly fire' or in even more modern parlance 'blue on blue'.

We lost fourteen killed and seventy-three wounded, with two others missing in action. Compared with many other battles that the regiment has seen, this was not perhaps a very great amount; but in international terms its importance was immense. For the first time the world realised that we, the British (or the Scots if you prefer), were involved to the hilt in Korea. In the days of major political discussions that followed, we had put our chips on the table, and they were powerful ones.

We went into rest for a short time after the battle, and were joined by the 3rd Battalion the Royal Australian Regiment, some 600 strong. At last 27 Brigade was a balanced organisation. We had no Sappers, artillery or guns yet – they would come – but in the run-up to the winter months that we faced, we reckoned that we were now a proper operational unit.

On 5 October all three battalions of the Brigade were flown by Boxcar to Kimpo airfield. Transport had to follow by road, and I think it took them five days, which we spent sleeping, eating and bathing. There was a Marine Corps airwing at Kimpo, which took us under their protection, and they did us proud: why does the Navy always seem to be better off than the Army? The war went on; the transport arrived, and one night we left for Kaesong, the small town on the borders of the Koreas. It was here that we received some very welcome reinforcements from home: John Sloane, who took over in Kenny Muir's place; Colin Mitchell, later to link his name with Aden; George Howat, who had left the battalion just weeks before we sailed for Korea, and some very experienced NCOs and men. The First Eleven were back in action.

We stayed in Kaesong for about a week. We had to fit the reinforcements back into their companies, put the many tradesmen back into their places left by casualties, and practise our new signallers. One day we were visited by Sir John Harding, C.-in-C. Far East, and one of the most charming and delightful generals around.

But there were disturbing rumours about the future. Originally our job under the United Nations was to get the KPA out of South Korea. Now it seemed that this was enlarged to sorting the KPA out completely, and that meant going right up to the Yalu. We wondered what the Chinese might think of that.

27 Brigade started off from Kaesong, on the 38th parallel on 16 October. We linked up with our tanks for that move so that we could put together some sort of cohesion and get the communications working. Next day at

least we and the tanks' crews could speak to each other reasonably well. We got to a place called Sinmak, about twenty-five miles south of Sariwon, and harboured there that night. There had been no opposition during the day.

I think it was about 8.00 next morning that we started off, with my company 'A' leading. The order of march was: first, a section of three tanks; then another four or five, each carrying a section of Jocks, with a platoon headquarters; then another platoon in US Army 30 cwt trucks, a mortar section, a Vickers MMG section, and our third platoon. Following were other tanks and the remainder of the battalion. 3RAR – to their disgust – were behind us, and the Middlesex brought up the rear. Somewhere behind was a company of US artillery, but they took no part in the battle.

Most unfortunately my faithful Land Rover with our proper communications threw some sort of 'wobbly' and refused to start that morning, so I had to travel with my three signallers and their sets in the leading 30 cwt truck, which was something of a drawback. The Land Rover eventually recovered, and joined us later.

We didn't know much about the enemy, except that Sariwon itself was a military town, and we were very likely to run into a hot reception when we got there. So we set off. What I had not realised was that we had been joined by representatives from the world's press, and a US major general with his own Jeep and a small escort. I thought he was some sort of liaison officer, but he turned out to be a kind of referee to see fair play between us, who were 'spearheading' the First Cavalry Division, and their rivals, the 24th Division, who were approaching Sariwon from farther west.

The column rumbled on. After about an hour the leading tank must have seen something suspicious, because it let fly with its gun – to the astonishment of my driver, a black sergeant of the US Transportation Corps.

'Say, Major,' he said, 'is this where you and I hit the dirt?'

As nothing was coming back in our direction, and the tanks were still rolling on, I suggested that there was nothing to worry about quite yet. This impressed my driver no end.

'Sure is great to be with the British – you're all real professionals, and I guess you've seen a lot of shooting!'

It was great to be so complimented, but I didn't want to disillusion him by admitting that my three platoon commanders were barely 20 years old, and that a good half of the Jocks were National Servicemen who had perhaps just a year's service in, and – until they had landed in Korea – had never seen a shot fired in anger! Mind you, the rest had seen a bit of action in the Second World War and in Palestine.

A few miles farther on we did run into some sniping going through a village, and we had to dismount to clear it, with a casualty or two. One was Private Kinne of my company headquarters, who was killed at almost point blank range two yards away from me by a North Korean sniper firing from a shack by the side of the road. It could so easily have been me.[2]

After a delay of perhaps half an hour we had cleared the village and were driving on, when there was an outburst of firing just behind my truck. It was the US general and his men, shooting chickens for their supper! I was struck dumb, but the situation was saved by my company sergeant major, who told the shooting party in no uncertain terms what to do with their weapons. I don't think any of then had heard some of the adjectives he used in their lives before! Shamefacedly they climbed back into their Jeep, and in US Army usage we 'barrelled on'.

By 1400 hours we were within four miles of Sariwon when the front tanks came under quite heavy fire from both small arms and anti-tank weapons. Two men on the leading tank were hit, and Ted Cunningham, the leading platoon commander, led his men forward to secure the road.

The problem was on the left flank, where fire was coming from an orchard some 500 yards from the road. We had to take it, as it could enfilade all traffic coming up from behind us. At that point my Land Rover – with my command set – was still not with us, so I and my two signallers legged it up to the point to see what was happening.

I managed to get 2 and 3 Platoons forward off their vehicles. I used 3 to reinforce Ted Cunningham and hold the road, and directed 2 onto the orchard, covered by our tanks, mortars and MMGs. It was led most ably by Owen Light, and in some ten minutes had sorted out the orchard with hardly any casualties, captured some ten LMGs, and killed forty or more North Koreans; the rest fled. They had not realised until it was too late that we would be able to get round their left flank and come in behind them, and the MMGs, tanks and mortars kept their heads down. It was a most spirited and successful little action.

By this time Leslie Neilson, my CO, had come up and told me to consolidate where I was. He sent B Company and the rest of the battalion into Sariwon, followed by 3RAR, who were not happy at missing the fun until then. (Their turn was to come that night!) This was the occasion, with 3RAR driving through our position, when some joker leaned out of his truck and shouted, 'For crissake mates – leave some for us!'

Up to then the whole affair had been the sort of encounter battle that one reads about in all the Staff College books and papers, except for one incident just after 2 Platoon's successful attack, watched by the US general, his retinue and the world press corps following close behind. Seeing the opposition melting away, the general came up to me and suggested that I and 'A' Company should press on immediately to capture Sariwon. By then I had been ordered to stand fast and consolidate, and this I told the general, but he was most put out, because to him the most important thing was to be in Sariwon before the 24th Division's column

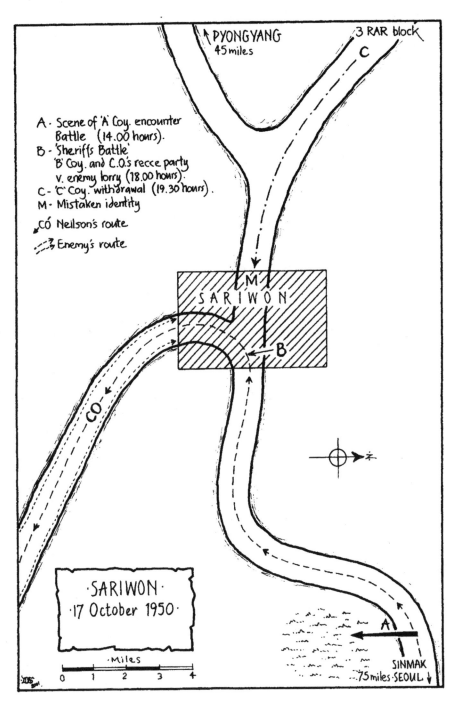

A · Scene of 'A' Coy. encounter
    Battle (14.00 hours).
B · 'Sheriffs Battle'
    'B' Coy. and C.O.'s recce party
    v. enemy lorry (18.00 hours).
C · 'C' Coy. withdrawal (19.30 hours).
M · Mistaken identity

→ Neilson's route

--→ Enemy's route

PYONGYANG
45 miles

3 RAR block

C

M

SARIWON

B

CO

SARIWON
17 October 1950

·Miles·
0   1   2   3   4

A

SINMAK
75 miles SEOUL

coming up on our left. We were the 1st Cavalry Division's point, and if we beat 24 Division into Sariwon, 1st Cavalry would have the road clear to Pyongyang; it all depended on 'A' Company, and it was my personal duty to capture that vital town!

How on earth can a mere major of some fourteen years' service deal with a general with some forty years behind him? In vain I pointed out that we were spread all over the countryside, that I had my orders anyway, and that I really couldn't care tuppence for the historical rivalry between two distinguished Divisions of the US Army. But luckily the issue was settled by 'B' and 'C' Companies driving through, which swept the general up with them to Sariwon and victory.

In due course I was bid to an 'O' group, which was to take place in the centre of the town, and having nothing better to do sat down in a small barber's shop, round which the personnel of the 'O' group were gathering. Suddenly there was a shattering outburst of noise, and the mirror behind me disintegrated.

From nowhere a North Korean truck had appeared, carrying a lot of very bellicose soldiers, who were discharging their weapons in all directions. It was all most confusing, and just at that moment my Sten gun jammed!

Somewhere in the middle of this mêlée was Alastair Gordon-Ingram, 'B' Company Commander, standing like an old-fashioned US sheriff, picking off targets with his pistol, and shouting 'Stand clear the Argylls!' He then lobbed a couple of 36 grenades into the truck, which effectively silenced the racket.

When we gathered ourselves together, the 'O' group had ceased to exist, and the CO, Adjutant, Intelligence Officer and Second in Command had mysteriously vanished, nowhere to be seen. We searched high and low, but found nothing.

What had happened was that, just before the bellicose truck arrived, they had started driving away from the centre of the town, in two carriers, and found themselves between two enemy columns moving in the opposite direction. The North Koreans had never seen British carriers and vehicles before, and as they were coming from the north thought they must be friendly. After some four miles the party found themselves clear, turned off the road and lay up uncomfortably for the night in some huts until daylight the next morning.

In the meantime 'C' Company, which had been sent north of the town, was withdrawing south as ordered, and met what must have been the same North Korean column going in the opposite direction. Again surprise was mutual: the North Koreans had never seen Scottish bonnets and cap comforters before, and thought we were their Russian allies coming to their aid. Chocolates and cigarettes were exchanged; Robin Fairie somehow found a North Korean comfort girl in his Mortar

Command Jeep, and exchanged hats with her; our American tank crews were told to take off their helmets and keep their mouths shut; and the two columns had just about passed each other in suspicious silence when someone gave the game away, and there was a furious outburst of shooting, just as they were about to separate! There were no casualties to us, but there were some to the North Koreans, who continued their withdrawal to be put into the bag by 3RAR.[3]

Eventually we all collected in the centre of Sariwon, less the CO's group, and held what I can only call a 'soviet' of company commanders. Next morning a shaken and rather shamefaced lot appeared, having lain undiscovered all night in their hideout, out of touch with the world!

What a way to run an army! But it had been an interesting twenty-four hours for 27 Brigade. I think we had all merited the opinion that my black transportation sergeant had of us earlier, at the start of the operation, particularly my three young platoon commanders, whose average age was then on the short side of 20. Two are still alive: Ted Cunningham, with a CBE after a distinguished career with the World Bank; and Owen Light MBE, who served with the Foreign Office, but for the last twenty years has been with the Ex Services Welfare Society, and is head of our operation in Scotland and Northern Ireland, looking after people who cannot help themselves. It's odd to think he earned his nickname at Sariwon – 'Killer'! The Jocks don't often get it wrong.

After Sariwon, resistance on the 27 Brigade front virtually ceased to exist, and we closed up to Pyongyang, the capital of North Korea, which had been taken by the 6th ROK Division. Here we thought we might be given a rest, but the Higher Command had different ideas. Our objective was to be the town of Chongju, some seventy-five miles away on the other side of the Chongchong River, and about thirty miles south of the Manchurian border. We were now under the command of the US 24th Division, but as they were some way behind, 27 Brigade was told to lead off. As usual 'A' Company led, 'spearpointing' as our American allies called it.

To cut off North Korean forces retreating in front of us, a whole parachute brigade was to drop to secure two routes. Our route, the one nearest the west coast, was called DZ William, and was to secure the town of Sukchon, so this was where we headed for. We had some difficulty in getting over the river at Pyongyang at a sandbagged bridge, but by 4.00 pm on 20 October we were in open country, having the odd encounter with snipers, which we and the tanks easily dispersed. It was beginning to get dark, and Brigadier Coad told us to stay short of the town, as there could have been the risk of blundering into the paratroops of 187RCT, and possible casualties. So we stopped about three miles short of Chongju, with orders to clear it next morning, when 3RAR would pass through us and the parachute battalion. I sent a small patrol forward, which contacted

Captain Claude H. Josey, their company commander, to let him know where we had got to. We then settled down for what turned out to be an exciting night.

Unknown to us most of 239 Regiment of the NKPA was in the area, full of fight. We had quite a few contacts with them, but their main effort was against the parachutists, who fought back with considerable skill and gallantry. Grenades, flares, machine guns and goodness knows what else went on all through the night. We had no wireless contact with the parachutists, and were unable to assist in any way; they had to fight it out on their own. We were being harassed by odd parties of North Koreans; I lost one killed and three wounded in a very confused situation.

The next morning we and C Company were told to clear Yongju and establish contact with the parachutists, but we found it difficult to get through the town as it was a nest of snipers. We were ordered to 'burn them out' – literally – which we did to great effect, so that others following us found it equally difficult to get through the resulting smoke and flames. Our Brigadier was not well pleased.

As planned, 3RAR now went up the road to the north. Their C Company, commanded by Mike Denness, had a dramatic encounter with some belligerent North Koreans in an apple orchard; they killed some 150 KPA and captured 230. Including those killed or captured by us – over 200 of 239 Regiment NKP – that made a total of nearly 600 in just twenty-four hours. They had, effectively, ceased to exist.

The next few days saw 27 Brigade close up to the Chongchong River, which the Middlesex crossed with some difficulty, partly because the US Engineers had forgotten the paddles for half the assault boats, partly because the river was swiftly tidal, and finally because they found it difficult to deal with the crowd of local dignitaries and citizens who were on the far side waiting to welcome them.

Battalions took it in turn to lead the Brigade column. 3RAR cleared Pakchon on 25 October, and it was just north of here that the Brigade had its first encounter with NKPA tanks (T34s). Intelligence sources suggested that the 17th Tank Brigade of the NKPA had been ordered to defend Chongju, which was our objective.

On 28 October it was our turn to lead A Company at the head, but this time we had a Mosquito (spotter) aircraft as our eyes. This was just as well; he spotted four T34s on our line of advance, and called down very successful airstrikes, which knocked them out. We got to just short of Chongju when 3RAR took over, and found themselves seriously opposed by tanks and infantry. Sadly it was during this battle that Lieutenant Colonel Charles Green, their commanding officer, was killed by a stray shell.

The battle for Chongju marked the limit of 27 Brigade's advance; they were relieved by 21 RCT, who continued up towards the north. This was the high point reached by 27 Brigade; we were moved sideways with the

Middlesex to cover a town call Taech'on. It was a rather eerie spot; nothing much was happening, but there was a disturbing menace in the air. We were out on a limb, with no artillery support, no transport, and not much news. It was just as well we did not know that our Brigadier had been summoned to 24th Division Headquarters, to be told by the Commanding General: 'Coad – the Chinese are in. World War Three has started!' He was then given orders to withdraw the Brigade, and transport was allotted to get us back from our very exposed position.

In this confused situation Colonels Neilson and Man took it on their own initiative to start the withdrawal on foot. It was as well they did; from what we know now, the Chinese were close behind in considerable numbers, 3RAR was out of contact, and the Brigadier was somewhere on the road between them and 24th Division, out of touch by wireless.

There was something very unreal and upsetting about those couple of days. It was more than uneasiness; there was the feeling that all was not well, and that something had gone very wrong. We didn't really have any orders, and we didn't know what we were doing at Taech'on, but we had the nasty feeling that someone was creeping up from behind. Goodness knows what Leslie Neilson, my CO, was feeling at that time, but he never let on, and he never showed any unease. There is so much more to command than the badges of rank on your shoulders. I can only hope that for my part I behaved in like manner, and that my platoons felt some sort of confidence in me. Once we started to move, things were better.

In due course our transport arrived. We drove south through the gloom towards Pakchon. There we were told that we would act as longstop to the Brigade. As I and my company settled in for the night, we could hear gunfire and see the flashes of artillery somewhere to the north. There was quite a battle going on at a place called Unsan, held by the 8th Cavalry Regiment. There was no question now that the game had changed: the Chinese were in with a vengeance.

A week earlier we had been part of a successful army: the enemy had been routed, and complete victory was in sight. Now came the first smell of defeat. What were we fighting the Chinese for? Why had they joined in? What sort of soldiers were they? No one really knew. We had previously heard that 29 Brigade was already in the country, and that as soon as they had organised themselves we would be sent back to Hong Kong. Now that plan seemed to be a dead duck. What is more, it was freezing cold at night, but as we had originally been sent from Hong Kong for only a few months we didn't have any sort of winter clothing; how did anyone expect us to operate without it?

If that is what we all felt inside, no one showed it. One splendid Australian of 3RAR leaned out from his truck and said as he drove past my company: 'Get stuck in Mates – you wont see Hong Kong for a long time yet!' You can imagine the reply he got.

We had about two days to settle into our new company position south of Pakchon. We were on our own, with one section of MMGs commanded by Corporal Danny Campbell, and one section of 3 inch mortars under Sergeant Clarke, but I was missing Owen Light (by now a very experienced platoon commander), who had fallen into a ditch at Chongju and broken his spectacles, without which he was nearly blind. He was whisked off to Pyongyang to get a replacement pair. It was all very peaceful and quiet; by night we watched across the Chongchong to see the headlights of the convoys carrying reinforcements on their way to us.

Winter usually comes quickly in North Korea, and November 1950 was no exception. By the first week the padi fields were frozen and there was a white rime on the roads and foliage. For those of us in 27 Brigade without proper winter clothing it was getting bloody cold. In those days the British Army's idea of a sleeping bag was two ordinary blankets fastened together with a bit of tape to tie yourself (and your shivering) in! The excellent airborne sleeping bags that we had four years earlier in Palestine had somehow never reached the Far East. So, on Sunday 5 November 1950 I woke up to the First Light Stand To, with my teeth chattering like castanets, to make the rounds of my company of Jocks. They were in like condition, but then the rum came round and we just about revived.

In cricketing terms, A company, 1st Argylls, was acting as longstop to 27 Commonwealth Brigade. We were on our own by the side of the Taryong River, guarding its crossing, with a detachment of 7th Cavalry, a battery of artillery and a few tanks, all commanded by a young major of the US Army. Behind us was a much larger river – the Chongchong.

The rest of 27 Brigade, the Middlesex and 3RAR were ten to twelve miles north of us; the remainder of the 1st Argylls were some five miles away on the other (east) side of the Tareyong. Parallel to this river the main road ran north to the small town of Taechon, and what had once been the main railway line from Pyongyang to the Manchurian border some forty miles to the north-west. As usual, communications were scrappy: I was just about in communication with battalion Headquarters, who in turn were just about in touch with Brigade.

The war had changed in the preceding seventy-two hours. Until then we had been pursuing a defeated North Korean Army, which could man a few rearguard positions, but was gradually disintegrating. Now a strange new menace had appeared from Manchuria: the Chinese. We hadn't actually seen any ourselves, but there were rumours and stories, and we had heard that two battalions of the 8th US Cavalry had been seriously attacked at a place called Unsan, and had had to withdraw in some disorder. There was a smell of uncertainty in the air. This was disturbing, but we in 27 Brigade reckoned we could handle any nonsense that might occur. So we did – but it was a near thing.

While I was wandering round our positions, I could see in the distance what looked like the smoke of shells exploding on the frozen padi fields north of us, between our position and the rest of the Battalion. But there was no sound of gunfire, and I could not hear anything on the wireless.

Gunfire is strange. Sometimes you can hear it miles away; sometimes the sound goes elsewhere over your head. I decided that there was nothing to worry about, and as I had been asked to have breakfast with the American battery, I walked down the hill to their lines, where I was given a large plate of bacon, hot cakes and maple syrup. (The US Army is pretty good at dishing up breakfasts under all sorts of conditions.) I had hardly got stuck into this when the Captain commanding the small tank detachment came dashing up and said that my CO wanted me urgently on his tank set.

It was indeed Leslie Neilson. He was very agitated. Someone had infiltrated a large force between him and me; I was to take everyone I could and clear the roadblock immediately. He and B and C Companies were going to have to cross the Tareyong and do what they could, but I was to attack the block from the South. I had to leave one platoon behind in my present position to guard the US detachment there. He did not know where the roadblock was, or how strong it was, but if I and A Company could not clear it, the whole brigade might be cut off.

It was a pity about the breakfast. I swallowed a last mouthful or two, and mobilised the Jocks. I could take only two of my platoons, two 3 inch mortars and my section of two Vickers MMGs. I persuaded four of the US tanks to come with me, and with one platoon on them and the reminder in trucks we drove north for about three miles, to come across a most astonishing sight.

Unknown to us, C Battery of the 61st Artillery battalion had moved into a harbour area during the night. As dawn broke they were attacked by a considerable force of Chinese, who were making for a small bridge on the main road that they were intending to destroy. The battery Commander, Captain Howard M Moore, formed his six guns into a semicircle and engaged the enemy over open sights at almost point blank range. In older days he would have had 'canister'[4] to use, but instead he depressed his guns so that his shells bounced off the frozen padi and exploded in their faces. As we arrived we could see his gunners being shot down behind their gunshields. It was like something from Napoleon's time.

Luckily we had arrived in the nick of time. The enemy could not face our four tanks, and fled. We pursued them, and something like a snipe shoot took place, with Chinese emerging from their hiding places in the padi and zigzagging away into the distance, and Jocks and tanks shooting them down. It took half an hour to clear the padi fields, and then we moved up to a smallish hill about 1,000 yards from the road. When we got to the top we could see more Chinese running away, but they were now out of range.

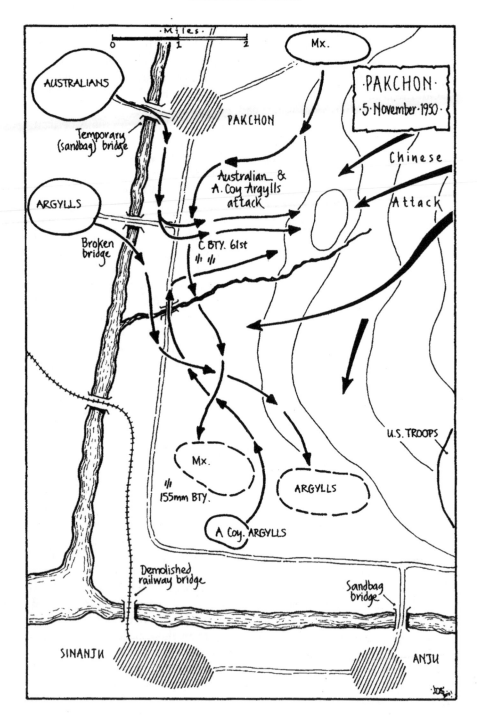

Now came the problem. The hill that we had secured, and its ridge, were too long for just one platoon to hold, and I could not afford to put my whole force on it. I had no artillery support; C Battery had fired its last round. I had no communication with Battalion. So I left just one platoon with Sergeant Clarke, the mortar NCO, who could call down fire to help them, and withdrew everyone else back to the road, where with the two Vickers and the tanks we had a good supporting position. So far so good: we had cleared the block, and it was just nine o'clock in the morning.

While all this was going on, Battalion headquarters and B and C Companies were crossing the Taeryon, with difficulty: one company commander wounded, other casualties, and communications out of action.

About 10.00 am things started to go wrong in my part of the world: the enemy put in a vicious counter-attack on my lone platoon. In the first few minutes Sergeant Clarke was killed, and without him they were blind. The platoon had suffered heavy casualties, with another three killed and six wounded. They could not stay there, so I ordered the young platoon commander to get his men off and down to a layback position where he could be covered by the tanks and the Vickers guns.

By 11.00 am we had reached a position of stalemate. The Chinese could sit on their hill provided they did not show their faces over the top, where they would be murdered by our firepower from the road. Equally we could go nowhere, and we were beginning to run out of ammunition. Had the Chinese realised that, we would have been sitting ducks. But at last the wireless started working again, and Battalion got through with exhortations to hang on where we were, as the whole Brigade was withdrawing to come to our aid.

At about 2.00 pm our friends 3RAR appeared and put in a two-company attack, which by 4.00 pm had regained the hill I had lost. I went along with them to see how our wounded had fared. I found to my surprise that the Chinese had done what they could for them: they had put on what dressings they had, and moved them into shelter. It was very different conduct from what I remembered of the way the Japanese Army had behaved some five years earlier. I helped carry Corporal Paterson, one of my section commanders, off the hill. He was badly wounded, but our Medical Officer reckoned that he would be OK. Lance Corporal Starke, his No. 2, had been killed trying to get him under cover; Sergeant Clarke and the others were dead.

We got back to the road, reorganised, and – with the rest of the battalion – went back to my original position, leaving 3RAR and the Middlesex in our area, where they had an exciting night. The Chinese came at 3RAR in strength, and a most confused battle took place. It left 3RAR with sixteen killed and thirty-two wounded – more casualties in one engagement that they had in any during their service in Vietnam.

As a result of this very confused day's operations 3RAR and the Argylls carry in a bit of silk embroidery on their colours the battle honour Pakchon. It is unique in the whole of our two armies; no other regiment bears it.

Some time during the night the Chinese broke contact, and at dawn next day they were nowhere to be seen. Patrols were sent out, tentatively at first and then at increasing range, but there was no trace, so we started moving forward again – very cautiously, but slowly and thoroughly. In the middle of all this came the news we were expecting. We were not to return to Hong Kong: whatever was to come, we were committed to Korea.

During one move forward there was some sniping, and our mortars came into action to cover us. Then I heard the ominous whistle of a broken tailfin. The errant bomb descended directly on one of my platoon headquarters. Ted Cunningham, the platoon commander, lost a leg, and his sergeant was badly wounded. It was a sad accident, which lost me two valued and experienced leaders.

Then came 23 November: Thanksgiving Day. As we were under American command we celebrated in style, but how does a company in a forward position cook eight enormous turkeys? This was no problem. We made ovens out of 50-gallon oil drums dug into the side of a river bank, with a space for a fire underneath, and fashioned a chimney out of ration tins. Our friends the 5th Infantry, who had the latest in US Army kitchen equipment, could not believe what the Brits were up to; I am sure our turkeys were better cooked than theirs.

About this time the first of our winter kit appeared. It was in fact courtesy of the US Army. Their parkas and jackets were streets ahead of ours, but our jerseys, string vests and socks were a class above theirs. Our boots were a disgrace. They were originally designed for operations in Norway in 1940, and had been in store ever since; they fell to pieces! Nevertheless, at least we could now keep reasonably warm and dry.

After our monumental Thanksgiving feast the Brigade went into reserve, for the first time since we had arrived in Korea. There was a cinema, baths and the chance of properly cooked meals. There was also a concert party, but the jokes were American, and the Jocks didn't understand them. Morale was soaring, and there was talk of another advance to the Yalu. The Chinese had vanished. Things were looking up – but not for long.

It was on 26 November that things started to go wrong. The whole Brigade was to concentrate round IX Corps Headquarters, at a dismal spot called Kunu-ri. None of us had seen a Corps Headquarters before. It was a collection of large tents, with chimneys protruding from the space heaters that kept the temperature inside at summer heat. Those of us who were allowed inside boiled in our cold-weather kit (the Staff Officers were working in their shirtsleeves). The atmosphere was depressing – and so were the maps. Everywhere there seemed to be large red arrows pointing through the gaps in our line, and question marks as to the whereabouts of our own side. There was an enormous void between the right flank of IX Corps and X Corps, who had been landed on the East Coast, and the ROK divisions seemed to have disintegrated. It didn't take us long to work out that we were in deep trouble. What were the three battalions of 27 Brigade going to be asked to do about it? I've never felt so far from home.

We were camped alongside this centre of doom and despair. Luckily we had no idea of some of the plans that were thought up for us, which our Brigadier successfully shot down. A bitter yellow wind blew down from the hills of Manchuria. The ground was rock hard; we were in a frozen riverbed, and it was nearly impossible to dig slit trenches of any sort – not so much to fight the enemy from as to get out of the freezing wind. The barometer of morale was sinking every minute, not from inaction but from the total lack of information and the rumours of disaster everywhere.

After some twenty-four hours at this ghastly spot the Brigade was ordered to proceed south to Sunchon, to guard the main supply route. There would be no transport; we would march. The battalion war diary for that day read:

> 1345. The Battalion moved off with
> 'A' Company leading and the pipes playing.

After about three hours it was dark, and I regulated the halts at ten minutes to each hour by my hunting horn, which carried the length of the column through the bitterly cold air. We did not really know where we were going, what we were going to do when we got there, or what lay in the future. But we were in fighting formation, ready to deploy on either side of the road if anyone tried to ambush us. We were climbing up to a pass along a winding road where such an ambush was very likely, and we had the feeling that unseen eyes were marking our progress, waiting to pounce. The Jocks later called this 'The Death March'.

Bernard Fergusson, Black Watch, leader of two Chindit expeditions and eventually Governor General of New Zealand, like his father and grandfather before him, wrote some lines about pipe music as he trekked through the Burmese jungle:

> Oh for the piper striding towards the morning,
> Half hidden in the gloom,
> Playing my choice –
> 'Steamboat', 'The Gypsy's Warning',
> 'The Wee man at the Loom'.[5]

In the same poem there is a magnificent line about the friendly stars that guided him and his men:

> Those soldier stars that pace the beats of heaven.

In November 1950 I had not read those lines, but I know so well what he felt, even though he was on his own away from his regiment, and I was leading mine towards some sort of destiny.

So we marched on through the night to the sound of the pipes for nearly twenty miles. At last, just as we got over the pass, we saw our transport, and all piled in for the last twelve miles back to Sunchon, where our cooks had prepared the best and hottest stew I have ever tasted.

There was one sinister episode. Just about the place where we embussed, there was a small Korean hamlet in flames, and two US Army Jeeps, badly shot up. In one there was a dead colonel, with his driver and escort. We had heard some firing ahead; perhaps this was the result, but we had made it to comparative safety.

Eight hours or so after we had marched through the pass, a large column of the US Second Division followed us in transport, with tanks and guns. They had hardly got halfway up when they were well and truly ambushed. Somehow they failed to get out of their trucks and up the hills on either side. As tanks and trucks blocked the road others tried to drive through, making the blockage worse. It was a dreadful scene of disorganisation and carnage, watched with horror by the Middlesex, who had been left at the top of the pass but were powerless to help the column through.

Farther down the road we watched as a few survivors drove by in their trucks. Descriptions of old time naval battles tell of 'blood running from the scuppers', and that was what we saw: trucks full of dead and wounded, with blood oozing along the sides and tailboards. We did what we could to help, which was precious little.

The US 2nd Division lost over 4,000 officers and men in that disastrous withdrawal. If it had not been for the Middlesex, who held the head of the pass at Yongwon Ni, it could have been even worse. What might have happened to 27 Brigade if *we* had tried to drive through in trucks the night before? The same thing, I believe. It would have been so easy to shoot up a convoy of trucks, but engaging a marching column in battle order might have made the Chinese stop and think – and what were the extraordinary instruments they were playing, making such an outlandish noise?

On 2 December we were detached from the Brigade to what was called 'Task Force Harris', a unit composed of part of the 7th and 8th Cavalry Regiments. A and B Companies, with me in command, was sent up the highest hill yet. It was a sort of flank guard, and there was no opposition.

There we sat for a day, and then late one afternoon we were suddenly told to withdraw. Korean porters came and collected our bedding and heavy kit, and I was given a map reference rendezvous that meant nothing to me at all. It was on a map we did not have, some two miles off the sheets we were using.

In vain I protested to Leslie Neilson that I had no idea where to go, or what to do when I got there, but he said that he was ordered to withdraw by that route. Somehow I had to get along the spine of the hills I was on, and after five or six miles come down to join a road that I had no idea existed. In famous last words, he added: 'You can't miss it!'

It was now dusk. We moved cautiously along the ridge, with the wireless gradually fading, and our artillery set out of contact with anyone. As we moved there were signs of enemy occupation not many hours before – slit holes, warm ash in the fireplaces, signs of branches cut for camouflage – but thankfully no enemy.

I had two very experienced officers in B Company: Colin Mitchell – an old and trusted friend – commanding, and Bob Wilson, one of his platoon commanders, who had been with me in Palestine four years earlier, but by now was actually in the Highland Light Infantry. It was largely due to the skill and leadership of these two that we found our way off that dreadful hill: had anyone fallen and broken a limb I don't know how we would have managed to get the casualty down. This was the 1937 Iblanke in reverse: something seemingly impossible that we managed without the loss of a single man or piece of equipment.[6]

Suddenly we were down and on a track. There was a dark village with barking dogs to the left, and though it didn't seem like the road described to me by Leslie Neilson four hours earlier, it just might lead somewhere, so cautiously we set off – without any maps. After a mile there was a road with a Land Rover on it, and inside the Land Rover was John Slim. Were we pleased to see each other! But he had problems too: C Company and Leslie Neilson had lost themselves somewhere down the road, he had no communication with either, and there was desultory shooting going on in the direction in which they had vanished. At least we had two companies and headquarters of a battalion, and it looked as if I might be in command. But it was not for long: Leslie appeared, having found C Company, and there were new orders. We were to withdraw back the way we had come. I and my two companies had flogged our way up and down hills for 36 hours to absolutely no purpose whatsoever. It was now 2.00 in the morning, and it had started to snow.

Then a remarkable scene occurred. Ted Marley of the US Artillery had joined up with his Jeep set, which was with battalion Headquarters, and had received orders to withdraw immediately. He and all the transport were to go down a different road from us: we were going to walk across a frozen river (if the ice was thick enough – we wouldn't know until we tried).

Ted came to Leslie Neilson to ask his permission to go. He was very reluctant to, as it could leave us without any communications with any artillery.

'Do you know where your guns are?' asked Leslie.

'No, Sir.'

'Can they support us in any way?'

'Not here, Sir, but maybe on the way back you might need them; without me you have no contact!'

'Well,' said Leslie, 'I think you must obey your orders and get back to wherever you have to go.'

'Sir,' said Ted, 'I will do that, but I did not want to without your permission. I would not wish you to think that the US Artillery would let the Argylls down!'

And he saluted and left. The next time I saw him was when we had lunch in Washington, some forty years later.

Sometimes I hear those who have never fought with the United States armed forces talk disparagingly of them. I remind them of this very young second lieutenant of artillery, all on his own, attached to a strange Highland Regiment, who set those of us who saw it a fine example of training, tradition and courage.

The march back along the track to the river was through snow, which got progressively heavier as we went along. Then we came to the river. Would the ice hold? If it did not we were in trouble. We sent a medium-sized volunteer with a rope round his waist. He made it, and then we followed, one at a time, at ten-yard intervals, very cautiously and slowly. There were ominous noises, but no creaks or cracks, and after about an hour we, and the Battalion of the 8th Cavalry that we were with, were across on the far side. We posted some pickets for local protection, then lay down in the snow by platoons and companies and went to sleep. We were exhausted.

The next day we heard we were to withdraw south of Pyongyang, but we had to wait for our transport, which we boarded early one morning. The rumour was that we were going all the way south of the Parallel. After thirty miles the town was in sight, and there were proper-looking British soldiers, British tanks, British guns and British trucks. It was 29 Brigade, businesslike in their berets and camouflaged winter kit. (It looked smart, but was not very good in the Korean winter that was to come.)

What a sight we must have made, in American troop-carrying trucks, battered signals vehicles, Land Rovers that looked as if they should have been on a scrapheap, and the most extraordinary selection of uniforms you have ever seen: partly American, with British boots and jerseys, and precious little in the way of badges of rank. We were filthy, unwashed, and mostly unshaven, after being on the go from frozen riverbeds to mountains for nearly two weeks. We looked more like a collection of tramps and layabouts than soldiers.

As we drove along I saw a smart young Ulster rifleman obviously wanting a lift, so I stopped by him in my battered Land Rover, and he hopped in beside me in the front. In the back was the usual clutter of sets and kit, and my two signallers, both of whom were Gaelic speakers, and were quietly nattering away to each other. This confused our passenger greatly; eventually he turned to me and said, in his splendid Ulster accent, 'Say – are youse the Turks?'

Once we were through Pyongyang 29 Brigade took over rearguard, and we headed south to Uijongbu, a small town about twelve miles north of Seoul. Here for the first time we went into Army Reserve, prepared a defensive position, and made ourselves as comfortable as possible. It was rumoured that, with luck, we would be spending Christmas there. 3RAR and the Middlesex were close at hand, and there was time to visit each other and get to know our opposite numbers. There was a lot of sorting out to do: kit was worn out, vehicles were in a parlous state, wireless sets needed maintenance, and reinforcements needed to be distributed round companies.

On 23 December the 8th Army commander, General Walton Walker, was killed in a road accident almost opposite our area. He was driving to Brigade Headquarters to present 27 Brigade with the South Korean Presidential Citation, when a badly driven 3 ton truck hit his jeep. His death was to have a great influence on the war. His successor was Lieutenant General Matthew Ridgeway, a parachute soldier of great distinction. He was warned for duty on 24 December, saw General MacArthur on the 26th, and was in post in Korea on the 27th. He took the 8th Army and all of us by the scruff of our necks, and within six weeks had us well and truly sorted out.

But first there was the small matter of General Peng Te-Huai's Third Phase Offensive to be dealt with. Some twenty-four Chinese and four KPA divisions were let loose on 27 December on the ROK Army, and by 31 December 29 Brigade were involved. On 1 January 1951 we were moved out of our area at Uijongbu to some ten miles forward at Tokchong to cover the retreat of the 6th ROK Division, and then to take up a rearguard position to cover the withdrawal from Seoul. On 4 January we, the Argylls, were left as the final rearguard to the two bridges over the Han River. At 1.00 pm that day they were blown. The UN had abandoned Seoul for the second time in the campaign.

'A' Company and I were the last over the main bridge across the Han River, except for a small party of American soldiers watching us from the bank. One of them had two grenades fastened to his webbing. He wore the badges of a parachutist, and the three stars of a lieutenant general. It was our new C.-in-C., Mathew B. Ridgeway. He was accustomed to leading from the front, but as this was a rearguard, he himself would see it over. Then things would happen: under his command we were to be transformed from a roadbound, somewhat dispirited army into a proper force able to fight in the hills.

Once over the river we joined the stream of refugees going south. We were bound for Changhow Won Ni, about fifty miles south-east of Seoul. There we would halt and reorganise. 27 Brigade was to grow a bit: we had our own British transport company now, 60th Indian Parachute Field Ambulance would join us, as would the 16th New Zealand Field Regiment, and we had acquired the 2nd Chemical Mortar Battalion of twenty-four 4.2 inch mortars from the US Army. We were now a very different force from the two understrength units that had landed from Hong Kong back in August, and we had gained a very great deal in experience.

The war was to change in the way we fought it. Up till now we had been fighting from roads, as we were dependent on them for all our supplies. If we had to take to the hills we could operate only at a very limited distance from the roads, as we had no means of carrying forward reserves of food and ammunition. The Chinese and North Koreans did not suffer from this disadvantage: they had the numbers to spare, and they could take to the hills more easily that we could, but for limited distances only. The UN withdrawal of some fifty miles gave us a breathing space to reorganise before the enemy could bring their main forces forward, and with our complete dominance of the air, any movement by them by day was very difficult unless the weather was bad.

The answer to our mobility problem was the use of our excess man-power – the Korean people themselves. They were conscripted and used by units as porters. Each company was allocated some twenty or so, and with their A frames they followed us up hill and down dale, carrying reserves of rations (not water – we could get that from melting snow or the hill streams). So instead of roadbound columns snaking forward into positions that were easily ambushed, the 8th Army and ROK forces now spread right across the country, from one coast to the other. Not one hill was missed out. If enemy forces tried to delay on one feature they would be outflanked by others.

This was a hard grind, and in some ways monotonous work. Day after day we slowly won back the real estate we had lost. From time to time there was a battle, 3RAR and the Middlesex were involved, but never seriously ourselves. From February until April we steamrollered back. And by this time another battalion had joined the Brigade: the Princess Patricia's Canadian Light Infantry. 27 Brigade had four infantry battalions, the 16th New Zealand Field Regiment, the US Chemical Mortar Battalion, the 60th Indian parachute Field Ambulance, our own British Transport company, and we were stronger than the US Army equivalent, a regimental combat team. What is more, we were a very battle-experienced unit.

We were to spend the next eight weeks up the hills, in the open, and February and March are the coldest months of the year in Korea. At least we had adequate winter clothing now, mostly of the American pattern, but our boots, underwear, and – particularly – our socks were British. And socks mattered. We had four pairs each: two you wore, the other two you stuffed inside your jacket or shirt. At evening Stand To you changed them over, so that you had a reasonably warm, dry pair to last the night and next day. At the end of a week or so they could get a bit high, but there was always a chance of rinsing out the spare pair at some time. It was a small but vital ritual, which saved us many casualties of frost-bitten feet.

As a result of these eight weeks' hard slog we had gained some thirty miles and were almost up to the 38th Parallel. We ourselves had a few skirmishes only; the other three battalions seem to have had more contacts. In that period the Brigade had some twenty killed and seventy wounded.

By this time a leave scheme, R & R (Rest and Rehabilitation) had been introduced – five days in Tokyo! (There were some who came back after the experience admitting to being more tired on return than when they left.) My turn came up at the beginning of April, and I handed over my Company to John Macdonald, my second in command. Various people came up to wish me farewell, amongst them Michael Cawthorne, my senior and quite my best platoon commander. He was an outstanding young man.

He asked me whether I would look after a letter he had written to his father, and I said that of course I would; I would post it the first opportunity I had in Tokyo. But that was not quite what he meant. Would I keep it in case anything happened to him, and then post it? All this was said quite calmly; there was no mention of possible death or anything like that. Then he left to catch up with his platoon, who were on the move, turning to wave to me as he went.

I spent five days in Japan with Gordon Skinner, the No. 2 in Shell Company, who had a lovely house in Yokosuka, and I saw a lot of the country. Just as my five days were up there was a change in the weather; everything was grounded, and I arrived back at Rear Battalion Headquarters forty-eight hours late.

There was an atmosphere of sadness and loss about the place. I found out why, when Andrew Brown, our Quartermaster told me: 'Mike Cawthorne was killed three days ago.' Now I knew why he had given me the letter, and strangely enough he had given another to Owen Light, one of his fellow platoon commanders – it contained a string of Mikimoto pearls for a very great friend.

It had happened on 4 April, on a mountainside near an insignificant little village called Karim. Mike and his platoon were leading A Company up a steep spur, when his leading section commander spotted movement above them. Quite rightly he got his men down into a covering position, his Bren lined up on where they thought the enemy was lying in wait. Mike, impatient of delay, came storming up, telling them to get on, but his section commander was adamant, pointing out where he thought the enemy were in position. Then Mike did what was typical of him, a natural leader from the front. He took his glasses out, walked forward in front of the Bren gun, masking its fire, and proceeded to survey the scene for himself. A sniper got him stone dead with one shot.

If I had been there, could I have stopped him? For all the time I had him in Korea I had tried to make him realise that his job was not to act as the leading scout, with his men following behind him. Of course he was their leader and commander, but there are other ways of getting men to follow you. But that was against his instincts. We had lost someone who could have risen to the highest ranks of the Regiment and the Army, and for the third time in my career I felt that I was somewhere else at a crucial time (I should have been with my platoon in Waziristan in 1937, and with 2 A&SH at the start of the Malayan campaign).

A couple of days later Gerry Hadow, second in command of B Company, came across some of 3RAR brewing up. One of them offered him a mug of steaming tea, and said to him: 'We were all sorry to hear about Mike Cawthorne, skipper; he was a good bloke.' That was the soldier's highest compliment to a brave comrade, but coming as it did from men of another regiment, it was something very special. What the speaker did not know was that he was speaking of a fellow Australian. Michael's father and mother were both Australian born. After a distinguished career in the Indian Army his father, General Sir Walter Cawthorne, went back to Australia after Indian Independence and ended up as Australian High Commissioner in Canada. We never realised that Mike was himself a 'Digger'!

That was about the end of our actual fighting in Korea. There were a few more mountains to climb, but no more actual contact with the enemy. By this time we had heard that we were being relieved by the King's Own Scottish Borderers, and would be back at Hong Kong within a fortnight.

On 19 April our advance party left. We were by now in a reserve area near Kapyong, and gradually we were stripped of all our operational kit, leaving us just enough to fight with. Two days later, on the Saturday, we held a farewell party for all our friends. The main refreshment was Atholl Brose, which did for Charlie Snow and his merry men of the 2nd Chemical Mortar Battalion, who were unaccustomed to this type of refreshment. 'Moose Milk' Charlie called it, but next morning his face was as green as his fatigues, and he confessed that he was suffering from a serious attack of the 'dry heaves'. I am glad to say that we also did for some of our friends in 3RAR, in return for their 'buttered rum', which they had given us at Christmastime in far-off Uijongbu all those months ago.

That Sunday our New Zealand gunners invited the whole battalion for a special barbecued bullock, cooked New Zealand style on hot stones in an enormous hole in the ground. But just when the party was going well, panic stations set in: the Chinese were on us again. The party packed up in record time, the Kiwis got their guns into action, and we went back to our camp wondering 'What the hell?' – we were used to foul-ups by now, but this seemed to be on another plane altogether. Next day we occupied a defensive position round our camp, while the ominous stream of refugees started through our lines. To the North we could hear the New Zealanders' 25 pounders firing in support of the ROK Division, who were in contact.

Our transport arrived at noon on 24 April, and we drove ten miles or so south to meet the KOSBs, past the New Zealand guns firing as hard as they could. This was the second time I had 'bugged out' of a battle – under orders, admittedly. Singapore had been the first, some eight and a half years earlier. What did I feel then? It is hard to say after this length of time: a mixture of relief at going, and shame at leaving my friends to face the music. It was 3RAR's turn now, and they dealt with the Chinese as they always had. Whatever else was happening around them, 27 Brigade held firm at Kapyong. It was their last battle; with the departure of the Middlesex and ourselves they were renumbered 28. 27 had passed into history.

We embarked on the USS *Montrose*. There was just time to hear the news that the Gloucesters and 29 Brigade were fighting for their lives at Solma Ri, defending the main road to Seoul against impossible odds, and then we were off. HMS *Belfast* was anchored off Inchon, and as we sailed past her the whole ship's company lined her side and cheered us. A solitary piper stood on B Turret playing our regimental marches, and the marine band was on the quarterdeck. The Royal Navy was seeing us off in style, with the highest compliment of 'Cheering Ship'. Even after all these years the memory of it can bring a lump to my throat. I wondered if we had really deserved it. Was it all worth it – what Prime Minister Attlee called 'a distant obligation but an obligation none the less'? I thought so at the time, and nearly eighteen years later I was to have that belief confirmed.

In 1968 I was back in Korea as a Brigadier with three different hats: Defence Attaché, Member of the Armistice Commission, and Commander of the Commonwealth Liaison Mission. In late October each year there is a remembrance ceremony at the UN Cemetery in Pusan, where British lie alongside Australians, Canadians, New Zealanders, Indians, Turks, Thais, French, and all the dead of the men from many nations who fought in the Korean War. The service is very much the same as any other remembrance service, but with one significant difference. Beside every grave stands a young Korean schoolboy, dressed in the same Germanic dark blue uniform of his school, or a schoolgirl, with the mandatory bobbed hair, all dressed in sailor suits of the Victorian age. Each holds one lovely red flower, which the Koreans call the 'never ending flower', as it stays in bloom for such a long time. During the two minutes' silence, each pupil puts their flower down on the grave they guard. It is very impressive, and very touching.

As we flew back to Seoul that afternoon I mentioned this to a friend sitting next to me, Major General Liew of the Korean Army, but added that I thought it a bit of a shame that so many young children had to wait for so long in the bitter cold in their thin uniforms, in a ceremony for men of completely different nationalities and races. The Koreans are a very civilised people. The General never let on that my question showed how ignorant I was of their culture and customs. He very quietly explained to me how wrong I was. I cannot quote him exactly after all these years, but this is pretty much what he said:

'In Korea, all members of a family have a duty to look after their family's graves. This happens at Chusok, the first New Moon in September. The whole country takes a holiday, and it is in many ways a happy occasion: the young are reminded who their parents and grandparents were, and it is a reunion of cousins and brothers and sisters of all ages. And it is a duty to tidy the graves after the long summer, and to replace plants that may have died. It would be dreadful to neglect this duty.

'But here at the UN Cemetery, these men are far from home and their families cannot come, and so they would feel lonely if no one came to take care of them. So each child adopts one soldier for this day, and they are proud to do so. And also they thank them for giving their lives for Korea.'

I should have known. I felt ashamed for asking what must have seemed a very stupid question, and I remembered that we, the Argylls, have a motto that echoes that very same sentiment:

Ne obliviscaris – 'Do not forget'.

NOTES

1 This was the lightest form of bridging material, for foot soldiers and bicycles only. It consisted of 'kapok' floats linked by a wooden treadway.
2 There is a strange twist to this story. His brother came out to Korea with the Northumberland Fusiliers in 29 Brigade, was captured in the Imjin Battle in April eight months later, and received the George Cross for incredible endurance and gallantry whilst a prisoner of war.
3 See Major General David Butler's account on pp. 27–29 of the June 1995 issue of *Duty First*.
4 This was much used by muzzle loaders in earlier wars. It consisted of a thin-cased shell, filled with lead balls, which exploded almost instantaneously; the effect on attacking infantry was deadly at short range.
5 From Bernard Fergusson's 'Lowland Soldier'.
6 See Chapter 2, p. 23.

CHAPTER 11
Bernard
Field Marshal the
Viscount Montgomery KG GCB DSO

It was a typically dismal, drizzly March day in 1957. The headquarters of the 8th Argylls was situated in a back street of Dunoon, where the Commanding Officer and the Adjutant shared a small office with the regulation army fireplace, which was specially designed to produce more smoke than heat. In the absence of the Commanding Officer, Lachlan Gordon Duff, a regular soldier turned Territorial after the Second World War, who lived up in Appin some eighty miles to the north, I as training officer occupied his chair.

The telephone rang. It was Bobby Smith from Scottish Command, acting Assistant Military Secretary: 'David, the Field Marshal wants to see you next Wednesday. You are to be his new Military Assistant, if he thinks you'll suit him.'

I was nonplussed. What on earth was he talking about? Which Field Marshal? I didn't know any at the time!

'It's Monty, you twit! You're to have lunch with him at the Mill next Wednesday – you're to take over the job in May if all goes well.'

You could have stuffed me, as the saying goes, with a ripe banana. I'd never met the man, though I had heard him lecture twice: once to my Staff College course, just before the Rhine Crossing in 1947, and the second time in the Whitehall Theatre in London, to all of us who were then serving in the War Office. But I was in Bill Slim's 14th Army, and it was there my loyalties lay. How on earth had anyone selected me? I learnt later that I had to thank two soldiers of my own regiment for that.

My predecessor as Monty's MA, Denny Esmonde Whyte, had been suddenly posted to command a gunner regiment, so the War Office had sent Monty a list of possible replacements. My name was not on it. But when Monty saw the list he exclaimed that it looked a pretty average, almost useless lot, and would the War Office produce a better selection? Which they did, and this time my name *did* appear. Monty exploded, saying that this second list was worse than the first.

'Well, what do you expect, Field Marshal?' said Brigadier Michael Dewar. 'You turned down the First Eleven; this is the Second Team!'

Monty was adamant, and asked, 'Is there anyone at all in this Headquarters who knows any of these useless officers?'

There were two Argylls at Headquarters: Colonel John Sloane, of Monty's own Strategic Studies Section, and Regimental Sergeant Major Paddy Boyde, the senior British warrant officer at SHAPE, with two DCMs, one of which Monty had personally pinned on him. They were hastily sent for, John Sloane first: he gave me an excellent character reference, but then made a most unfortunate remark when he was asked what spare time and recreational pursuits I followed. John listed cricket, hockey and rugby, and had he stopped there all would have been well; but then he added, 'He plays the bagpipes.'

Monty recoiled in horror.

'What? A mad bagpiper? That won't do at all. He might play the bloody things in my office!'

John retreated hastily, and sent in Paddy Boyde, who Monty knew well.

'Mr Boyde, do you know an officer called Wilson in your regiment?'

'I know two, Sir. One was my first commanding officer in 1933 in Edinburgh, and his son was my platoon commander in 1938 when we were in Secunderbad.'

'Ah,' said the Field Marshal, 'it's the son I want to know about. Was he a good platoon commander?'

'Well I thought so, Sir,' replied Paddy. 'He gave me my second stripe!'

'Excellent. Thank you, Mr Boyde. Obviously a good judge of men – he'll do for me!'

So I got the job. It was a classic example of regimental skulduggery. Much later I heard Monty say about the affair: 'If you want to find out about an officer, ask an RSM!'

I still had to pass my interview and inspection at Isington Mill, Monty's home, which I reached at the appointed hour via that lovely Pullman train, the *Queen of Scots*, which ran from Glasgow to London down the East Coast. It was not a very fast train, but it was very comfortable, and the food was delicious! Next morning I took the rattle-and-bang electric train to Bentley Station. There on the platform was the familiar, somewhat dishevelled figure of the great man – sweater, corduroys and all. He took me to his car, which he drove himself to the nearest post office. There he produced his pension book and drew his cash over the counter, explaining for all to hear that he didn't trust the banks!

We then went back to Isington Mill, where I was given an excellent lunch, and subjected to what we got to know as a 'good talk': a very detailed inquisition, in which you felt like a butterfly pinned to a wall, while every secret was quickly and efficiently drawn out of you. During that lunch I was put under Monty's microscope in a most charming way. He brightened up when the name of General Jock Burnett-Stuart came up, and I told him that my father was one of his senior staff officers at Wellington in Southern India in 1922, and that I and his daughter Kax had almost been brought up together. It was not till much later that I found out that General Jock had been his superior officer twice, and twice had somehow saved the Field Marshal's bacon from the frying pan.

After lunch I was taken round the house, the garden, the caravans, and the Rolls-Royce. Suddenly he said, 'You'll do me,' and proceeded to give me a list of dates and places and people to whom I would report, and the date on which I would take over the job. He had also had arranged for me and my family to take over a lovely house in France, Le Blanc Moulin at Seraincourt, about twenty-five miles from SHAPE, where all his military assistants had lived. The whole thing was cut and dried in about twenty minutes, and then he drove me back to Bentley Station. I got back to London and eventually to Dunoon feeling as though I had been put through a wringer, but at the same time I was very excited. It was going to be one hell of a good job.

Two months later found me and the family installed in Le Blanc Moulin, a lovely old water mill, in the little village of Seraincourt. It was about thirty miles east of Paris, and five miles or so from Meulan, situated on the Seine. Just down the road was Flins, where the big Renault factory dominated the area. The mill itself was not in working order, though most of the machinery was in place, in the big room that we made into an entrance hall. The stream and lave[1] were well maintained. The property belonged to a great character, M. Louis Français, ex Adjutant-Chef of the 6ème Chasseurs Alpins. After the Second World War he had gone into what he described as 'assurance'; he had made a packet, and bought his parcel of land with the profits. Rent was payable by me monthly, in cash (so no cheques that could be traced by the taxman), and there was a little ceremony ending with what he called '*Un petit coup de Calva*': a large glass of his own home-brewed Calvados, which effectively put an end to any other worthwhile activity for that day.

The Field Marshal was away in the United States and Canada at that time, so I had a week or so to take over the job, but I wasn't very clear about just what the job was to be. I was nominally in charge of his staff, though he had a Major General as his Chief of Staff. Unfortunately he and that individual did not get on, which was a problem. There was an ADC, Sandy Cheyne of the Royal Warwickshire Regiment, whose job was to look after Isington Mill and the London office, but who frequently came over to France, where he had a room in what the Americans called the BOQ (bachelor officers' quarters). There was a chief clerk, and two other clerks (one of whom was the Field Marshal's personal stenographer), a soldier servant of his own regiment, and three drivers for his three cars, one of which was permanently mine, but could at times be called on for special duties.

At Isington Mill was another soldier servant, a cook/housekeeper, and Sergeant Parker, who drove Monty's rather special 16-cylinder Rolls-Royce. There was also one very special person: Capitaine de Fregate Claude Delacour of the French Navy, who had succeeded Jean Costa de Beauregarde[2]. He ranked equal with me as a military assistant, and dealt with all the domestic and travel problems on the French side. Claude had been sunk three times in World War II: first by the Germans at Dunkirk, then by the Royal Navy during the Syrian operation, and finally – and to Claude the ultimate disgrace – by the Italians in 1944. Claude and I became great personal friends, and we worked together closely.

I discovered to my horror that one of my jobs was to keep Monty's personal diary: the record of his meetings, doings, sayings and correspondence, which was completed in draft form every two months, given to him for his approval, typed up by his staff, and then taken home by him and deposited in his bank. A routine job? There was a catch. From time to time you would be handed some specially secret or confidential document, and told that it would be required for the next edition of the diary. This was in complete breach of every security rule in existence. Worse, each edition of the diary showed all too clearly who had compiled it and written it up – you! All of us who held the job of his military assistant have had the diaries hanging over their heads like the sword of Damocles.

Records of meetings that you attended had to be written up that day and the draft handed to him first thing next morning for his approval. There was one problem: you were not allowed to take any notes whatsoever. You had to sit and concentrate on what was being said. This was not as difficult as it might sound. After about a month you got to know all his views on particular problems, as he would tend to restate them again and again, so usually you knew roughly what he would say; all you had to remember was what the actual reply was.

Eventually the great day came, and 'Father' – as his staff irreligiously called him – arrived on a Sunday afternoon at Orly in his Dakota. I met him in the No. 1 car, with all the English Sunday papers and his brief for engagements for the next week. He asked me a few searching questions. How had I and my family settled in? How had the handover gone? What did I think of various members of his staff? This was a poser. I had yet to learn that his habit was to ask very direct questions and expect a very direct answer. If he caught you bluffing you were for it. I managed to avoid the trap, and we arrived at his hotel in Versailles, where the French government had provided him with a suite of rooms.

Next day, punctually at 10.00 am, he arrived in his office. His stenographer had already been down to the hotel, and the letters he had dictated were ready on his desk for his signature. At 10.30 precisely the first of his visitors or appointments commenced, and this went on till 12.30, when there was a break for lunch. On most days he would have it in his small private dining room, with just one guest; it was usually a business affair, although occasionally it would be social. But it always ended sharply at 2.00 pm, when he would come back to the office and sign any papers that needed attention. Then he would depart – unless there was something else on at 3.00 – and go back to the hotel to take a long walk, on his own, in the lovely woods round Versailles.

There were of course variations to this routine, particularly when he was planning the big annual SHAPEX[3], which he ran with the help of his Strategic Studies Section. At this time the Section was headed by Colonel (later General) Dick Stilwell of the US Army. Dick was a great chap, who took a delight in twisting the tiger's tail with convoluted Americanisms in his papers. This acted like a red rag to an infuriated bull. Monty's own English, written in his very clear but somewhat childish and rounded handwriting, relied on short, simple words. Sentences that included multisyllabic words such as 'extrapolate' were ruthlessly suppressed! But they were a very high-grade team, and everyone – including the Field Marshal – enjoyed the verbal fencing that went on.

On some days there was also a change in the routine when we, his immediate staff, had to accompany him for lunch in the Officers' Club. This was quite an occasion. First, there was a sort of royal progress down the corridors of SHAPE, as he greeted friends, and particularly the younger officers of all nations. He was so very good with the young. But then came the crunch. Food was not the object of the exercise at all. He would grill each of us on some particular subject, which he expected us to know all about. Heaven help us if we didn't! So Claude Delacour, Sandy Cheyne and I tried to work out a plan whereby we would choose the subject, so that we could defend ourselves on our own ground. Occasionally it worked, but often we found ourselves pinned to the wall, racking our brains for a successful riposte.

On one such occasion Monty told me that no Highland regiment had ever produced any soldier of any distinction whatsoever. We were just a lot of bare-arsed tribesmen: good fighters, but with no brains at all! In vain I racked my brains. 'Sir Ian Hamilton,' I suggested. 'Quite useless,' was the damning reply; 'look what happened at Gallipoli!' Almost everyone else I suggested was consigned to the military dustbin. The Field Marshal had an expression for proper higher commanders: *Grands Chefs*. We had never produced a *Grand Chef*.

Then I had an idea. I mentioned the name of Ian Stewart of Achnacone. Monty had never heard of him. This was not surprising; they had never served near each other in their careers. When I mentioned that Ian had passed brilliantly into the Staff College, but refused to go because he didn't agree with the system, it was as if a salmon had taken my fly. Had I anything about Ian? Indeed I had: the History of the 93rd that he had written about the Malayan Campaign. Next day I gave Monty the book, and feeling rather like someone who has lit the blue touchpaper of a firework I stood back and waited for the explosion. But it never came.

About three days later he came into his office, and as he passed my desk he gave me back the book, saying: 'Most interesting. I've written something for you and your regiment in it. You were right – he could have been a *Grand Chef*!'

When he had vanished through the double doors of his office I looked at what he had written:

Human endeavour by Scots

This is a marvellous story, It shows what the British soldier can do when properly led, and how he responds to a challenge – giving of his best when asked to face up to hard conditions.

I know better than most to what heights the soldiers of Britain can aspire. Their greatness is a measure of the greatness of our national character, and I have seen the quality of our race proved again and again on the battlefield.

No better example can be found than the story of the 93rd Highlanders unfolded in this book.

Montgomery of Alamein FM
August 1957

It is only a small history of just one battalion in the ninety days or so of the Malayan campaign, but it remains one of my most treasured possessions.

The Strategic Studies Section was a very important link between the Field Marshal and the SHAPE staff, particularly the American Forces on it, who in fact ran the whole machine. Although he was called D/SACEUR, or Deputy Commander, Monty had made his own niche in the organisation as the Future Planner in Global Terms. He saw far beyond the boundaries of NATO: hence his many visits and contacts with people of influence outside the merely military and political organisations in the direct line of command, or even in the organisation. For example, whenever he was in Italy he always visited the Pope and – surprisingly – the Superior General of the Jesuits. No written record of these meetings was ever put in the diaries; they were completely private, and only he attended.

He also saw himself in a very personal role in Anglo-American relations. He had served alongside all the US's senior commanders in

World War II, and knew them personally. He had no hesitation in speaking or writing to them if he thought they were setting off on a mistaken course.

I once queried a paragraph in a paper he had prepared for General Norstad, his C.-in-C., on the grounds that it was a bit tough and outspoken, even rude. But he would not have it.

'Is this not the truth?' he asked me. 'Are the facts not completely accurate?'

I had to admit that they were, but perhaps he might put it a bit more tactfully. He would accept no watering down. He had a very firm belief that he wrote plain and unvarnished truth.

He always felt, though, and very strongly, that our relationship with the government and armed forces of America were paramount, and that he was one of the mainsprings of liaison. This had been put very severely to the test by Suez.

Some time in 1956 the Field Marshal was in the UK, and was sent for by Anthony Eden, then Prime Minister. At that meeting the question of the Suez operation came up, and Monty was asked his advice and opinion. At that time he was in no way connected with British planning (and never was for Suez); he was a NATO officer, and therefore could act as a sort of referee.[4]

The Prime Minister had given a rough outline of events, and of the action that Britain was going to take to secure this very vital waterway.

'What is the aim of all this planning?' asked Monty.

'The aim is to knock Nasser off his perch,' was the reply.

'But where is the "perch"? It is at Cairo – but nowhere does the plan mention Cairo.'

Eden agreed, but said that such an operation was neither politically nor militarily possible; the opening of the Canal would do the trick.

The Field Marshal answered: 'Prime Minister, you have an excellent aim, but your plan has nothing to do with it. Therefore it must fail, and I think you have forgotten the first rule of war.'

'What is that?' asked Eden.

'If you start a war, make sure you win it,' was the devastating reply.

The results of Suez are all too well known. Perhaps not quite so well known were the reactions of bitterness, mistrust, even anger, between old friends – British, French and American – who all felt that each had deceived the other, and in the end had let each other down badly.

At SHAPE and elsewhere the Field Marshal's extensive and valued contacts did much to repair the damage. He never let his private thoughts dominate his public duty and loyalty to his country and its leaders. He did his best to ensure that Britain's point of view and her vital interests in the Canal were properly known and understood, particularly by Generals Gruenther and Norstad, who were Commanders in Chief at the time.

I have already mentioned one particular part of Monty's organisation: his personal aircraft, a Dakota normally kept at RAF Odiham, and piloted by Squadron Leader Joe Haughton. It was entirely for Monty's own use, and no one else was allowed to set foot in it without his permission. Monty would write out his own flight timetables for his trips (after consultation with Joe), in his own particular way using one expression throughout. For example:

Doors Close ORLY 1600
Doors Open ODIHAM 1800

That meant exactly what it said: the time he would step into the aircraft, and the time he would emerge. I do not know where he got the expression from, but like so many other things he did, it made life very simple for his staff. Of course, headwinds and tailwinds could alter things!

One problem was that of HM Customs at Odiham. They were rather suspicious of what might be imported in this peculiar aircraft – a specially fitted Dakota! The Field Marshal was adamant that there should never be any 'nonsense', and that everything should be properly listed and declared. This was the job of his aide who flew with him; on occasions that was me! As a VIP representing his country he had to be meticulously careful. On one occasion the Swiss government gave him a beautiful Rolex watch, together with a similar one that they wanted him to give to Sir Winston Churchill. Naturally both were declared on arrival at Odiham. About a week later, HM Customs sent the Field Marshal a letter, with a swingeing bill for import duty and tax, etc. It was a considerable sum. Coolly, the Field Marshal wrote out a cheque for the whole amount and enclosed it in a letter to the Head of Customs, adding that he would be delighted to hear that they had also received Sir Winston Churchill's payment. He got his cheque back!

Then there was the small matter of a beautiful gold filigree galleon, a parting gift from Dr Salazar, President of Portugal. It was so delicate that we had to strap it into a specially cushioned seat, and I had to carry it off the aircraft at Odiham as if I was carrying the Holy Grail! No one had ever seen anything like it before. How can you value a gift that has no sales invoice or other paperwork to authenticate it? HM Customs could not send a note to Dr Salazar to ask him how much he had paid for it. As far as I know, no duty was paid on that either.

I went on five trips with Monty, and they were hard work. Apart from writing up the various interviews, I was baggage master, communications officer, and holder of the privy purse (for tips). Monty had made it very clear to me that he did not believe in tipping anyone at all. Instead I carried a portfolio of signed photographs, which he would hand to his valet or the house butler on departure, and I had to have enough of these photos on hand for each occasion. I knew that, for example, Sir Robert Laycock's Royal Marine house sergeant had a suitcase full of the things, and in desperation I rang Sandy Cheyne at the Mill and asked what to do. He answered that I should take from the privy purse enough money to disburse at the right and proper scale.

'But I have strict instructions not to give anyone any money at all!' I protested.

'Forget that,' said Sandy, 'but don't let him see you do it!'

'But what happens when he does his monthly check of the accounts?'

'It won't bother him. He knows very well what goes on, but he makes a pretence of not wanting to know!'

And so it proved. After one period when we had done two visits, I produced the books, all properly entered up, and stood quaking as I waited by his desk. He gave it all a very cursory look through.

'Hmm,' he said, 'rather a lot of outgoings this time. I'm not a rich man, you know.'

And that was all!

Of all the visits, the most interesting was the last trip he made to Belgrade. It was quite short: we landed in the late afternoon, and left after lunch the next day. The appointment with Marshal Tito was set for 11.00 am, and was to be followed by lunch. Tito and the Field Marshal were to meet on their own, with just one interpreter, but I was invited to lunch. Tito's palace/residence was not large, but it was beautifully furnished. The silver and china on the table were exquisite, and so was the food. However, I wasn't able to really enjoy the food, or take much part in the conversation, as I had to concentrate on what was passing between the two principals. The conversation was mostly in German, which I could understand and get by with. There was one memorable exchange, when they got on to the subject of education, and of training the young for a particular career or trade.

Tito had explained that he was proud of being a qualified electrician, and that he held a series of certificates to prove it. If Yugoslavia kicked him out as President, he was quite capable of earning his living.

'Where did you learn your trade?' asked Monty.

'In prison, just down the road from here in Belgrade.'

'Ah, a prison that educated people – it must have been a good prison!'

'No,' replied Tito, 'it was a very bad prison, but I think it is better now!'

That evening two charming senior generals of the Yugoslav Army took us to a very smart restaurant for dinner. Part of the entertainment was a band dressed in the most colourful gypsy clothing, complete with violins and czimbaloms. The walls of the room were decorated with scenes of the Second World War: Germans being well and truly shot up by partisans, gallant resistance leaders, and young boys and girls taking part. It was all very colourful and most exciting. Inevitably the leader of the orchestra came and fiddled at our table, right in the Field Marshal's ear. When his performance had finished, he asked Monty what he would like the orchestra to play.

Whatever talents Monty had (and they were many) music was not one of them, but nevertheless there were tunes that he remembered and liked. He said:

'I remember very well a tune that we in the 8th Army in the desert loved. We listened to a girl singing it every night . . . "Lili Marlene", that was it. Please play it for me.'

The result was like a Bateman cartoon, in which everyone in the picture is struck dumb with horror except the innocent who has made the offending remark. The Field Marshal was quick to realise all was not well, but could not understand what had gone wrong. He had forgotten that it was from Belgrade that the tune had been broadcast so long ago. Of all the tunes that he could have asked for, that one was at the bottom of the Yugoslav list. But nevertheless that wonderful band hammered it out full blast, and the old man was delighted. When we got back to our residence I told him what he had done. He roared with laughter. To this day I do not know whether he deliberately asked for that tune. It would have been so like him to have done so, and to have played the innocent.

I have a souvenir of that visit: a lovely silver cigarette box, given to me by Marshal Tito. He also gave me a dozen bottle of various Yugoslav liqueurs in a beautifully fitted-out box. I hadn't touched a drop from them by the time I returned to the UK eight months later, and when I and my car were decanted from the night ferry early one morning at Dover, I had to explain the liqueurs' presence to the Customs. I had always made a point of having a complete list of possessions with me, and I handed it to the examining officer. He had never seen anything quite like it before.

'Where did you get these?' he asked, pointing at the bottles, snug in their case.

I ventured that he would not believe me if I told him.

'Try me,' he said, 'we're used to all sorts of strange stories here!'

'Well, actually, there were a personal gift from Marshal Tito. He gave them to me in Belgrade.'

'I don't believe it – I've never heard anything like that before!' – and then he burst out laughing. 'But can you prove it?'

Oddly enough I could. My passport showed the date I was there, and I had kept a copy of the menu at President Tito's lunch party, which had on it the names of all those attending and the seating plan.

The effect was magical. The Customs officer took a special interest in the bottles, as one by one he examined them minutely. There were three bottles of Yugoslav slivovitz, three of cherry brandy, three champagnes and three brandies. I could feel my chequebook slipping from my grasp.

'This is the most interesting stuff I've ever seen,' said the Customs officer. 'This slivovitz stuff – really a sort of cider, I reckon – the cherry brandy is a cordial, and so there is no duty on either of those. You're allowed one bottle of brandy and one of the champagnes in free.' He took his cap off and scratched his head. 'I've never seen Yugoslav champagne before; I don't think it is on our list! But I will have to charge you duty on the two last bottles of brandy' – which he did, at the lowest possible rate. He never bothered even to look at anything else. There aren't many Customs officers of his ilk around at 6.00 am!

Once you were accepted by the Field Marshal, you became a sort of honorary member of his family, and he took a personal interest in your private affairs. How were the children doing at school? How did they enjoy living in the French countryside? Did they have any French friends, and if so who were they?

To the delight of my landlord, M. Français, he insisted on a full-scale inspection of the mill, followed by a similar visit to M. Français' house, and the village school! This last operation was a roaring success in Anglo-British liaison.

Occasionally, though, his interest could go a bit far. At that time Sandy Cheyne, his ADC, had a very nice girlfriend, whom he later very happily married. One day, when Sandy had been in France and was about to return to the Mill, Monty sent for both him and myself.

'Now, Sandy,' said the old man, 'are you going to marry this girl of yours?'

'I'm not quite sure, Sir.'

'Haven't you asked her yet?'

'Well – not exactly.'

'What do you mean, "Not exactly"? That's what I call mucking about, and I won't have it. You must make up your mind now, and this is what you will do. When you get home tonight, ring her up and have her to dinner at the Mill. You can have a nice bottle of my wine from my cellar. After dinner get her on the sofa, tell her you love her, and get yourself properly engaged! And what is more, you will ring me up first thing on Friday and report to me that you are engaged. If you don't, back to regimental duty you go. That's all quite clear, isn't it now? Off you go.'

So out of the office we both went. Sandy was gasping like a sprinter who has just run the hundred metres in even time. I cannot remember what I felt like.

So there it was; Sandy and Sue lived happily married for years. Sadly they are both now dead.

Monty had a very strong streak of possessiveness. No one was allowed to lay a hand on or use anything that belonged to him. Even if they asked permission he would usually refuse. The 1958 SHAPEX was the culmination of his ten years in SHAPE and Western Union/NATO, and it was to be attended by just about every chief of staff and ambassador to be found. The British Embassy was stretched to the limit to provide accommodation and cars for the British contingent. Shortly before they all assembled, someone high in the Embassy telephoned me and asked whether they could borrow the Field Marshal's No. 2 Humber saloon for Lord Louis Mountbatten, then Chief of the Defence Staff. I could not of course give permission myself, but I saw no reason why it should not be lent and went in to ask. I should have known better.

'Certainly not,' was the abrupt reply, 'I might need it myself. If the Ambassador invites guests to stay with him, it is up to him to provide their transport.'

In some ways this was a rather childish reaction: 'You're not going to play with my toy.' But there was a sequel. When the great day came, and the high, mighty, learned and distinguished arrived, the Field Marshal was watching from his side window to see the fun. In due course Lord Louis and his staff in their Embassy car drove up – straight onto the flower bed in front of the main entrance, coming to a shaky halt right in the middle of it. The front wheels were all askew; the steering track rod had broken. Had it done so just five minutes earlier on the autoroute we would have been needing a new Chief of Defence.

The Field Marshal's eyes glittered with delight at their misfortune.

'Typical of our Embassy and the useless crew there,' he said as he turned to Sandy Cheyne. 'Go straight to Lord Louis now. Tell him that he can have my No. 1 car for the whole of his stay, and I guarantee it won't let him down!'

The CPX[5] (his last) was a great success. Claude Delacour and I excused ourselves from the duty of handing round the specially ordered cough drops on the grounds that we were too senior – we managed to get away with that particular bit of insubordination – but as on all previous briefings unnecessary coughing was 'out'.

It started somewhat unusually, with a projection showing a view of NATO from Moscow, and the Field Marshal's appreciation as a Russian considering that view. There was the usual map of the Atlantic on the floor for further discussions. (When, some years before, Monty had been striding over the middle of the sea to illustrate some point, Maréchal de Lattre de Tassigny was heard to say in a loud aside that there was only one person who would walk on water, and he had been dead for nearly 2,000 years!) There were the usual receptions, parties, private and public meetings. Claude and I hardly had time to breathe, but three days later all had gone well, and 'Father' was well pleased.

It was getting near the time for departure. There were four main events:

the presentation in the Invalides of the Medaille Militaire, a final lunch with President Charles de Gaulle, a guest night at SHAPE, to which General Al Gruenther was coming, and the final departure from Orly.

When France lays on a parade, she does it with a special sense of panache, and the Invalides has an air about the place that makes for a magnificent setting.

It was a showery day, and there had been a slight disagreement with Claude and myself about a tatty mackintosh that the Field Marshal wanted us to carry. Like the business of the cough drops, we both flatly refused to have anything to do with it. The Field Marshal protested that if it did rain, he would get soaking wet, almost certainly catch 'flu, and die! On this somewhat disagreeable note we arrived at the Invalides. In the end Claude Delacour relented, and I have a photograph of the distinguished gathering – Maréchal Juin, General Ely and all – with, in the background, Claude distastefully holding the tatty mac over his left arm: all watched by the statue of Napoleon from his position high above the Court d'Honneur.

Then it was off to the Matignon for the farewell lunch with the President. It was a small party – not more than twelve people – and Sir Gladwyn Jebb (Ambassador to France) and Sir Frank Roberts (Ambassador to NATO) were the only civilian guests. It was all very informal. De Gaulle and Monty were pulling each other's legs, and those of their subordinates! One particular jibe from the President was prompted by the green Foreign Legion ties that Maréchal Juin and General Koenig were wearing. All other officers of the French Army wear a plain black tie in uniform, but the Legion has to be different, and takes great pride in doing so! The President denounced the wearers of the green ties as *mercenaires*. Monty, not to be outdone, drew attention to me in my kilt, as something of the same breed! At least he did not use the expression 'bare-arsed savages' on this occasion.

The party ended when the President made a charming speech in which he, on behalf of France, bade farewell to the Field Marshal, and thanked him for all he had done, both as a soldier in the war and as a leader and trainer at SHAPE. It was very short, very sincere, and delivered in his impeccable French. We then got up from the table and went into an anteroom for coffee and liqueurs. In the course of this, de Gaulle came up to Claude Delacour and myself, who were standing a little apart from the rest. He said he hoped we had enjoyed ourselves, and then turned to me and wished me a pleasant trip home with the Field Marshal the next day. When I explained that I was staying at SHAPE to serve General Sir Richard Gale, his replacement, he looked genuinely surprised.

Claude explained that, on the day he left the Army, the Field Marshal would retain no military staff at all; he would become a private individual.

De Gaulle was horrified. 'Disgraceful! We in France know better how to look after our distinguished soldiers. Consider Maréchal Juin over there. He has an office in the Invalides, an *aide militaire*, a small staff, an official car, and a driver. Yet, like your Field Marshal, he is on the retired list.'

And then he broke into a slight roguish smile. 'Do you know why we take such trouble to provide all this?' he asked.

Claude and I together admitted that we hadn't a clue.

'Non, mon Général,' I answered.

'*Pour les surveillez!*' he replied, which loosely translated could – and indeed did – mean 'To find out what they are up to!'

That was a prophetic remark. Four years later, in 1961, Maréchal Juin would find himself under house arrest and eventually jailed for his part in the Algerian troubles. He was one of General de Gaulle's oldest friends and companions in arms.

We had some four hours to relax before the final guest night at SHAPE. This was an entirely military affair, and was great fun until, as the party was dispersing, Claude Delacour appeared. He was the bearer of distressing news. Did I realise that our Master was departing France the next afternoon at 4 o'clock, and had not written one single letter of thanks to anyone in the French government, who had done so much for him over the years? And that already he had heard on the grapevine that many in high places were very distressed, and there was talk of many who would not come to Orly to say farewell?

It was now getting on for midnight: what were we to do?

Claude had it worked out. He and I would drive to the mill where I lived, and where I had my typewriter. Sylvia would be roused as cook and coffee maker and additional interpreter (she was bilingual in French); together we would compose the ten or so letters required for ministers and generals. In the meantime we would rouse the Field Marshal's clerks and have them ready for the draft letters, which would reach them at about 3.00 am. They would have them ready typed by 7.30, when I would take them to the Field Marshal's hotel, for signing punctually at 8.00 am. Claude would organise a team of dispatch riders and staff cars to deliver the letters personally to each addressee.

Down to the mill we went. Fortified by endless cups of coffee, to counter the effects of our guest night intake, we got down to writing the official letters of thanks and farewell. At precisely 8.00 the next morning, accompanied by his personal stenographer, I entered the Field Marshal's bedroom – something I had never done before.

'Good heavens, David, what on earth are you doing here?'

'Sir, I have brought you some rather important letters to sign, which I think you would wish to send to people like Maréchal Juin, General Ely, and one or two ministers, to thank them for all the arrangements at yesterday's parade, and so forth.'

'Letters? I haven't written any letters – and in any case I shook them all by the hand and said "Thank you" yesterday. What more do they want? Very curious lot these French. Oh very well, give them to me.'

With bad grace he signed them all, barely bothering to check the text. We rushed them downstairs to the waiting teams of cars and motorcycles, who roared their way into Paris and the ministries. And that was that.

Later I heard via Claude Delacour that the result was quite remarkable. The recipients thought it incredible that, on his very last morning in France, the Field Marshal should have taken the trouble to write to them all personally, with all the other things that must have been bothering him. Little did they know! But that is why, in one of the last photos taken of the Field Marshal's departure from Orly, his two military assistants look as if they have been on some sort of prolonged thrash, lasting for perhaps a couple of weeks.

There was one last guard of honour, one last general salute, and then the Dakota took off. A very significant part of my life was over. I had never worked so hard for anyone before (or since for that matter). For eighteen months, for twenty-four hours of the day, I had been part of the Field Marshal's life. Even when I was on holiday he wanted to know where I would be, and where he could contact me if he needed to. Sometimes, to test communications, he would do just that.

I think he taught me three things. The first was trust. As part of his staff, you were completely trusted to get on with the job, to use your own judgement, not to bother him with small things, and to take responsibility for everything you thought he would wish you to do. He never checked up on what you were doing, but he expected it to be done exactly as he had directed.

Second, he taught me the art of reducing any problem to its ultimate simplicity. He had an astonishing knack of doing this, and writing it all down in his plain but very simple handwriting. He could reduce a lengthy staff paper to perhaps half a sheet of foolscap, with everything that mattered clearly stated. He took great pride in this.

Finally, he taught me what I would call the direct approach: the business of asking a very direct question to which there can only be a direct answer. It was disconcerting at first to be handed a list of senior officers and asked 'Do you know any of these?' and then, if you admitted you did, 'Is he any good?' If you hesitated, you were lost!

Many people have tried to describe this very remarkable man and have run out of adjectives. He was both the easiest and the most difficult man I have ever served under. He could be incredibly kind, and the next minute equally rude or unfeeling; he could be generous and he could be mean. I could go on and on about the contradictions of his make-up and character. When Nigel Hamilton published his massive work[6], many of us who had served the Field Marshal met in the Imperial War Museum, and of course we talked our heads off. But there was one thing about Monty on which we all agreed: if he looked at us and crooked his little finger to summon us back to his service, we would drop everything we were doing to join him.

NOTES

1   The lave of a mill is the channel down which the water is directed to turn the wheel.
2   Costa de Beauregarde was a distinguished officer of the Chasseurs à Pied of the French Army. Before World War II he had been the French instructor at the RMA, Woolwich, and he spoke perfect English. He had been of the staff of Marshal de Lattre de Tassigny, who 'lent' him to Field Marshal Montgomery for liaison purposes. He was one of the Field Marshal's most loyal servants.
3   This was the annual SHAPE Exercise, which usually lasted three days, and at which matters of high political and strategic policy would be discussed by the C-in-Cs of subordinate commands, and by the Nato diplomats. It was the Field Marshal's yearly *tour de force*.
4   It was on one of our trips abroad that he told me of this meeting; no one else was present, and it is not recorded in the diary.
5   Command post exercise: in effect a Signals and Staff exercise without troops deployed on the ground – similar to a TEWT but on a larger scale, with Signals actually working.
6   Nigel Hamilton, *Monty: The Field Marshal 1944–1976*, London: Hamish Hamilton, 1986

CHAPTER 12
BRIXMIS

I commanded 125 (West Lancashire) Infantry Brigade from September 1962 until my posting to BRIXMIS (the subject of this chapter) in June 1965. Headquarters were at Liverpool, but my Brigade was a very spread-out affair: it stretched from there to Barrow-in-Furness, Carnforth, Preston and Rochdale. One of the farthest-flung units was my RASC company, based at Rochdale, in what had been a Territorial Lancashire Fusilier drill hall in its early days. It took nearly two hours to get there from Liverpool by staff car.

I was due to go there with Derek Brown, a Gordon Highlander who was my Brigade Major, for the unit's annual inspection. We were to arrive at 4.00 one afternoon, and the whole affair would last until nearly midnight. I had gone into my office as usual at 9.00 in the morning, but I wasn't feeling all that good. By midday I was in a dreadful state – so much so that Derek ordered me home and cancelled the inspection.

Sylvia had gone out for the day with some friends. She was not expecting to get home until late that night, and knew that she was unlikely to see me until 2.00 the next morning. In the meantime I had somehow crawled upstairs, got into bed in the spare room, and passed out.

Next day, Sylvia awoke to find herself – so she thought – alone in the house. Fearing the worst she rang Derek to find out if anything dreadful had happened. To her surprise she was told that I had been back at home since lunchtime the previous day.

'But he isn't here,' she said, 'I've looked everywhere' (everywhere, that was, except the spare guest room, where the door was shut). So Derek summoned his car and drove to Formby to join the search, which included questioning our neighbours and friends Pip and Barbara Bell: had they had seen any trace of me absconding during the night? At last someone thought to open the door of the guest room – and there I was, out for the count. The doctor was called.

'Mumps!'

It seems funny now, but it was not funny at the time. I have never felt so rotten, and it lasted for a week. Kind friends would ring up and ask tenderly about my symptoms; get well and joke cards arrived by every mail. Talk of dreadful after-effects was bandied about. I was injected with horrible substances, which after a time worked, and I began to recover. The dreaded after-effects never appeared, but for some ten days I was as weak and helpless as a kitten. And some time in that period Bernard Penfold rang to see how I was, and to give me some news as to my fate.

Bernard was deputising for my Divisional Commander. He had been a fellow pupil at Wellington, and in the same company at Sandhurst: there he had passed out three places ahead of me, which gave him the right to assume command of the Division over my head. (But he did become a proper Major General in his time, and ended a distinguished career by running the Hong Kong race course.)

Bernard told me he would not come within a mile of my infected quarters for fear of catching my foul disease, but he thought I would like to know that the No. 2 Selection Board had nominated me to command BRIXMIS – and that it was a good job. I had never heard of BRIXMIS. It sounded like the name of some patent breakfast food. Where was it, and what did it do?

Bernard did not enlighten me (I am not sure that he knew much about it himself), but he did tell me that in ten days' time, when I was due at a Western Command exercise at Chester, I would be staying with the C.-in-C., General Sir Edward Howard Vyse. Also staying there would be General Douglas Darling, an ex-Chief of Mission, who would brief me, so I had better get operational quickly.

I have met one or two Generals whom I have disliked, and I suspect their regard for me was much the same, but all the rest have been great characters. Ted Howard Vyse was one such: a typical Horse Artilleryman, he was a charmer with a delightful family, a great horseman, and a great soldier. You found yourself immediately at home with him.

I had met Douglas Darling briefly before. He was a rifleman, highly decorated, a tough dedicated leader of men, and a very experienced soldier. He gave me a detailed account of what BRIXMIS was, what it did, how it did it, and how he led it during his two years of command. When he had finished I seriously wondered whether I was going to be up to the job: it was something I had never really been trained to do. I had never served anywhere near Intelligence, I had never served in Germany, I had never seen a Russian, and knew nothing about them or their Armed Forces. I was the squarest of pegs for this particularly round hole.

But they had not finished with me yet. In the next two months I was to be briefed at the MOD and the Foreign Office, with two days at Maresfield (the Intelligence Corps Centre), and I was to fly to Germany for briefing at Rheindahlen (GHQ), with four days in Berlin staying with 'Bala' Bredin, the then Chief of Mission.

Bala was a legendary character. He had won his first Military Cross with the 'night squads' under Orde Wingate in Palestine in (I think) 1937. These were the highly trained young men of the Jewish race, originally trained by the British Army to protect the oil pipelines running through the desert to the refinery at Haifa. From the night squads came such men as Moshe Dayan, the founders of today's Israeli Army.

Bala's hospitality was also legendary, and the four days passed in a dream, punctuated by visits and briefings of a more serious kind, and meetings with the fifty or so characters that made up the Mission, the full title of which was 'the British Commanders in Chief, Mission to the Soviet Forces in Germany'. (Note that there were two British Commanders in Chief – one Army and one Air Force.) BRIXMIS was actually a signal abbreviation for this ponderous title.

I found out that I was to take over, amongst other things, a palace by a lake in Potsdam, a mansion (no. 10 Stuhmerallee) in West Berlin, this small but very select unit (of which my deputy and one third of the staff were Royal Air Force), and twelve specially converted Opel Kapitan cars, with strange yellow number plates. And I would be responsible to three very senior Masters, with resounding titles:

- The Commander in Chief, British Army of the Rhine
- The Commander in Chief, Royal Air Force, Germany
- The Commander, Group of Soviet Forces, Germany.

According to the Bible, 'No man can serve two masters'.[1] Clearly this did not apply to the Chief of BRIXMIS – and in fact, as it turned out, I managed to serve three, to their evident satisfaction. There were to be times when I would encounter their imperial displeasure, but thankfully not all at the same time.

Not many people know about BRIXMIS, and many who served in Germany had not the least idea who we were or what our job was. Perhaps this is just as well. What started as a purely liaison unit became something very different – perhaps one of the most successful gatherers of intelligence since the 'pundits' of the Survey of India in the Great Game days,[2] when the opponent was the same: Russia and her ambitions.

When the war in Europe ended, it left chaos in its wake. Whole populations were on the move; food was scarce; starvation and disease were all around. Families were split up, their homes destroyed, and the military governments of the occupying powers faced near-impossible tasks in restoring communications, light, and all the infrastructure that had been ruined. In particular there was a need for liaison and communications with the Russian military, who controlled much of the territory. Such a need for military liaison missions had been thought of in 1944, in an agreement called 'The Control Machinery in Germany'.

On 16 September 1946 the Chiefs of Staff of the British Control

Commission of Germany and the Soviet Group of Forces, Generals Robertson and Malinin, formally signed the agreement. It allowed reciprocal arrangements for travel and circulation in each zone, guaranteed wireless and telephonic communications, and granted couriers diplomatic immunity. Each mission was to be administered by the zone in which it was stationed in respect of rations, petrol and accommodation. The object of each mission was to maintain liaison between the staffs of the two Commanders-in-Chief and their military government in the Zones.

Initially the headquarters of BRIXMIS was in Potsdam, with a rear headquarters in Berlin with the British garrison, but by the time I arrived in July 1965 the main headquarters was with the British headquarters in the Olympic Stadium buildings. There was an outstation in a lovely villa (a small palace in fact) at 32 Seestrasse in Potsdam, where the RSM of the Mission and his wife lived permanently, where we maintained a duty officer, and from where all tours began and ended. In the twenty or so years since it began as a purely liaison organisation the Mission had changed out of all recognition – and this was what I was expected to command, with the grand but somewhat strange title of 'Chief'.

In July 1965 I arrived at the *autobahn* checkpoint at Berlin, my car laden down with uniform, family silver and personal possessions, after a journey that I can best describe as a GMFU (which can be – politely – translated as a Grand Military Foul-Up). It had been caused partly by a violent North Sea gale, and partly by the sudden desire of both Commanders-in-Chief at Rheindahlen to see me en route, after they had previously said that they did not want to. I was beginning to think the evangelists in the Bible were on the ball with their 'two masters' comments.

Immediately – before I had even unpacked – I was a guest at one of Bala Bredin's lunch parties. It was a small one, with only eight guests, and as he was getting married in the garrison church next day there was yet another party that evening. On the day after – Saturday – he was married to Anne, and there was a reception. They were elsewhere during the weekend, but others took me in charge. I soon realised I was not trained for Berlin life.

On Monday the serious business started. I was to be introduced to my third boss, the Soviet C.-in-C. I handed my kit to Bala's batman, and on Monday morning we set forth for Zossen Wunsdorf, once the headquarters of Hitler's army, but now under a very different regime. It was about an hour's drive from Berlin, via the Glienicker Bridge and Potsdam, and the combined Soviet-GDR checkpoint at the south end of the bridge. Just before we reached the bridge, our driver stopped and put the car's Union Flag in its socket on the bonnet. Only Army commanders and the Chief BRIXMIS had the right to display such a flag.

Zossen was the original headquarters of the pre-1939 German Army, and we stopped in front of an imposing, pillared block. At the entrance were two of the tallest Russian soldiers I had ever seen, standing as if frozen in an impeccable salute. I felt very small as we walked between them into an enormous entrance hall with chandeliers, red carpets stretching into the distance, and an imposing flight of stairs, up which we were led by Colonel Pinchuk, Chief of the Soviet External Relations Bureau, whom I was to get to know very well indeed. We walked up the stairs, along another endless, red-carpeted corridor, passing a whole lot of what seemed to be deserted offices. There was no one in sight, and not a single nameplate on any door, and yet this was the headquarters of a very considerable and powerful army! It was all rather disconcerting but, as I later found out, was the normal Russian practice.

Eventually we came to a door that led to a small ante-room. A smart young ADC took our hats, and ushered us into the presence of his C.-in-C., General Koshevoi. The General welcomed Bala, myself and our interpreter warmly, and motioned us to sit down at a table where there were glasses and titbits that the Russians call *zakuski*. Another surprise – there was not a map or paper in sight. Koshevoi's desk was completely clear of papers, but there was what looked like a complicated telephone console by his desk, the only sign that it was some sort of Commander-in-Chief's office.

Champagne and brandy were brought, healths were drunk, and the conversation was animated and very welcoming. Where had I served? What had I done? What sort of family was I bringing to Berlin? It was the sort of talk that one would expect from any senior officer. After about forty minutes we left. It had been an interesting visit, and was to be the first of many, some of them in less favourable circumstances!

The next day Bala left, and I was in charge: Chief in my own right, and feeling (at first) very much out of my depth. Then Peter Badger of the Leicesters, my GSO1, and Derek Hargreaves, my Adjutant, appeared in my office with a detailed programme of my doings in the next two weeks. There were visits to be made, conferences to attend, and my training as a tour officer to start.

This last was the most important part. Touring was the lifeblood of the Mission: it was on tour that one picked up the intelligence and information that was the essence of our job. One of my most experienced officers, Nigel Broomfield, once likened it to rock-climbing, in that as one got more experienced one was able to tackle increasingly difficult and dangerous pitches. I would have compared it to stalking in the Highlands.

We toured in a team of three: the driver, the tour clerk (an NCO) and the leader, usually an officer. The tour clerk and the leader had excellent maps of the area, with the restricted areas and signs on them; the leader had the cameras and lenses. In my day this was the Leica III, and my own assortment of long-range lenses. In latter days, night vision and video kit altered the game greatly in our favour. But when one started from scratch as I did, it was exactly like being taken stalking, with the tour clerk as the gillie, the driver as the pony boy, and myself as the rifle being taken where the gillie knew best, and subject to his guidance. Instead of the rifle with its telescopic sight, I had my camera. It was the tour clerk's job to get to the right spot and hope I didn't make a mess of my shot! Like all novices on the hill I frequently did at first. There was the same excitement of the stalk when the game came into view; the difference was that they were armed and could shoot back, and sometimes did.

There was another hazard – the East German police in plain clothes. We called them the 'narks'. They would follow us around, and try to catch us in some nefarious breach of the rules, so that they could detain us. There were occasions when physical violence was used, with cars deliberately rammed, and other unpleasant methods employed.

As I did more tours, I began to know the countryside: the little tracks though the woods, small wooden bridges over streams that the Kapitans could traverse, hidden lay-bys where we could hide and lie up for our quarry. By the time I had got to the second year of my tour I was able to pass on tips to a new tour clerk who had only just arrived in the Mission, and so I became both gillie and rifle. Then I really started earning my pay as a tour officer.

Once I was on the job, rank went a bit out of the window; what counted was experience. I might wear the badges of a brigadier, but my sergeant and driver knew far more about the countryside than I did, and though the final responsibility for the tour was mine, any success was theirs. We took turns to brew up, and the crew would not be impressed if their Chief was useless at turning out edible food in the snow with a wind whistling it into drifts round the car.

There was one disadvantage in being the Chief on tour. To start with my car was shining black, with a star in the front and a Union Flag flying from the bonnet: easily recognisable by all. But as Chief, I was accountable for the behaviour of all my Mission. If a tour was clobbered[3] – perhaps deliberately for a political reason – it was my job as Chief to go to the External Relations Bureau and convince the Russians that the tour was in fact innocent of any illdoing. But if I had frequently been guilty of illicit acts, I would be in a difficult position to argue. So I had a problem. How far could I personally stick my neck out? And if I did not at least have a try, what would those I commanded think of me?

This is where the rock-climbing analogy comes in. There were areas and places that were difficult to get at, situations when a bit of quick thinking and brass neck paid off, and incidents that caused great amusement afterwards. The Chief who had the most legendary record was probably the present Duke of Norfolk, then Brigadier Miles Fitzalan Howard. He had the reputation of being confined by more Kommandants than any other Chief before or since, but he charmed his way out of every situation, and everybody – British and Russian – admired the way he did it.

I never knew what I might find when I went off in the very early morning. One Sunday (in my second year) I was rung up and asked if I would take over a tour whose officer had gone sick. As I had nothing on, and my family was away, I agreed to take over. We found ourselves in an area we called the Zerbst Gap, about forty miles south-east of Berlin. It was a favourite hunting ground for the Mission as it was between two permanent restricted areas, with tracks that were frequently used on exercises. As it was Sunday I thought we might be in for a dull trip. I was quite wrong.

Halfway through the Gap we came across a nest of traffic regulators, or 'Reggies' as we called them: soldiers used as a sort of human signpost by the Russian Army to direct traffic on exercises. There was considerable movement on a track crossing the road we were on, and the Reggies halted our car while vehicle after vehicle drove past us at some thirty yards range – point blank indeed for my camera. Better still, some of them were machines we had never seen before. I nearly ran out of film!

Suddenly an officer in the armoured column crossing our front saw us, and turned his BTR50 (an enormous eight-wheeled APC[4]) out of the column towards us with evil intent. We had to get out of it very quickly indeed, but this was through a field where his cross-country performance could easily outrun our Kapitan. However, I had been there before; I remembered that there was a very wide, deep ditch that ran through the field, crossed by a wooden plank bridge, which a previous tour clerk had shown me. I knew that the bridge would take the Kapitan, and was pretty certain that the BTR50 would perish. And so it proved. We made it, the Sov didn't, and went nose first into the mud. It was one of my better photos: a ditched BTR and a furious officer shaking his fist! It was incidents like that that made life in the Mission such fun.

There was another memorable occasion, early on in my time. We had had a long and not very productive day in the Dresden/Halle area, with nothing very much to see. Late in the evening we were about five miles out of Potsdam on our way home. The road crossed a railway, and there below us an interesting-looking train had halted. It was carrying an assortment of tanks, APCs and sundry Russians. This was too good to miss.

My tour clerk was Captain Nigel Broomfield of the 17/21st. He knew of a sandy track that ran alongside the railway line, which was in a deep cutting, so down the track we went, stopped at a suitable spot out of sight of the train, and crawled up the bank with our cameras and lenses. Twilight was falling fast, and although we were using very fast film, I wondered whether it could cope, as the train was in deep shadow. We spent some five minutes happily snapping away, and then crawled back to the car – only to find that it was completely bogged down in deep sand. This was only a minor problem. We got out the TIRFOR (our trusty winching kit), but there was no suitable tree stump to which to attach the far end. We had to use our ground anchor. This was a large steel plate, with eight holes into which went eight steel spikes, which you hammered into the ground with a sledgehammer. This made quite a bit of noise, which would be clearly heard by the soldiers on the train. And though our car was hidden from them, they could just about see the sledgehammer at the top of its swing.

The TIRFOR cable would stretch for about twenty yards, but we had about 100 yards of soft sand to get through, which meant five separate hammering jobs for the ground anchor, with the path rising all the time, giving less cover for us as we slowly hauled the car back. We had successfully completed three such hauls when it became obvious that the soldiers on the train realised something was up, but they did not dare leave their flats, in case the signal came off and the train moved on. Glasses were trained on us, there were excited voices, and an officer arrived. Then, just as a posse was being assembled, the signal did come off, the engine gave a series of hoots as it moved away, and the incident was over – except for the fact that we still had to complete the unditching of the car.

I arrived back two hours overdue, covered in oil and dust, late for dinner, to be asked by an anxious but slightly peeved Sylvia: 'Where have you been, and what on earth have you been doing?'

And I couldn't tell her. Later on, as an experienced BRIXMIS wife accustomed to tours that vanished from time to time, she knew better than to ask such a question. The photos *did* come out – in quite reasonable detail. I had gained a rung or two on the ladder of experience.

Late one evening, when I was returning to Potsdam, I and my car got caught in the middle of a major traffic jam. The local motor rifle division was moving out for an exercise, and two of their traffic regulators directed us down a diversion that put us right in the middle of the whole thing, with no way out. The Russian soldiery thought this was the funniest thing they had ever seen – the Chief's Mission car completely surrounded by every sort of weapon and tank, quite unable to go forward or back. Two senior officers were hopping mad, but they could do nothing about it. Interesting and highly secret items of kit were outside my car at point blank range, and I had run out of film! I could have kicked myself.

There was a great deal of opencast mining for the brown coal that was the main fuel for the GDR; enormous areas of country were reduced to what looked like a lunar landscape. On one occasion, in an effort to elude some Narks, I found myself in one such area. It was not marked on the map, there was no clue to entrances and exits, and because we were effectively below ground level there were no landmarks to give us any sort of clue as to navigation. For an hour we drove around aimlessly, trying to get back to civilisation. Suddenly a Vopo[5] car appeared, apparently out of nowhere, with two uniformed police inside. We were in trouble.

Police all over the world behave in very much the same manner. If you look guilty, they will rightly suspect you are up to no good, and will act accordingly; but if you politely ask for help, they will change completely, and become the protector of the public. I thought I would put this to the test.

I got out of the car, held up my hand, and walked over to the Vopo car. In what I thought was my best German, I apologised for wasting their time, but explained that we were completely lost; we had followed a traffic diversion sign (that wasn't completely true, but there were an awful lot of *Umleitungs* around the area), and now the signs had run out and we wanted to get back on the road to Halle.

It worked. The *Oberwachtmeister* got out of his car, saluted, and said: '*Zu befehl, Herr Brigade General.*' Telling us to follow him, he led us out of the maze, apologised for the mix-up over the diversion signs, and saw us on our way. My tour clerk and driver were speechless with astonishment. Officially we did not recognise the GDR, and officially we were instructed not to have anything to do with their police (except of course for traffic directions). To approach them for help was something neither had ever seen before. Their normal contact was when Vopos and Narks drove them off roads and blocked them in for a detention!

BRIXMIS was the largest of the missions, with thirty-one pass-holders. The French and American missions had fewer. This meant that our tours always consisted of three people. The extra pair of eyes was a tremendous advantage. It also meant that if you were out of your car on a 'stalk', the third man could watch your back in case someone appeared without warning from a different direction. With only two in the car, there was no reserve driver, and it also meant that at times the tour officer had to drive himself.

Each mission had its own ways of handling the detailed organisation of tours, but our operation officers kept in very close touch, as did the three Chiefs, so there was no overlapping. But I did catch Commandant Alain de Germiny of the French Mission flagrantly poaching in our area one day, when he should have been miles away. He had only a partial sighting of my car, and thinking I was a Russian general, departed hastily in a cloud of dust and black smoke, much to the delight of my crew.

On another occasion a BRIXMIS tour on a railway watch found a French Mission car, with both crew asleep, in a wood near a signal-box. Suddenly the German signalman came out of his box and woke the occupants of the French tour car in good time for them to catch a troop train as it steamed past. What excellent service! We had never thought of that dodge.

Relations between the three Missions could not have been better. We were all friends, and we all wore the same tie, dark blue with little miniature 'Mission signposts' embroidered on it. It was very much an international team, working for a common cause. Perhaps Colonel Gerard Milliet, Infantrie Coloniale, of the French Army could express this feeling for all of us who served together in the late 1960s. He was the operations officer of the French Mission, and he and his family were great personal friends of ours. In 1996 Tony Geraghty wrote a magnificent account of the work of BRIXMIS,[6] and many of our friends in the other Missions wished to have copies of it, since it included a great deal of their own work. I happened to sign the copy which Gerard received. He sent me a letter of thanks, from which I quote direct in the original French:

> Merci infiniment d'avoir apporté votre signature sur le livre *Beyond the Frontline* que John m'a si gentiment envoyé. Cela a fait revivre en moi-même chez tous les 'Missionaires' ces moments exaltants dans une carrière militaire.

That expression, *moments exaltants*, says it all, because although the excitement of touring was perhaps eighty-five per cent of the business, the purely liaison side of our job also had its 'moments'.

Most of the liaison took place at the Potsdam office of SERB, the Soviet External Relations Bureau, about five minutes' walk from our Potsdam Office. During my period there were two senior Russian Colonels, Pinchuk (who had been a tour officer with SOXMIS[7] in the British Sector) and Grischel (a big bear of a man, with a charming smile and a sense of humour). They had two interpreters, one of whom was French-speaking, and a small staff. They had a direct line to all three Mission houses in Potsdam, which they or we could use to call meetings. Most of these were on minor matters, such as aircraft or helicopters straying from their appointed flight-paths, or sometimes over the border. These small affairs were dealt with by my GSO1, but in more serious cases my Royal Air Force Deputy, Ted Colahan, might go if I was away, or if the meeting concerned an air matter. Whoever went took one of our interpreters with him, all of whom were tour officers. (In the early days some of the original Chiefs were Russian speakers, but none of my successors was.)

For more serious affairs I was called to Zossen, to be given the works by either the Russian C.-in-C. or his Chief of Staff, and this happened when a very serious incident occurred at 3.30 pm on 6 April 1966. A Russian fighter – their latest – suffered an engine flame-out over Berlin, and came down in the Havel River inside the British Sector.

That day Nigel Broomfield and I were about to play in an inter-unit squash match against the Greenjackets, when we heard the air raid sirens, and the telephone recalled me to Headquarters. This was easier said than done: Berlin traffic had gridlocked itself, as the police had closed the Heerstrasse for security reasons. After about an hour we got to Headquarters and, in our squash kit, attended a council of war run by Peter Hayman, the Foreign Office Minister, who was the titular Second in Command of the British Sector, as our General, Sir John Nelson, was in the UK. Clearly BRIXMIS was going to be heavily involved in dealing with the Russians, so we cancelled all tours, and stood all our interpreters to for whatever duties might come their way.

While all this was going on, Maurice Taylor, one of our RAF tour officers, had got into a small boat with his camera and had taken photos of the tail of the aircraft, which was sticking out of the river. When we developed the film at our office, he and another RAF technician noticed a very unusual aerial protruding from the back of the tail fin. They compared it with a photo taken by the US Mission a week before, and confirmed that the plane was indeed a Firebar – the code name for the YAK25. Immediately HQ BAOR and the MOD were alerted; this was a catch indeed.

I had a dinner party on that night, which I did not wish to cancel, and in any case there was nothing I could do at the time; all the wheels for dealing with the Russians who flocked to the scene were put into motion. I and my guests enjoyed our dinner as if nothing had happened. They knew that an aircraft had crashed, but they had no idea how sensitive the situation was, nor what was at stake.

After everyone had gone home, Angus Southwood – my senior Operations Officer who had been down at the river bank – told me of the considerable goings-on that had taken place during the afternoon and evening. He also told me that a senior Russian Air Force general was on the site, making something of a nuisance of himself, and that SERB were there in strength!

I then made an unfortunate decision. I reckoned that if some of the top brass of the Soviet Air Force were on the river bank, that was where I ought to be, with one of my Russian-speaking officers, so I got two large Thermoses of soup and a bottle of Laphroaig whisky, called up Aldridge (my driver), and set off for the scene of the crash. Sylvia, wiser than me, thought I was an idiot. I disregarded her advice, and I now know she was right.

I was welcomed, if that is the right word, by a posse of Russian Air Force officers, who were in a pretty inflammable state. Between them and the Havel River was a thin line of white tape on screw pickets, and about three British military police, who had strung it up. Fifty yards or so farther on was the bank of the river, and perhaps one hundred yards in was the tailplane of the Russians' latest fighter.

'That's it, gentlemen; no one beyond the tape please.'

The sergeant of the Corps of Military Police had just one pistol in his white, blancoed belt. In front of him was the might of the Soviet Air Force, powerless to do anything except stand behind the tape. They were in the British sector, where they had to do what they were told. They didn't realise – and neither did I – that we were being covered by a whole platoon of the Inniskillin Fusiliers, armed to the teeth, but out of sight. I am glad I never knew what their orders for engagement were.

A few cups of hot soup and drams of Laphroaig reduced the temperature, and we passed the night happily enough until the Russians counterattacked with what they called 'breakfast'. This consisted of caviar, cloves of raw garlic, and vodka. By 4 am, as dawn was starting to break, the situation had cooled off a bit. I decided to retire from the unequal contest and go home to bed.

At 7.30 am the telephone woke me up. It was my duty officer at Potsdam: I was required to see the Russian Commander-in-Chief in Zossen at 11.00 precisely.

I got on to Peter Hayman, acting GOC Berlin. I had to have some sort of brief. Clearly the Russians were very angry, and would be waving a big stick or two. What was I to say? At 9 am we met at Berlin HQ, and I was given an official statement to read in reply to whatever they had to say. I was not to depart from this statement; I was to answer no questions, and to give no excuses no matter what they said.

The gist of the statement was that one of their aircraft had landed in the British zone of Berlin. We – the British – would recover it, and would then hand it back to them. In no way would the Russians be allowed to interfere in what would be a British operation on British territory. If their plane had landed in the British zone without permission it was their fault!

Armed with this, and supported by Nigel Broomfield as interpreter, we set off for Zossen Wunsdorf. On the way through Zossen village we were nearly stopped by two Reggies, who must have been left over from some exercise, as there were no others to be seen anywhere along our route. Luckily they were looking in the opposite direction as we drove past them, but there were menacing shouts and brandishing of weapons as we swiftly went out of range.

We arrived at Zossen to be greeted by the usual enormous statues of sentries – and by Colonel Pinchuk, who looked as if he had spent the previous twenty-four hours on the thrash in a night club and had just been put through a mangle. He was unshaven, and looked desperately tired, after a night of dealing with all the top brass. I might have felt a lack of sleep, but Pinchuk showed it.

We marched up the red carpeted stairs, and were ushered into General Belin's office. It was the same office that Koshevoi had met us in some eight months before, but this time there was no champagne or caviar – just a very angry, senior Colonel General of the Russian Army. We were treated to a long tirade about British obstructionism and our illegal refusal to allow the Russians to recover their own aircraft, and a stern warning that if we did not cooperate at once the situation could become very serious indeed, and we would be entirely to blame.

During this performance the telephone rang. Belin picked up the phone, and a long conversation in Russian ensued. We could only hear half of it, but when Belin put the telephone down he explained that the caller had been none other than General Koshevoi himself, requiring an urgent answer to the Russian demand to be able to handle the aircraft.

He asked me if I had anything to say, and through Nigel Broomfield I read out our prepared statement.

Stalemate.

I assured Belin that we were doing everything possible to rescue the pilots, but most of the aircraft was buried in deep mud, and the explosive charges for the ejector seats had to be disarmed. We were doing the best we could under the circumstances. As soon as the pilots were recovered, their bodies would be properly handed back to the Soviet delegation on the river bank.

The atmosphere eased a little. In reality there was little more to be said, but I asked General Belin if he could provide an escort to take us past Zossen village, and explained about the two Reggies: having let us slip through their fingers once, they would not make the same mistake again. We could be properly held up, with all the subsequent delays to getting his protest back to Berlin and to my own Commander-in-Chief.

The general roared with laughter. All we had to do was to mention his name to the Reggies, and they would speed us on our way: there was no need for any escort!

As we were leaving the office, Nigel Broomfield said to me: 'Well, Brigadier, that was just like a good swishing from the Beak in our young days!' Pinchuk, whose English was good but not all that colloquial, heard this remark without understanding it, and asked Nigel what he had said. We didn't enlighten him.

So it was back into the car and straight into the arms of the Reggies, who were delighted that they had got the top *Angliske spion*, but weren't sure what to do with us. By mischance they had fairly buggered up the works for their side. In vain Nigel tried to explain who we were, and when we mentioned the name 'Colonel General Belin', they gave the normal soldiers' reply: 'Never heard of him.'

Eventually, after about an hour, Nigel persuaded the Reggies to let him get to a telephone in a local house, and with some difficulty managed to get through to SERB to report the detention. He might just have well have triggered an atomic bomb in Potsdam.

There was a howl of horror from Grischel, who answered the telephone, and we were told that immediate help was on the way. And about twenty minutes later, with a roar like a Formula 1 car, a Gaz 69 appeared from Zossen. The two Reggies were delighted. Their efforts were going to be rewarded at last: now the Brits would get what was coming to them! They were disappointed. The Colonel tore up to the senior and knocked him cold, while the wretched junior stood dithering by the side of the road.

Now it was my turn. Through Nigel I told the colonel that because of the idiocy of his soldiers, and the reluctance of his Commander-in-Chief to give us an escort, the protest could not now be in Berlin before 3 pm, and by then GHQ BAOR would have shut down for Easter. I very much doubted whether anyone would be around to bother our Commander-in-Chief with the Russian protest until the following Tuesday.

The Colonel was appalled, but undertook to deliver the message. We drove off as slowly as we decently could, wasting another hour in Potsdam at SERB to complain about the incident and underline its consequences. Eventually got back to Berlin, where Nigel and I wrote up our account of the meeting and the day's affairs and sent it back to Rheindahlen on our teleprint. With the help of the two wretched Reggies we had gained four days' breathing space.

Meanwhile things had been happening on the river bank. By evening the pilots' bodies had been recovered, and at midnight they were handed back in a rather macabre ceremony, with a guard of honour and a piper from the Inniskillins, and a guard and band from the Russians. There was a cooling-off of tension.

Two days later I was again summoned to Zossen. The atmosphere was quite different. Belin thanked us for the way we had treated the bodies of the pilots, and apologised for my hold-up. He promised that whenever a Chief of Mission visited Zossen again, an escort would be provided from the village to the camp. He said with a wry smile that he was sure the two Reggies concerned would know who I was when they next saw me, and would salute when they went by, but he laughed when I wondered aloud whether they would still be around to do it.

He then asked what progress had been made with the recovery. I said that it was coming along satisfactorily, but it was not an easy job. We would keep SERB completely informed as to how and when it could be handed back. At some time during this much more friendly affair the massed bands of GSFG[8] struck up on the parade ground outside the building, making conversation difficult, so we stayed and listened to them until an ADC was dispatched to tell them to pack it in. We left the Russians in a much more friendly mood. They were no longer anxious that the pilots might be alive, and possibly prisoners. They realised that we held all the cards, and that although they could stall a bit, the game was in our hands.

This went on for a fortnight. While Group Captain Ted Colahan, my deputy, dealt with detailed affairs on the river bank, I dealt with the higher command. Meanwhile intelligence and other experts took the Firebar apart under the Russians' noses, and put it together again, and we finally handed it over in the middle of the Havel.

There was one small hiccup. Some days after the handover, a small party of Russians camped on the river bank by the site, presumably in the hope that there might be bits and pieces still to come. Though we assured them that everything was finished they still hung around. Eventually General John Nelson, GOC Berlin, got fed up and sent a most undiplomatic message to the Chief of Staff GSFG, requesting him to tell his stupid soldiers to get lost! I never saw that message – it was not passed through BRIXMIS channels – but it had the desired effect: the small party left.

About two days later Colonel General Turantaev, Chief of Staff GSFG, summoned me to meet him in the Zossen Kommandantura. This was a strange place for such a meeting. It was dark, poky, and ill-furnished: a slum compared with their main building.

Turantaev was an interesting man, with distinguished looks and a charming smile, unlike so many of his comrades in arms. We wondered whether his family had originally been of high aristocratic birth, but we were never to know.

It was an extraordinary meeting. Turantaev started: '*Gospodin* Brigadier, do you know why I have called you to this dingy place for this meeting?'

I said I had no idea; none of us had ever been to the Kommandantura in Zossen before.

He continued: 'Your General sent me three days ago an extremely rude and peremptory message. He may be Commandant of Berlin, but he is junior in rank to me, and I am not prepared to receive such messages from a junior officer. Go back and tell your General that if he treats me with such little respect, then I will treat his staff with the same discourtesy. That is why I have called you here today'.

And there the meeting ended. When I subsequently told John Nelson about it he laughed, but I think he took the point. I certainly did.

Relations between the Russians and the East Germans were strange. On the face of it they were good, but the DDR was beginning to flex its muscles a bit, much to the suspicion of its overlords, and one such incident took place just before I finished my time in April 1968.

The Elbe River marked the boundary between the British Zone and the DDR. Normally such international boundaries run down the centre of rivers, but for some reason we – the British – were responsible for shipping and navigation down to where our boundary ended.

At a place called Havelburg the local East German *Gauleiter* thought he might have a bit of fun with the West German navigation and river patrol boats, who were carrying on with their normal job of seeing that the buoys were in their right places, and that no new sandbanks or other hindrances to navigation were appearing. But East German Vopo boats began interfering – indeed began shooting at our boats – and eventually I received a protest from BAOR addressed from our Commander-in-Chief to Commander-in-Chief GSFG. I rang SERB and made an appointment; it was in fact Turantaev that I saw.

I explained what the problem was and handed him the protest, which set it all out at some length. The sting came in the tail. The protest concluded by stating that – at a certain date and a certain time – a whole regiment of British tanks would line the bank opposite Havelberg, and if any East German boat so much as poked its nose out into the water, it would be sunk without warning. Turantaev was clearly shocked. Obviously no one had told GSFG what was going on, and someone in the East German government was going to be for it.

He asked me: 'Is your Commander in Chief seriously going to order British tanks to fire on unarmed boats?'

I replied that my information was definite that he would, that the East German boats were indeed armed, that they had been interfering illegally with our river patrol boats, that I personally knew the Brigadier who would be in charge of the operation, and that I had no doubt that he would obey his orders to shoot. There really was little that Turantaev could say in reply, apart from issuing the usual warnings that the British were causing unnecessary aggravation to a situation, and that we would be responsible if anything went wrong that might lead to serious results.

It was a businesslike meeting. The Russians were obviously worried: a local East German official had clearly overstepped the mark, and they had known nothing about it. Three days later, as promised, British tanks lined the edge of the river, our patrol boats carried out their routine navigation tasks without any trouble, and no East German boat was to be seen. And there was no protest, or any other reaction, from the Russians.

About a fortnight later the Czech press ran an article complaining of aggressive British tactics on the border of the Elbe, and so we stood by for a summons to Zossen, which in due course arrived. I and one of my RAF interpreters attended General Turantaev again, and as expected were handed an official protest.

It was quite the wettest protest I had ever seen, and what was better someone had made a mistake. Instead of *Britanskaya* (British), they had used the word *Angliskaya* (English), which translated spoke of 'English' tanks and 'English' warlike provocations, terrifying the peaceable East Germans and provoking warlike movements.

At the end of this interesting document General Turantaev added the usual request that I should immediately forward this important protest to my Commander-in-Chief. Usually it was my business to dismiss the whole thing as nonsense and reply with a counter-protest of sorts, but the mistranslation had played right into my hands. I replied that I would be delighted to do so. Turantaev could not believe his ears.

I went on to say that both I and my interpreter were Scots (I was indeed wearing the kilt at the time), that as Scots we had had centuries of trouble with the English, and that what was reported in the protest was typical of the aggressive way they had behaved down the centuries! Turantaev suddenly smiled, gripped my arm, and said, '*Gospodin* Brigadier, you and I understand each other!'

With that the meeting ended. Protocol had been observed: GSFG had made an official if somewhat useless protest to keep their East Germans happy. We knew that they didn't mean a word of it. Later we heard that there had been one hell of a political row: the Russians had put their feet very firmly down on those who had started the affair, and the local *Gauleiter* responsible had been summarily sacked. It had been an interesting bit of liaison.

Part of the liaison side of our role was the social scene. Most of our entertaining took place in the Mission House, but knowing the Russian love of parties and music, I organised a Scottish Dance party in Stuhmer Allee. We rolled the carpets back, got hold of pipers from the Queen's Own Highlanders plus suitable records, and invited SERB and their wives, with guests from the French and American Missions as well.

The problem with inviting Russians was that one never knew just who or how many would come. But there was one officer who always came: Major Minaev, a small, tough man with a rather jolly, bubbly wife. The problem was that he was the 'minder' of SERB, being undoubtedly either KGB or GRU (the Soviet Intelligence Corps). He was highly decorated, and wore the black badges of the Soviet Tank Corps.

So you always laid off for eventualities. Perhaps some would come, perhaps they would not, and whoever did come it was Minaev who set the time of departure: when he said they would leave, they said their goodbyes and left! But they loved music and they loved dancing, and once the initial coolness was over, lubricated by whisky, they would have a whale of a time. Not for nothing do the Russians have a toast 'We shall meet under the table!'

The main thing was to sort Minaev out, and in this I found a great ally in General Sir John Nelson, GOC Berlin, Grenadier Guards, and eager to enter into any sort of fun. Once when he and his wife Jane were at one of these parties, around midnight Minaev signalled that he and SERB would leave, but John Nelson got hold of him as planned, and told him that in his (the British) army no one could leave a party without the permission of the senior officer. The night was still young, everyone was enjoying themselves, and in any case he had not really had the opportunity to talk properly to Minaev about his service in tanks, in which he, John, had also served. The SERB members watching this scene were delighted at Minaev's discomfiture. They did not want to go home, and while Minaev was filled up with whisky, they continued to enjoy themselves. It was interesting to see how the iron grip of the KGB could be prised open, if only for a short time, by a combination of British cunning and hard liquor.

There was not much Russian reciprocation as far as entertainment was concerned. I think this was because they had nowhere to do it. We never saw where they lived, or the inside of any of their own married quarters; they may have felt diffident in asking us back. There was one occasion when they asked all members of all three Missions to their Officers' Club in Potsdam, to see a showing of their version of *War and Peace*, a magnificent film that took two nights to show, with a prolonged interval for refreshment! That was fun, but sadly no wives were invited.

The Russians did not observe Christmas then, but New Year's Day was a different affair. We used to ask the whole of SERB round to the Mission House for a midday drink, with refreshments – what are sometimes now called 'finger eats' (a horrid expression). It was mandatory to start with vodka, and this we had in plenty from the Russian equivalent of the NAAFI, where we were allowed to purchase goods, vodka and caviar being the most favoured items.

The first New Year I was there I suggested that, after the welcoming toast of vodka, they try out our Scots custom of drams of whisky. For that we had a plentiful supply of Laphroaig, which they had never had before, and didn't realise what a powerful brew it was. The result exceeded all my expectations: they fell for it in a big way – in both senses of the word.

When after some two hours SERB left in complete disorder, Colour Sergeant Clark, the NCO in charge of the Potsdam Mission house at the time, said: 'That was some party, Brigadier. I was proud of you: Colonel Pinchuk couldn't get into his car, and Colonel Grischell trod on his hat! They didn't care whether it was Easter or Christmas!' Luckily he didn't ask me how I was feeling.

There were so many sides to the Russians. Once the ice and the language barrier were broken, many of us felt that we had so much in common. In many ways we reckoned that deep down, despite all the years of communist education, they had never lost their religious beliefs: they would come out in little incidents time and time again.

One November day when I was on tour in the southern part of the country, I came across a Russian war cemetery where there was clearly some sort of remembrance parade on: a guard of honour, a band, senior officers, the lot. We couldn't just drive past pretending not to see: that would have been rudeness and bad manners of the worst sort. So we stopped and got out, and I asked whether we might attend the service as past allies. They were delighted. We might have looked a bit scruffy in our tour uniforms, but at least we had the BRIXMIS flash on our shoulders and our uniform hats, and as we had not been up to any skulduggery our boots were clean. And there was the Union Flag on the bonnet of my car to lend a proper British presence.

The service was in much the same form as anything we do. Wreaths were laid; we had none, but I went up and saluted the central memorial stone instead. When the service ended the senior general, a local Tank Division commander, came up and thanked me for coming, as a reminder of the comradeship of the 'Great Patriotic War' as the Russians call it. It was all rather moving. When we moved away, we carried out rather a desultory tour; somehow we were not quite in the right mood.

About three days later, at a meeting at SERB, I happened to mention the incident to Pinchuk. I told him how impressed we had been with the ceremony, and asked him to pass on our thanks to whoever the Divisional Commander was. But I added that I found it all very strange. How was it that the Russians, who officially abhorred Christianity, seemed to be carrying out a very Christian service of remembrance?

Pinchuk explained that Christianity had nothing to do with it. What was happening was that Russian soldiers were remembering their comrades who had fought and died against the enemy in the war. As long as their comrades and the Russian people remembered them, they would never die in their hearts. I had to tell Pinchuk that, to my way of thinking, that was a fairly Christian thought. But he would not agree.

For all of us, particularly the families and children, life in Berlin in those days was marvellous: a throwback to what the British Army had been like in foreign garrisons fifty years before. Unlike today, when everyone goes home on Friday afternoons and doesn't come back to barracks (except for the special dutymen), we had no homes to go to, and so Saturdays and Sundays saw every form of sporting and social activity, and we had the Americans and French to help. Then there was the marvellous Opera in East Berlin, where every Christmas they put on *Hansel and Gretel*, to which all the families went. We might have been a beleaguered garrison, but it had its advantages, even though there were times when the atmosphere got claustrophobic. But at least we in the Missions could get out of the circle, and that was a great advantage.

My two years passed in a flash. Apart from the major incident of the Firebar there were lots of minor ones. Three of my tour officers were declared 'persona non grata' in my time, for what the Russians called 'hooligan acts' (they loved to describe officers whom they caught in restricted areas as 'hooligans'). One tour was severely shot at, but no one was actually hurt. Cars were broken into. There was one bout of fisticuffs where the Narks lost! But by and large there was nothing like the rammings of tour cars and shootings that occurred after I left.

Eventually I handed over to David House of the Greenjackets (in later years Lieutenant General and Black Rod). Together we went to Zossen for me to say goodbye and introduce him to the Commander-in-Chief. He was dressed as a Riflemen – black cross belt, black buttons and all – and I was an Argyll.

We went through the usual routine, and were shown into the Commander-in-Chief's Office. This time there was champagne and brandy on the table. After the official introductions, we all sat down and had a most interesting conversation with Turantaev, who in the absence of General Koshevoi on leave was doing the honours.

Somehow we got onto history, and the Russian and British Armies. I think it was Turantaev who talked about casualties in the last two wars, and the appalling losses of the Russians in both – over twenty million in the second, and they did not really know how many! How many had the British Empire had?

I knew the answer: four million in the first and just over a million in the second.

'You see,' said Turantaev, 'we are not talking about the same Germans, are we? That is why we are determined they will never have the chance to start another war in our lifetime.'

Then he had something to say about the British Army: a ridiculously small affair compared with what the Russians had, but an army they admired greatly, particularly its Regiments and their traditions, and laughingly he wondered how such an army could afford to let itself be dressed in such diverse uniforms as David and myself were wearing.

And then he said something very unexpected. He talked about the terrible problems of the Russian Army when it was first formed: how they tried to break with everything the Czarist armies had, and built up a new Red Army, but then the dreadful purges of the late 1930s almost destroyed all their senior ranks of command. Luckily he had been in the Far East, and had somehow escaped the purges and shootings.

He ended by pointing to his badges of rank, which he said were, with small alterations, the same as those that Russian generals had worn down the ages, but he added that it had taken a terrible struggle and many lives to achieve that, and something like fifty years in time. Then he said something very wise, which I had never thought of before: 'We are all proud of our uniforms and traditions, but in the long run, if you read your history, you will find that, in battle, the Russian and British soldier will fight the way they always have, no matter what uniform they are wearing. We are both very patriotic people, but we sometimes don't realise it until our countries are in grave danger.'

And then we said goodbye.

We drove back to Potsdam, past the place where the Reggies had clobbered us, and over the railway where Nigel and I had got stuck in the sand. I said to David, 'If you look over this bridge, it is a good place to catch a train or two.' He did look, and there was a train loaded with tanks. But of course we were on an official visit, and with nothing so lethal as a camera!

Anyway it was his job now, not mine.

NOTES

1 Matthew 6:24; Luke 16:13.
2 The 'Great Game' was the title given to British and Russian intelligence activities on the boundaries of India and Central Asia from the early 1800s, as described in Rudyard Kipling's novel *Kim*.
3 This was a bit of BRIXMIS jargon. In effect it meant being detained or caught by either the Soviets or the East Germans, with a subsequent detention at the local Kommandant's headquarters, and – if the matter was serious – a possible 'PNG', which meant confiscation of the individual's tour pass, and removal from the unit. This could be a serious matter if it resulted in the loss of an experienced officer.
4 Armoured personnel carrier.
5 The Vopo were the *Volkspolizei*, or East German police. Sometimes they were uniformed; sometimes they were in plain clothes and unmarked cars. These latter we called the 'Narks'. They were for the most part a tough and pretty nasty lot; their job was to watch and frustrate our efforts.
6 Tony Geraghty, *Beyond the Frontline: The untold exploits of Britain's most daring Cold War spy mission*, London: HarperCollins, 1996.
7 SOXMIS was the Soviet equivalent of BRIXMIS. They had three missions, in the British, French and American zones of West Germany.
8 GSFG was the Group of Soviet Forces in Germany. It was the equivalent of BAOR (British Army of the Rhine), but much bigger. Its headquarters were at Zossen.

CHAPTER 13
Panmunjom

I left Berlin on a hot July afternoon by myself in the Rover. I was laden with the family silver and the Meissen china that I did not care to entrust to the Army to transport (after bitter experiences of what could happen when their movement control got their hands on my possessions). I drove down the *autobahn* to Helmstedt, where a BRIXMIS tour saw me through the barrier. This was quite unofficial – I had nothing to do with them now – but it was a nice gesture.

I made my way towards Hamburg, and stayed the night with the Queen's Own Highlanders who were on one of the British Army training areas near Luneburg Heath. I did not know it then, but it was to be the last time I was to sleep in a tent and be woken up by reveille on the pipes. That afternoon I drove to Bremen and got on the ship to Harwich. I had been given a very comfortable suite, befitting my rank, but I cannot think why! It was a comfortable but lonely voyage: once again I was leaving behind a lot of friends, and a way of life that was almost pre-war in comfort, servants, entertainment and general ambience. You would think that by now I had got used to these partings, but somehow I never did. I always felt that I had left something of myself behind: something that was lost in the past for ever.

We docked early next morning at Harwich and I set off for London, hoping that somehow there would be a space opposite my mother's house in Chelsea where I could park the car and unload my possessions. There would not be much time, as that evening the Scottish Division were Beating Retreat on the Horse Guards, and I was one of the regimental party who were gathering in the Banqueting Hall afterwards to entertain the Queen, our Colonel in Chief. This meant stowing all the contents of the car in the limited space of my mother's house, and getting changed into a respectable London suit. It was a particularly hot afternoon; it always seemed to be hot whenever I landed up in London from abroad, and this day was no exception.

The Retreat went well. In the whole mass of men and regiments we just had two: Pipe Major Ronnie McCallum (Pipe Major of our 8th Battalion, and in private life the Duke of Argyll's Head Gardener), and the Senior

Drum Major, David Legge, who I remembered many years ago joining the Regiment as a boy soldier. It was a sad occasion in that it was the last appearance of that great regiment the Cameronians, who were soon to disappear from the line of battle. Looking at the picture of it all thirty years later other regiments have gone too. It was I think the last occasion when men of all the regiments of the Scottish Division played together on a brilliant summer's evening, but we were not to know that then.

Afterwards we all trooped into the Banqueting Hall, where we were marshalled in various regimental groups so that the VIPs could circulate and meet us all. The Queen was somewhat astonished to learn that I had left Berlin only two days before; she had indeed heard of BRIXMIS, and I suspect she knew quite a bit about what we were up to.

So at the end of a pretty hectic forty-eight hours I got home and crashed out. Sylvia was due by air next day – she had stayed for two days with friends in Berlin – and then we collected ourselves together and drove down to Charity House to get it ready for the family and the summer holidays, which were now just about two weeks ahead. Our tenants had left it in pretty good order, and there was little to be organised except getting our own furniture out of store, and cleaning up the kitchen. The garden was in a pretty good state as well.

The Army had not told me anything of my future, although I knew I had six months or so to wait for any appointment, so I enrolled myself in the Crawley College for Further Education to study for the final part of the Chartered Secretaries Exam. I had already passed Parts 1 and 2. Part 3 dealt with company law and accountancy, two subjects of which I knew very little, and it would be fairly hard and detailed work. I was signed on for four days a week, which meant leaving the house at 8 am and getting back at 6 pm from Mondays to Thursdays.

The long-suffering Sylvia accepted this with good grace. She had got herself on a dressmaking course, and I suspect was in some ways glad to see the back of me for four days in the week. My son Sandy had just started at Downside, and Maggie was at her teacher training college at Roehampton, so for the first time in many years Sylvia was her own mistress, and – within reason – could do as she liked: no generals or diplomats' wives to look after, and no regimental families with all their problems to cope with. I wonder now whether she did not feel a bit lonely, but she never complained. In any case she had many friends in the area, as well as her aunt and her father, so her time was pretty well occupied.

For nearly six months this pleasant but somewhat humdrum life went on. I learnt quite a bit about law and accountancy, Sylvia turned out some very smart suits and dresses, and the children seemed very happy at their schools. We all awaited the telephone call, and one day in February it came, from the Military Secretary's Office at Stanmore, while I was away at my college. I was to ring him back personally. By the time I got back home it was past six in the evening and it was too late to ring, so we spent the night apprehensively, wondering what fate had come up with this time.

It was mid-morning before I managed to get through, not to the Military Secretary himself, but to one of his staff whom I knew well – a Major General. His message was a bit of a shaker:

'We've got an interesting job for you, David. We want you to go to Korea as Commander of the Commonwealth Liaison Mission, and as Defence Attaché, but – most important of all – as Commonwealth Representative at the Armistice Commission in Panmunjom.

'Have a think about this – it is a very important job, but there may be all sorts of family snags – and let me know next Monday if you think you can accept.'

I put the phone down. I could see Sylvia itching with curiosity at the kitchen door, wondering what it was all about, and I was not at all sure how she would take the news.

'They want me to go to Korea,' I said, 'but I don't have to make up my mind till Monday'.

She went almost white with shock. For a moment I thought she was going to burst into tears. Somehow Korea struck her as being the end of the world – away out of touch with her family, her children, and all her friends.

There was much to think and talk about. I had no idea what the job entailed, and indeed wondered whether there was any future in it for me at all. It seemed a bit of a come-down after BRIXMIS. When I left Germany my Commander-in-Chief, Shan Hackett, had more or less told me that my next job would be a two-star one, and that is what he had recommended in his final report on me. Had something gone wrong? Had I been consigned by No. 1 Board to the waste paper basket for clapped-out and useless Brigadiers?

The problems were entirely family and children. The latter could join us for two of the three holidays in the year – summer and winter – but from January to July we would not see them, and somehow we would have to make arrangements for someone to look after them. Sylvia's mother was dead, her father was an invalid in a home, and her aunt was getting on in years and living with a companion in Suffolk. My own mother was approaching her eighties. She had a large enough house in London but no car, and therefore she was somewhat immobile when it came to school half-terms and the like. What would happen if any of them, children included, fell seriously ill, or had an accident? The two of us would be miles away, and of little help to anyone.

For all the attractions of the job, the disadvantages seemed almost insuperable, but there was a way out. Down the years we had made a number of very great friends, mostly in the Services, whose children were about the same age as our own. If they were willing to keep a sort of watching brief for us, and help with the half-terms and holidays, we could go, trusting to luck that nothing would go amiss at home. So on the Monday morning, keeping my fingers crossed, I said I would accept, and discussed very fully all the problems. The Military Secretary's Office did everything possible to see that all sorts of safety nets were put in place to safeguard any family needs.

There then followed a seemingly endless round of briefings, meetings and planning for the move. (There was also the question of letting Charity House. Here our usually impeccable solicitors and estate agents failed us: they let it to a bigamist, who had the most impeccable references, but no fewer than three wives, which caused us endless difficulties two years later!)

Eventually briefing and packing were over, our heavy baggage was dispatched, the children were back at school, and Sylvia, her aunt and I (with all our documents in my pocket) caught the train from Jarvis Brook station to London. There we were to spend a night with my mother, before travelling on to Brize Norton, where we were to catch the RAF flight to Singapore the next day.

At Brize Norton we were given the start of a VIP journey. The Commandant, Group Captain Don Attlee, was an old friend from Berlin days. He gave us lunch in his house, we were relieved of all our baggage, and the check-in procedure, and after this we were driven in his own staff car to the steps of the VC10 that was to take us. I hadn't received such treatment since my days with Field Marshal Montgomery.

About an hour after taking off we were flying through cloud to our operational height, when there was a brilliant flash, a loud bang and a smell of burning. We had been struck by lightning! It had happened to me years before in 1945, in an old Dakota flying between Manus and Pelelieu Island, but it was still just as frightening. No harm had been done to the aircraft, but the electric discharge had knocked our navigation instruments out. We had to return to Brize Norton, bur first we had to ditch our fuel, which meant flying out to somewhere over the sea. After two hours we were back where we started, and it took another hour to transfer us all from our original VC10 to another that was waiting ready for us. Then we were well and truly off.

We stopped for refuelling at Bahrain, and the Captain asked Sylvia and me into the cockpit to watch the approach and landing, which was in the dark and most spectacular. Once on the ground we were whisked off to a VIP lounge, where drinks and sandwiches were ready, and there were particularly nice changing rooms where, had we wanted, we could have had a shower. After an hour we were back on the plane, and we slept fitfully until we landed at Gan, a small island in the Maldives. This was a most beautiful spot, but we had no time to look round before the final leg to Singapore, where we landed in late afternoon.

Dennis Beckett, a Major General on the Staff and a very old friend, was away in Borneo, and he had lent us his house and servants for our stay. It was part of a complex known as Alexandria, next door to Gillman Barracks, where we were first put up in 1939. It had not changed one bit, except that in those far-off years it had been a major's or perhaps a lieutenant colonel's quarter. I remembered as a very young officer going to parties there. It was like going back in a time machine. The places, the trees and the gardens had not changed; only the faces were different. In the evening light I walked with Sylvia the short way to Gillman, showed her the Officers' Mess and where my room once was, and the long, winding road up to the top of the barracks, where I had so gingerly led our new Bren carriers. She had never been in the East before, and the atmosphere and the evening colours enchanted her. Little by little the worries of leaving home were beginning to slide away.

After three days of more meetings and briefings we were on our way again, this time by Cathay Pacific to Hong Kong, and yet another surprise. Since I now held an official command in the South East Asia area, I was entitled to travel first class – and what a difference that made. No bother at check-ins, very comfortable accommodation, superb food, and the undivided attention of the Cathay Air hostesses, drawn from all the countries the airline served. They were the nicest, the most attractive and the most efficient cabin staff I have ever encountered.

The journey to Hong Kong, via Bangkok, took some four hours. We were met by Bobbie Smith, a very old friend. A Gordon Highlander, he was serving on the headquarters staff. His son was at Downside with Sandy, and he and Geila his wife would see them through Hong Kong when the holiday journeys were on. They lived in a beautiful flat overlooking Repulse Bay, not far from Stanley Barracks and the Repulse Bay Hotel, which I believe has now been destroyed to make way for yet more skyscrapers.

There followed more briefings for me. I also had to pick up my tropical uniforms at Mr Shan Tuck. I had sent out my measurements from home, and there only remained the final fittings. All was ready in thirty-six hours for me to collect before my flight to Korea: all beautifully made, and – by today's standards – amazingly cheap. I had to spend a morning with Lieutenant General Sir John Worsley, who was GOC Hong Kong, but my immediate superior as far as Korea was concerned. For purely military purposes I was under his command, but for diplomatic doings I was under our Ambassador. It was all getting a bit complicated. Sir John was Indian Army, and I had met him before; he and his wife gave us a delightful lunch in their beautiful house.

Early next morning we left Bobby and Geila's flat, crossed the harbour on the car ferry to Kai Tak, and got on the final Cathay flight to Seoul, which took a rather roundabout route via Taipeh and Tokyo. Taipeh was an interesting place: the British did not recognise Chiang's regime, and so we were confined in a sort of 'quarantine' waiting room. This was very comfortable, but we found the numbers of armed soldiers all over the place rather unnerving. Haneda looked very different from the deserted airfield I remembered on that early morning in 1950, but we did not get off the aircraft. Then it was the last lap: two hours or so to Seoul, where we stepped off into another VIP welcome led by Dawnay Bancroft (whom I was to relieve) and his wife Elisabeth. The welcome party included the Dean of the Attaché Corps, a delightful Thai colonel with his wife, the head of the ROK Army Protocol Office with his, and Lieutenant Colonel Bill Whyte of the Australian Army, with his wife Lillian.

We were led into a VIP lounge, where we were offered all sorts of drinks. Eventually we were bundled into one of my Mission's staff cars and driven to the US Army Mess in the South Post. The Defence Attaché's house in Seoul itself was adequate, but there was not room for two families to live alongside each other for the week's prolonged handover and the parties that attended it all. Dawnay and Elisabeth took us out to dinner that evening to introduce us quietly to the Embassy staff with whom we would be working. I was handed a long and complicated programme of events for the next week.

Although I had been briefed in London, Singapore and Hong Kong, I really had little idea of what I was being pitchforked into. I had three quite distinct jobs:

- Defence Attaché
- UK Representative, Military Armistice Commission
- Commander, Commonwealth Liaison Mission

This meant that I was responsible to three very different people: the British Ambassador (with the Australian and New Zealand Ambassadors thrown in for good measure); the Commander-in-Chief, Hong Kong (and, breathing over his shoulder, the Commander-in-Chief, Far East); and last but very much not least the Commander-in-Chief, United Nations Command, Korea – an American four-star general! Any one of them could at any time send for me, tell me what they thought, and expect me to make sense of it.

The job of a defence attaché is relatively simple. He is responsible to his Ambassador for keeping him in touch with the military situation in the country to which he is assigned. He is in some ways a sort of spy, but a perfectly open one.

The Commonwealth Liaison Mission was the residue of the

231

Commonwealth Forces that fought in the Korean war. There was an Australian lieutenant colonel, a Canadian major, a New Zealand naval lieutenant commander, and a young British major who acted as adjutant. We had a small clerical and pay section, our own post office (BFPO 3), and a clerical staff. We also had our own camp, messes and stores. If anything serious was to happen in Korea, we were the toe in the door to help Commonwealth forces redeploy in the country. We looked after the small British contingent of some thirty soldiers and a small Turkish contingent of two officers and about ten soldiers. There were two officers from Ethiopia to add spice to the mixture. All the officers were attached to the Armistice Commission and took part in meetings.

The Armistice Commission was an entirely American staffed and organised affair, but from very early days the British Defence Attaché (in his guise as Commander of the Commonwealth Liaison Mission) was allotted a seat at the top table, and was privy to the many plans and briefings that took place, but with certain exceptions.

So there were a great many people to meet, including the US, United Nations and 8th Army Staff, and the four ROK services (their marines are, like the US Marines, a completely separate organisation). There were ceremonial briefings, guards of honour, receptions of all types, and parties in individual houses until it was all over, and Dawnay and Elizabeth Bancroft left from Kimpo, the Seoul airfield, in a ceremony that was much the same as our arrival, but in reverse. After their plane had taken off, Sylvia and I moved into our new home to take stock of how we were going to live.

The solid, red brick house was one of an identical pair within a walled compound. It had been built in the 1930s by, I think, the Shell Oil Company. There was no garden to speak of: just a few flowering shrubs and a winding path from the wall gateway to the small plateau on which both houses stood. Downstairs there was a wide veranda in the front, and a large L-shaped room, part sitting, part dining. You could sit twelve down comfortably at the dining table, and there were three large sofas and sundry armchairs in the sitting room. Completing the ground floor was a good-sized kitchen and larder, with a cellar below. From the sitting room a staircase rose to the first floor, where there was one large bedroom, a smaller guest bedroom, a dressing room with a bed in it, and two bathrooms. There was air conditioning of a sort downstairs and in the main bedroom, and excellent central heating for the winter. It was tolerably well furnished, but with our own pictures and carpets, and the odd bit of Korean furniture, we made it look very reasonable in time.

If the house was not all that much to enthuse about, the staff we inherited were a very different matter. First and foremost there was Yi-Si, the cook. Large, fat and round, with a beaming face and a charming personality, she was a very good cook indeed. She was approaching her

61st birthday, which is a landmark in any Korean's life. On attainment of that age, known as the *hwangap*, the individual is honoured by his or her family and everyone else, and particularly if she is female she can really enjoy life.

Then there was Ahn Chong Ho. Technically, she was my batman! She had originally started as servant to the Commanders of the Commonwealth Brigade, but when that was disbanded stayed with the defence attachés. Her husband had disappeared in 1950, leaving her with a son, who was just starting at university. I have never known a better batman; she knew her way round every nuance of British Army uniform, and became a real family friend.

Mrs Kim Ae Sa, otherwise known as 'The Ant', was the third member of staff. (She really did have a face like an ant!) I am not quite certain what her duties were officially, but she never stopped working at something or other: furniture polish, vacuum cleaners, dishcloths and brooms were always in action somewhere in the house. She also looked after her husband, 'Guard' Kim, our so-called security man. He patrolled the grounds at night – when he was not asleep – and like the senior warder in the Tower of London was the keeper of the keys!

I have left the most important character to last. He was not a member of the household staff. Mr Moon Yung Sun was my driver, held on the establishment of the CLM, but he was much more than a driver: he was escort, interpreter, guide, philosopher and lifelong friend.

He had an extraordinary history. He came from the very top right-hand corner of Korea, almost from Siberia. When he was 15 or so in 1950, his grandfather gathered all his family together and told them he was worried that North Korea was bent on hostilities, and he wished his family to leave the North and make for the South, where they could re-establish themselves. Only two succeeded – Moon and one cousin. By the winter of 1950 Moon had somehow got himself attached to a British Army REME workshop in Pusan as a sort of general dogsbody and cleaner, but he was so obviously well educated and intelligent that little by little he found himself as a fitter's apprentice, then a fitter, and finally a driver. When the main body of the Commonwealth forces left at the end of the Korean War, he applied for and got the job of driving the Defence Attaché in the late 1950s.

By the time I took him on he had been in post for nearly twenty years, and he lasted right up to 1995: a Korean who had spent all his life in the British Army! You might have mistaken him for a Gurkha: he had much the same sort of face and complexion, and with his green beret and regimental badge he certainly did not have the appearance of a Korean soldier. He was a mine of information about the Korean Army, and he knew a great deal about the Americans as well. I think I learnt more about the Koreans, their history and their customs from Moon than from any lecture or book. Time and time again he saved me from appalling social gaffes, or put me right about someone, or some incident that otherwise I would have known little about. In 1998 all those of us whom Moon had served clubbed together and had him and his wife over here for six weeks as part of our thanks for all he had done for us.

The Embassy was a small one, in a beautiful house in its own grounds, and built by the Royal Engineers, who had made a good job of it. Ian Mackenzie ran it for the first six months of my tour until he was succeeded by Nigel Trench. The First Secretary was Fred Rainsford, transferred from the Royal Air Force, succeeded by Dougie Reid, and the Third Secretary was Michael Gore, who found time amongst his many other duties to write a comprehensive book about Korean birds. Except for Michael all the diplomatic staff lived in the Embassy compound, which enclosed the Chancery building where I had one of my two offices.

I did not have long to wait for my first meeting at Panmunjom – perhaps four days. My predecessor had briefed me on what I might expect, but it was still a strange affair, and I felt like a fish out of water. We were called into the MAC office in the North Post, where the Secretary, Colonel John Lucas of the US Army, briefed us on why the North Koreans had called the meeting. Then our Chief Major General G.H. Woodward told us what he was going to say. We were to meet at the small landing strip on the banks of the Han River at 8.00 the following morning. We would fly to the advanced camp, and the meeting would start at 10.00 am. Moon got me to the airstrip on time, where two large C54 helicopters were waiting, and we flew to the advanced camp – a journey of perhaps thirty minutes. We sat in the Mess there and relaxed with a cup of coffee, and then loaded back into our convoy of staff cars for Panmunjom itself, some three miles down the road (helicopters were not allowed to fly over the DMZ). On arrival we piled out of the cars and into the meeting hall. I followed the general and sat as directed on his left, with a Turkish colonel on my left, and two ROK generals on the right of General Woodward. In front of us was a green baize table on which were two flags, those of North Korea and the United Nations.

Facing us across the green baize were three North Korean officers, all of general rank, in the simple but very smart Russian-style uniforms that they wore. Behind them were their staffs, similarly attired, and with them on a table by themselves were two representatives of the Chinese Army, in simple uniforms with no badges of rank. As soon as we and our staffs had sat down, the senior North Korean, General Park Chung Kuk, started reading – in Korean – the complaint that we had been expecting about an incident in the Demilitarised Zone, or DMZ as we called it.

His statement lasted some ten minutes. When he had finished, one of their interpreters stood up and read the same statement in English, followed – when he sat down – by yet another interpreter, who repeated it all in Chinese. We had already been 'in play' for some thirty minutes and had not yet replied. Now it was our turn.

General Woodward read out his refutation of events, followed by the Korean and Chinese versions. One hour had passed to do twenty minutes of business, but there was plenty more to come. Eventually – after four hours – our two principals had run out of comment on what was actually a very insignificant affair, and it was back to the cars, a strong drink in the Mess, into the choppers and back to Seoul. I was assured that I was lucky to have had such a short meeting to cut my teeth on. Being unused to these goings-on I thought it was a complete waste of time, but I had a lot to learn about the MAC and how it all worked. I got back to our house in time for a late cup of tea (no lunch that day), and found Sylvia all agog to know what had gone on. In all truth there wasn't much to tell her: I just could not see the sense in any of it. It was all so different from my meetings with the Russians at Zossen and Potsdam.

The rather strange procedure dated back to July 1951, when delegations from the United Nations Command, the Chinese People's Volunteers, and the North Korean Army met at Kaesong to consider an armistice. It took months of talking and bluffing until the Armistice Agreement was signed in July 1953, and the shape and size of the Military Armistice Commission was finally agreed. Unfortunately the original negotiators for the UN side found themselves led into a series of procedural traps, including the use of three separate languages when simultaneous translations could have been adopted, and the odd custom that no member could leave the top table for any purpose during a meeting: to do so would be a sign of weakness and a lack of manners! We inherited these traditions some fifteen years later.

In 1968, when I joined, negotiations for the return of the crew of the *Pueblo* were still in progress, but this was a completely US/North Korean affair: the UN was not involved, and we were not informed of what was going on, though it was held under the cover of the Armistice Commission.[1] The talks were businesslike, and in no way cramped by the MAC's tortuous procedures. Both Generals – Park and Woodward – were able negotiators, and got on with the job. Park was in fact an experienced diplomat in his own right, and Gilbert Woodward was a Virginian, born 200 years too late, who did not care two hoots for anyone. I suspect they enjoyed knocking spots off each other over the green baize.

Initially I was there to listen and report back through the Embassy to both the Foreign Office and Singapore. In no way at any meeting could I open my mouth with any comment – nor could anyone else except the two principals on either side – but as time went on and I got the hang of things, I could pass notes to the senior member or the Secretary if I spotted some inconsistency or mis-statement in what the North Koreans were trying to say.

Many of the meetings were humdrum, and could be boring, but the sparks could fly sometimes. On one occasion there was the sound of shooting with automatic weapons and mortars very close to Panmunjom. 'Woody' seized the opportunity to suggest to Park that it was their joint business to leave the meeting at once with all their staffs, seek out the battle and stop it! The invitation was not accepted.

On another occasion the North Koreans, quite without warning, produced a large tank transporter bearing a bullet-holed and bloodstained small landing craft. From it they showed us remnants of lifejackets and kit, and photos of corpses allegedly caught off their West Coast. Clearly the ROK special forces had been up to no good without telling anyone, and had walked into a well prepared ambush. We had been badly caught out. What could we say except flatly deny all knowledge of any such operation, which was true enough! Later we found that there had indeed been an illicit operation by the ROK Marines, carried out without the permission of General Bonsteele, UN Commander-in-Chief, which had resulted in a major political row between the US and ROK governments.

Then there was the major incident in September/October 1968, when North Korean commandos landed some 180 highly trained and motivated young officers halfway down the east coast of South Korea to get into the mountains and create havoc. It took over six weeks to deal with the last of them, but very cleverly a complete radio and news blackout was imposed, and though there were guarded references at MAC meetings to tales of revolution and uprisings in the south, they never heard a thing from us until we were ready, and all but a few prisoners were left. One day they called a meeting to protest about some minor incident. We waited right until the end, when protocol allowed us to give our closing speech. We started this quietly, but then produced a detailed film showing the burnt houses, the murdered villagers, the casualties themselves, and statements by the prisoners. We handed over a casualty list, and reminded them that any further incursions would be dealt with in the same way. The effect was astonishing. Clearly the North Koreans knew that something had gone wrong with their plans – they must have picked up the odd signal from their commando force – but this total disaster was something they had never expected. There was little they could say, and they never tried anything like that again.

Part of the problem with MAC meetings lay in the use of the Korean language, which is complicated by its many modes of address, depending on who may be talking to whom. For example, a *Yangbang* or nobleman talking to a butcher (after the soldier the lowest form of social life in Korea) would use a particular form of address that would make it quite clear who was the master, and who was the servant. From time to time, if the North Koreans were really angry and worked up about some incident, they would frame their speeches accordingly, and our own interpreters could get a sense of their anger or frustration.

But even in normal complaints their speeches included some quite astonishing phrases. We were always referred to as 'the UN aggressors', which for them was the acme of politeness; more robust expressions were 'drunken devils dancing on heaps of corpses', or better still 'vile octopuses roaming the oceans with bloodstained claws'. There were many more. It was all routine stuff, mostly fit only for the rubbish bin, but sometimes – when the North Koreans' imagination went way out of bounds – the whole UN side, with the benefit of our instant translation, would explode with laughter. The North Koreans could not understand this, which drove them to further excesses of descriptive language. I came in for my share of abuse. Once, when a long-range signal detachment had come in from Hong Kong for an exercise with the US and ROK Armies, I was described as a 'lackey like a starving lapdog running after my American masters' heels for rotten bones'.

All of these proceedings were watched by the world's press through the windows that lined the side of the conference hut, but they had to be careful. The table lay exactly on the 38th parallel, and the ground outside was policed both by detachments of the North Korean Army, tough men with grim faces who never seemed to smile, and our own soldiers, including detachments from the British contingent of the Honour Guard, Thais, Turks and Americans. It was a relief to look up and see some cheerful faces looking at you, but they had to stay on their side of the international Tom Tiddler's Ground. There had been cases of abductions, fisticuffs and shootings from time to time.

In summertime the journey home by helicopter was usually in daylight, but sometimes the winter evenings' journeys posed problems. There was one really hairy escapade when a meeting had lasted until about 7.00 in the evening, and there was a thick fog. It really was well below flying conditions, but there was some sort of major conference the next day and Woody, our Chief, was anxious to get home. Neither of the C54 pilots wished to fly but, wrongly, deferred to the General, so we took off. We could not really see Seoul at all through the murk, and mistook one of its main roads for our small landing strip. Luckily our pilot saw it in time, and eventually we touched down safely, but our companion got completely lost and ended up at Suwon Air Base, some twenty miles south of Seoul, with only a few teaspoons of fuel left in his tanks. Some of our wiser colleagues, who had refused to fly, came down by road, and were not home until dawn the next morning! Next day there was a sort of minor mutiny meeting at MAC Headquarters, where a lot of us made sure that such an escapade would never take place again.

Part of the Armistice Commission included Poles, Czechs, Swiss and Swedes: four two-star generals, each with a small staff. They were known as the Neutral Nations Advisory Commission. The Swiss and the Swedes lived in a delightful camp in part of the Panmunjom area, the Poles and Czechs in North Korea near Kaesong. Their job was to act as international referees to see fair play, and a very valuable team they were as, in theory, they had free transit permits throughout the whole of Korea. In fact it did not quite work out like that, but through them we could get news at first hand of what was going on in the North, and equally the North Koreans could check the state of play in the South.

Once every two months the Swiss and Swedes would give an enormous Sunday lunch, to which we were all invited (although the North Koreans diplomatically refused), and a great deal of very useful information was exchanged. But sometimes there were diplomatic hiccups. In 1968 the Russians decided to put the stopper on Dubcek, then premier of Czechoslovakia, and the Polish Army was forced to take part. Our Czech general's son was caught up in the goings-on and imprisoned, and while this was happening the Czech and his Polish opposite number (who were great friends) had to pretend to the outside world that in fact all was well. It cast a bit of a sadness over one particular party.

The year 1968 was a particular busy time for MAC meetings, but when the crew of the *Pueblo* were handed over some of the tension eased, though the North Koreans were putting both military and diplomatic pressure on, and there was quite a bit of cross-border shooting. The problem for both Sylvia and myself was never knowing when I might be called at short notice to a meeting, and engagements – diplomatic or otherwise – had to be cancelled at very short notice. All this made life difficult for Sylvia, as she had little idea from week to week what I might be up to, and invitations to events, receptions and parties were legion. We also had to do our share of entertaining, which included giving a hand at Embassy receptions, and dealing with 'Visiting Firemen' from Hong Kong and Singapore.

Once every two months the Honour Guard Detachment changed over. The new guard arrived in a big C130 Hercules, which carried amongst other things supplies of drinks from the NAAFI, fresh meat from Hong Kong, and guests of all sizes, shapes and seniority. Four days of solid conferences, visits and parties followed until the relief was complete, the old guard and the guests flew back, and life went back to normal. Particularly high on the list for visits were Panmunjom, Gloucester Valley, The Hook, Kapyong, and all the sights round Seoul. Sylvia and I became accomplished tour guides, but we had the help of the CLM staff to take a great deal of the weight. My Australian GSO1's wife, Lillian Whyte was an expert on Korean culture, pictures and jewellery, and very knowledgeable on history and tombs. If a very senior officer was in the party, Moon would act as driver, very proud of a two- or three-star plate with flag to match; David Collins, my New Zealand sailor, could deal with the Navy; and we usually ended with a party for all and sundry in our CLM Mess in our own compound. When the plane left for Hong Kong we all breathed a sigh of relief, but sometimes not for long.

Any American Army camp starts the day by firing a gun off when the national flag is hoisted. This is a bit unnerving if your sleeping quarters happen to be near the gun. For some reason we, the British, had inherited that duty. The gun in question was a 75 mm pack howitzer on the big parade ground at the South Post, and each morning a British soldier would load it with a blank cartridge and, at the given hour, pull the trigger. Every time the Honour Guard changed so did the gunner, who took over the day the old guard left, which was very early in the morning.

On one such changeover some infamous member of the old guard had cunningly left a baseball in the barrel. The new gunner failed to look up the barrel, stuffed his cartridge in and pulled the trigger. With unerring aim the baseball flew across the parade ground and through a window of the mess hall on the opposite side, landing – so I was told – in the middle of the hash browns, to the fury of the duty cook. But the villains of this piece of nonsense were in their Hercules, blissfully on their way to Hong Kong far out of the reach of the law as it existed in Seoul, leaving a very embarrassed Brigadier to explain away the inexplicable to a very senior American general, who luckily liked the Brits and had a sense of humour.

He was General Charles H. Bonesteele III, the third generation of his family to serve in the US Army, a Rhodes Scholar, an engineer and a very distinguished man. At Oxford he had been a great friend of General Shan Hackett, my late Commander-in-Chief, Germany. He held the post of Commander-in-Chief, UN Forces Korea, and was also Commander-in-Chief, US 8th Army. He was a man of infinite good temper and patience (though his staff were scared stiff of him), and he had a very difficult job.

The South Koreans by now had large and efficient armed forces, some of whom were deployed in Vietnam, and the remainder were all ready to go for the North Koreans. But their back-up was completely dependent on the USA, who held the purse strings, and had problems enough in Vietnam without an additional shooting match erupting in Korea. In some ways the General was on a sort of military tightrope: one slip could mean disaster. He had succeeded in calming everyone down after the Blue House Raid in early 1968, when a body of North Koreans got right into Seoul, within 200 yards of the Presidential Palace. He had had the *Pueblo* on his hands, and a mere cannonball into the cookhouse was not going to upset him all that much!

But I saw the most efficient way he dealt with one of his many diplomatic pinpricks. This concerned the reinforced company from Thailand, some 180 officers and men, that formed part of his UN Command. They were attached to the 7th US Division on the DMZ, and as UN soldiers had the privilege of using the Post Exchange facilities. For their service in Korea the US Government subsidised each soldier's daily pay to the equivalent (I was told) of $10. But their company commander, a colonel, ran a sort of mutual savings society to which every soldier contributed, and when special offers came up at the PX, a horde of Thai soldiers would descend and buy up the lot; these contributions also went into the kitty.

In order to support this company a C130 Hercules of the Royal Thai Air Force would from time to time come to Korea via Hong Kong, and return via Japan. In addition to its purely military supplies it carried Thai silk, to dispose of in Hong Kong, where it picked up suitable goods for sale in Korea. It left with the PX special offers, which it disposed of in Tokyo, and there it picked up further trade for Thailand! On the face of it this was all perfectly legal and above board – the import/export company that the Thai colonel ran so efficiently profited greatly, as did his soldiers, who were shareholders – except that onward sale of PX goods was strictly forbidden, and as the plane was under UN command, it was exempt from customs declaration and search. Everyone knew this trade was going on, but there was no proof!

The Thais had part of our CLM compound where they held surplus stores, and one day their colonel, a most delightful chap with a son still at Sandhurst, came to me and asked whether they could take over an additional hut for stores that they were expecting off their next plane. There was nothing odd or suspicious about that, and the hut was duly handed over. From time to time a truck would draw up and stores would be unloaded, but one afternoon my Quartermaster Sergeant noted that most of the so-called 'stores' were very unmilitary: they looked to him rather like TV sets and radios from a PX offer that was in force at the time. Surreptitiously we had a peep through a window where a curtain had not been properly drawn, and lo and behold we saw an Aladdin's cave of all sorts of kit! Now the CLM compound was under my command, and I was not going to be hung for knowingly assisting in a large-scale smuggling operation, so I sought the Chief of Staff UN Command and told him of my suspicions. I was immediately marched into General Bonesteele's office. He was delighted. For some time his intelligence branch had been watching the operation, and now they had the evidence to scupper it once and for all.

The method he chose was a cunning one. We were strictly forbidden to use US dollars in Korea; the notes we used looked like dollars but were called 'scrip'. They had the same purchasing value, but could only be used inside Korea and Japan. From time to time the authorities would announce a change of scrip: all units and camps would be sealed off, and you had to change your old scrip personally for the new issue. There was a limit according to rank and pay on how much you could exchange without detailed information as to how you came to have the extra.

So when the day came – and it was kept a great secret – all the camps were sealed by the military police, and only the authorised paymasters were allowed in. The scene round the Thai hut was marvellous to behold. A body of soldiers were seen burning their excess scrip; no transport could move, so the cave was opened for all to see; and worse, a large Thai lorry was caught coming out of the Suwon PX loaded with contraband. Its crew's pockets were stuffed with US dollars to which they had no right, and carrying them was a military offence!

About a week later, feeling a bit like the school sneak, I was sent for by the headmaster, to thank me for what I felt had been rather a successful operation. A major black market hole had been well and truly plugged – or so I thought.

General Bonesteele looked at me with a grin. 'We didn't get them, you know,' he said. 'I sent for the Thai Ambassador to tell him a thing or two, but he took the wind completely out of my sails. He profusely apologised for the disgraceful behaviour of his men, and assured me that he would recommend to his Government that the whole Company should leave the United Nations force and be sent back to Thailand, but then he said that this would make our United Nations component look a bit thin on the ground!'

He added, wryly: 'There is an old saying I once heard. The Thais are the nicest people that money can buy.'

I was glad I was never a professional diplomat: the round of parties could become overpowering. New Year's Day was the worst, for in the Korean calendar this was the great day. It started with the official reception at the President's Palace at 10 am, champagne and all. You next called in turn on the Chairman of the ROK Joint Chiefs of Staff, and the Commander-in-Chief ROK Army, followed by the Navy, Air Force and Marines, and the UN Commander-in-Chief. At about 3 pm, when you were exhausted and filled to the eyeballs with liquor, there was a welcome lunch in the American Mission Club. By perhaps 4.00 you were back in your house for a brief respite, but not for long. Traditionally our CLM held a reception in our Mess. By midnight you had literally had it.

We had to learn the rules of Korean protocol, which was a strange mixture of American and oriental behaviour. For example, you must never refill your own glass – a friend will do it for you – and it is your job to see that your neighbour's glass is kept filled to keep pace with the numerous toasts that accompany each meal, to the expression *Gambai*, which roughly means 'your health'. Compounded with that was the Japanese influence of their near forty years' occupation of Korea, when they tried hard to convert the country into a sort of mirror image of Japan. There were endless social nuances, ranging from seating at meetings to exchanges of gifts, introductions and dress. Official parties were very formally organised, and could be very stiff and starchy at first.

The exception to this was a *kisaeng* dinner. This was strictly a 'men only' affair. The *kisaeng* was in some ways the equivalent of the Japanese *geisha* – a paid, professional entertainer, and very attractive girl, beautifully dressed, who sat next to you while the meal was being served, and saw that your plate and glass were never empty. After the meal the girls would entertain the company with Korean music and songs, some with very nostalgic and catchy tunes, and there could be somewhat childish games like 'Hunt the Slipper' and an Eastern variation of what seemed like 'Postman's Knock', and there could be dancing until it was time to go home. Sometimes a great deal of tact was needed, as some hosts still observed an old rule of hospitality whereby your partner was expected not just to see you home, but to entertain you there as well. To refuse such an offer point blank was considered bad manners, and so oblique excuses had to be hastily invented! I was only faced with this situation twice, when Sylvia was luckily in residence, and escaped the temptation with little difficulty.

In Seoul there was a Government-sponsored place of entertainment called Korea House. Whether it had survived the war or had been completely rebuilt in the 1950s I do not know, but it was a most attractive place surrounded by a large and well-kept garden. For what was in those days a very reasonable sum you could reserve it for a large dinner party or reception, complete with a troupe of professional entertainers who would put on an hour-long show after dinner was finished. The dinner was entirely in the Korean style, and the entertainment was similar to that put on by the *kisaeng* girls, but much more lavish and with many more performers.

Without exception our guests found Korean dance and music fascinating. Like their language it is of Central Asian origin, quite different from anything the Chinese or Japanese have. In particular there is an instrument called the *kayagum*. This is a sort of hybrid harp with a bit of double bass along the way, except that it is placed flat on the floor (or grass), and the strings are plucked – there is no bow. The player sits behind the instrument, also on the floor, and I have a photo of eight such instruments in action at one of our Embassy's receptions one summer's evening, with all the girls wearing their national dress and playing the most attractive music.

It is strange to think now that 'Arirang', which is perhaps the best known of all Korean tunes, was originally an anti-Japanese song, which, if you were caught playing or singing it, could result perhaps in imprisonment and very likely death. It is a lovely, haunting tune, and goes straight onto the bagpipes with no alterations to any notes.

The other place where we could entertain our guests was at Lake Chompyong, an artificial lake that was part of a major hydroelectric scheme. Here the CLM had the loan of a lovely summer house, complete with all mod cons including its own jetty, and we had a very fast motor launch which we kept on the lake in the summer. It was ideal for waterskiing and picnics, and in the hot summer it provided a welcome escape from the heat, dust and smog of Seoul. Just about one hour's drive got you to the jetty that was part of the maintenance road round the dam, the other side of the dam itself, and then you took the launch over and ferried the party across. On weekdays the men of the Honour Guard took turns to use the summer house and the launch for exercise and a breath of fresh air. Saturdays and Sundays were reserved for the officers and their families.

The first summer holidays came, and Maggie appeared looking as if she had stepped straight out of a San Francisco 'flower power' procession, despite our strict advice that such exuberance of dress was not regarded favourably by Korean society! She fell in love with the place at first glance, and immediately got herself a job teaching English at the local Sacred Heart Convent. If that were not enough, she made further cash on the side by taking pupils privately from some of the attachés and their friends. There was a delightful Vietnamese couple who had two small children whom their parents wanted to learn English, so she took them on as well, and most successfully.

There were two Sacred Heart establishments near Seoul: the school where Maggie taught, run by the American branch of the Order, and Chunchon University for Girls run by the British side. To see the 18- to 20-year-olds in their ceremonial national dress was quite something, but the nuns who ran the place were still very much in the traditional black robes of the Order. Their Superior, Mother Chu, was a delightful person. Though she was tiny, she had a presence and character that would have made her a Mother Superior anywhere in the world. I was told she came of a very old Chinese family of Mandarin stock. Her No. 2, also a great character, was Mother Thornton, otherwise known as 'Quacky' throughout the order. She was enormously tall, with eyes that drilled right through you, a considerable Chinese scholar who had faced down Chinese Communists and their like many a time, but had retained a great sense of humour.

These were the days when the reforms of Pope John XXIII were just beginning to permeate the religious orders, and the Americans were way ahead of their British counterparts. At an Embassy reception one hot summer evening, I was talking to Mother Chu and Quacky, dressed in their ceremonial black, when Quacky noticed Mother Rhode (the American Superior) attired in a very smart white silk uniform dress, with the nearest thing to a miniskirt I have ever seen on a nun. Quacky snorted in disfavour: 'I suppose one could vaguely recognise in that habit something of our Sacred Heart tradition – but not very much!'

243

On another occasion an aircraft carrier came up from Hong Kong. There was a great reception, and their Royal Marines beat retreat on the flight deck, but then a vicious storm blew up. The carrier was five miles off Inchon, so no one could disembark, and we had to spend the night on board. What were we to do with four nuns, in addition to the other guests? The Royal Navy, as always, had an answer for the problem, and we all left the ship next day after a great evening and a superb breakfast. Somehow beds had been found for everyone. Luckily there was no air group on board, so there were a few cabins to spare, but I have no idea where most of the officers slept!

Sylvia had found herself plenty to do apart from the purely social side. The high point was a club called the Bamboo Circle: its main object in life was bridge, which Sylvia could play, but of which she was not inordinately fond. However, the club organised all sorts of other things, and the Royal Central Asian Society, based on the British Embassy, ran educational trips to historic sites and places of interest. These were mostly day trips, but some of them needed a weekend. There is so much history to be seen in Korea. But Sylvia's real interest lay in a home for disadvantaged children, some of them orphaned, run by an American missionary society. Their main concern as far as the orphans were concerned was to try and arrange for their adoption by families in the USA. They worked under very strict rules to make sure that the adoptive families were suitable and would be able to look after their new charges, and it was very rewarding work. As a result Sylvia got to know Korea and the Koreans much better than I ever did: she had the chance to meet them as ordinary people rather than just those in authority.

In a strange way both she and Maggie gained great kudos amongst my Korean friends and servants for what they did. Protocol is enormously important to Koreans. Their traditional order of social rank puts the scholar at the top, followed by the student, the official, the farmer, the artisan, the merchant, the soldier (rather low, I fear), the *kisaeng*, musicians, dancers, and last of all the butchers. And even the butchers have their ranks: the beef butcher is the highest, followed by the pork butcher and – last on the list – the dog butcher! So technically, although in Korean terms I held the rank of General in the Army, I was way behind my wife and daughter on the Korean social scale.

The Commonwealth Forces had left behind them an enormous fund of goodwill after the Korean War ended. Somehow the bravery and behaviour of our forces had left a legacy that served us well: everywhere we went we felt we were among friends.

In April 1951, at a place some thirty miles north of Seoul called Solma-Ri, the 29th Brigade were attacked on the line of the Imjin River by the whole mass of the 62nd Chinese Army (equivalent to a British Corps). The brunt of the attack fell on the Gloucestershire Regiment, who most gallantly fought them off, but with very severe losses to themselves.

Some time after the war they put up a monumental stone on the side of Kamak San, the hill that had formed the nub of their defence, but by 1969 the small stream that ran along the side of Kamak San had begun to eat its way into the hillside and was threatening to undercut the memorial stone.

The ROK Army unit in that area, their 25th Division, was occupying the headquarters that our Commonwealth Division had used, and their General was a particular friend of mine, as many British visitors used to pass through to visit the memorial. One day he and his Chief of Engineers asked me to visit him as he wished to discuss a plan for the memorial. He produced some plans showing what could be done to ensure that the river could be kept under control, and the memorial itself made more accessible to visitors. His own engineers would do the work, but they needed money for materials. Could I get it for them?

Only a short time earlier General Tom Pearson, Commander Land Forces South East Asia, had visited Korea and had seen the memorial himself, so I sent all the papers, plans and calculations to Singapore, and asked for his help. I was not sure that any good would come of it, but it was worth a try. To my surprise, the next time our RAF Hercules came up with the Honour Guard relief, there also stepped out a senior Royal Engineers officer from Singapore, whose brief was to visit the site and 25th Division and discuss the matter. The whole thing was approved, and somehow a large cheque found its way into 25th Division's funds, and work started.

Their engineers and stonemasons did a brilliant job. Not only did they reline the banks of the errant stream, they also constructed a bridge over it, and laid a large memorial garden to its approach. There was a large notice at the entrance to the garden in Korean and English which read:

HERE SLEEP THE HEROIC SOULS OF BRITISH SOLDIERS WHO
FOUGHT FOR OUR COMMON GOOD, THE FREEDOM OF
MANKIND. LET US PAUSE FOR A MOMENT OF SILENT PRAYER

And in case anyone ignored that, on high days and holidays when traffic up and down that small country road was heavy, a soldier of 25th Division would be posted on the roadside by the notice to make sure that passers by *did* stop!

It was a long time before I found out why the Koreans took such pride in Solma-Ri and the Gloucesters' battle. It was one of the ancient invasion routes leading to Seoul, and down the ages enemies from the north had used it with success, but in April 1951 strange soldiers from a far-off country had held fast and – for the first time ever – slammed the gate shut.

*

We were due six weeks' mid-posting leave in June (not counting travelling time). The homeward journey was the same as our outward one, except that we caught the VC10 from Hong Kong, with the usual spectacular take-off from Kai Tak, and a welcome stop to refuel at Changi Airport, Singapore, where a number of friends were on the ground to meet us with refreshments. Our leave was timed to coincide with the end of the school summer terms so that Maggie and Sandy could fly back with us.

Just before that, there was a meeting at Panmunjom that we thought was going to be a record breaker. It went on and on and on. After seven hours had passed both sides got their second (or third) wind, and their respective secretaries started handing their chiefs statements that really had nothing to do with the original subject for which the meeting had been called. It suddenly became fun: we were going for the record, which was just over nine hours – and talk we did without stopping, for nine hours and thirty-four minutes! How we at the top table managed without leaving our seats I will never know; our staffs at the back could withdraw to 'freshen up', as the Americans say, but the four of us and our North Korean opponents could not. But we made it, and with sighs of relief but some hilarity got back to the advanced camp and its lavatories – and drinks!

Some weeks later a much more serious affair beat our record. It lasted nine hours thirty-eight minutes, but of that about four hours were spent in complete silence, as the North Korean side got in a muddle and refused to answer a particular question, and both sides sat glowering at each other until the North cracked. It was all rather like a poker game. Luckily I was not there; I heard about it when I returned from leave.

Leave passed all too quickly. We were based on my mother's house in London, as ours was let. All went well until the return journey, on which Maggie and Sandy were flying with us. The Royal Air Force had a hiccup: there was a dispute, which led to a shortage of cabin staff (I would have called it a strike, but you cannot have strikes in the Services). The shortage of staff meant that the aircraft could not carry its full load of passengers, and so Maggie had to be left behind to follow on a later flight. In fact she was only delayed for forty-eight hours; our gathering of friends in Hong Kong looked after her and put her on the Cathay flight to Seoul.

Seoul in July can be very hot and sticky, and even coming from a hot English summer we were not acclimatised to what we walked into. Our rather aged air conditioning could only just cope. During one dinner party the first course – a cold mousse – melted before our eyes, and became a sloppy mess of brown lukewarm porridge, much to the horror of Isi, our cook. Luckily the heat was off at Panmunjom; the last MAC meeting had taken the steam out of the opposition, and a certain quietness had fallen on the DMZ.

At the end of August we escaped for a fortnight's break at Chinhae, the Korean naval base, where there was a lovely guest house. The US Navy commander there, Captain Ralph Graham USN, was a very distant cousin of mine. There were expeditions in his launch to the lovely islands round the bay, sailing, all sorts of places in the surrounding countryside, and days watching the local divers, some in old-fashioned Siebe Gorman suits, but most diving for shellfish from aged fishing boats with just a mask. The actual base commander was a Korean rear admiral who lived in a house that had originally been built for the Japanese Commander-in-Chief in the days of their occupation. Chinhae was the harbour that Admiral Togo used for his battle fleet before he engaged the Russians at Tsushima in 1904.

We were asked to dinner by the Korean admiral, and I had carefully explained to Maggie and Sandy that sometimes their host might chose some delicacy and put it on their plates – in which case, they must eat it regardless. To my horror, the Admiral chose the biggest, blackest and greasiest sea slug, the size of a small squash ball, and tenderly put it on Sandy's plate. We loved most Korean food, even the hottest *kimchi*, but sea slugs are something that look horrid and, if you try to chew them, have the consistency of rubber. But Sandy wasn't brought up 'proper' for nothing. He somehow seized the slug in his chopsticks, and swallowed it whole. The honour of the family was secure. It was a memorable dinner!

There was some wonderful shooting to be had (the Americans and Koreans called it 'hunting'), particularly on the borders of the DMZ, which became a sort of game sanctuary. No one ventured into that disputed area for fun. Expeditions there were a sort of military patrol, as one had to be accompanied by an armed escort, and guides who knew where the wire and minefields lay, but you were dealing with genuinely wild pheasants, who knew much more about the country than you did, and could run a great deal faster.

There was wildfowl too in great numbers along the Han River, but again any expedition had to be carefully planned with the local military, who treated any armed party as potentially hostile. One had to adopt the American hunting practice of wearing very conspicuous hats and jackets for fear of being peppered by one's companions, as most of the shoots took place in low scrub over hills. The idea of a well-ordered 'line' of guns was foreign, and in any case impossible to organise. Luckily for me the friends who took me out were extremely safe shots, as otherwise the affair could have been potentially very dangerous, but all the same it did seem odd to be walking round the countryside wearing a fluorescent red hat.

The best shooting of the lot was on Cheju-Do, a large volcanic island about 100 miles south of Korea, but part of the republic. Once a year in late October, the Koreans organised what they called an international friendly shooting competition on Cheju-Do. There were teams of four from various nations – America, Korea, China (Formosa) and Japan. Somehow the British managed to raise a team from the CLM and the embassies, and for two years I found myself ex officio 'Captain'.

The whole thing was a cross between orienteering and sheer luck. Teams were given a map of their area, taken to a starting point, and told to rendezvous at the end of the day at a particular spot, where they would be picked up and the bag counted. No dogs were allowed, and you had to recruit your own beaters from any villages in your path, wherever that might lead. To make sure that you did not get completely lost, and to see that the rules were obeyed, a Korean policeman was attached to each team as guide and interpreter. You were let loose at 10.00 in the morning, and you had to be back to your rendezvous at 4.00 pm. It was a test of low cunning, marksmanship and endurance. Your relied on your team of locals to guide you where they thought pheasants might lie up; you then tried to surround the area, drive the birds out of their hides, and – hopefully – shoot them.

One of the few words I knew in Korean was that for pheasant, which was *kwong*, and throughout the day our small boy guides would take us to places that they assured us were literally honking with *kwong*. But the latter had usually taken off long before we got there, and we would walk for miles up hill and down dale without seeing any, but hearing their mocking calls in the distance. Somehow the Japanese always seemed to get the biggest bag, and the 'international friendly' bit rather tended to go out of the window, but on my second year the British team *did* get a prize, due entirely to me! A bird got up that I shot stone dead, and it was the most beautifully coloured thing I had ever seen, a cross between a Chinese Green Pheasant and the local wild breed, which was very similar to a British-bred 'melanisitic' variety. It won the prize for the best bird shot in the competition, and I had it stuffed and mounted by a local taxidermist in Seoul. It now rests in Argyllshire along with the other bird I bagged that day.

After our marathon march the parties ended up in the local hotel where we were staying and had to endure a marathon celebration. Endless speeches were made, and a myriad of toasts were swallowed, undoing all the excellent fresh air and exercise we had taken. Next day we all flew home.

Early one morning in October 1969 Sylvia, who had never been taken seriously ill in her life, suddenly complained of a severe pain in her stomach. We had been to the usual Sunday evening supper and film in our Mess the evening before, and she had been fine. Whatever had struck her, had come unexpectedly and very quickly. I rang the duty officer at the local military hospital (121 Evac of MASH fame), and was told to get her in as quickly as I could. So we bundled her into some warm clothes and drove in with Moon in my staff car, and in some thirty minutes she was in the hands of that most efficient unit. They told me there was little point in my hanging around; they would let me know what was up as soon as they found out.

About four hours later they did let me know. X-rays had disclosed a large tumour in part of her stomach, and they required my permission to operate, but I had better come and see her first, which I did. She had been told what was wrong, and together we told the head surgeon to go ahead. There was an alternative: he could arrange for her to fly down to the British Military Hospital in Hong Kong, but that would mean a delay of some ten hours, and he advised against it.

The operation was completely successful, and five days later Sylvia was back at home in the hands of Isi, Ahn and Mrs Kim, who transformed themselves into a highly skilled nursing staff. Within ten days she was able to walk around the house, and within three weeks – although she had to take life very easy – she was back with her Korean children. In the meantime we were overwhelmed with countless visitors of all races and all ranks. And the good news was that the tumour was not malignant. By Christmas Sylvia was back on form, ready for Sandy on his last visit before we returned home. We were not to know that it would be the last Christmas we would ever spend together as a family.

Meetings at Panmunjom had gone into a sort of decline. There had been a serious incident in which the North Koreans had shot down an EC121, a very sophisticated reconnaissance aircraft, into the sea without any warning. It was flying off the east coast of Korea in international waters when it was jumped by North Korean fighters and destroyed. The situation was understandably very tense, and we called an MAC meeting to protest.

Knowing the North's reluctance to answer questions directly we were strictly briefed as to how we should conduct the meeting. There would be a very brief statement outlining the circumstances of the case – time, date, position and last known transmission of the EC121 when it was attacked – and then the North would be directly asked to admit responsibility. If they refused to answer, or made some evasive statement about other matters, we would interrupt that statement and again ask for a definite answer. If they still refused, we would walk straight out of the meeting without a further word. No one had ever behaved in such a manner before at an MAC meeting, and it was thought that we might gain a point or two by such a tactic. It was a deliberate and well rehearsed gambit, which had the complete approval of everyone, from Washington, down through the Commander-in-Chief Pacific in Hawaii. Our Chief, Major General James Knapp of the US Air Force, got the final go-ahead in our Chinook helicopter as we flew from Seoul to the advanced camp.

Sure enough, the North Koreans put up their usual verbose reply, which had nothing to do with the incident. As rehearsed, Jim Knapp repeated his statement and his request for an immediate answer and acceptance of responsibility. Back came the North with more waffle. They had hardly got started when, at a signal, we all stood up, left the conference table and filed out of the room, leaving the North and their two Chinese colleagues sitting in astounded silence, totally lost for words, while the world's press took pictures of some very embarrassed negotiators and their staff officers. They had lost a great deal of 'face'. Everyone knew about the incident: the EC121's Mayday calls had been picked up all over the area, and the North themselves had bragged about shooting it down. Their MAC representatives had been shown up for what they were – the mouthpieces of a most unsavoury government. For the first time in many years the United Nations team had gained a bit of initiative. As a result it was some months before the North called another full meeting.

Each year the Armistice Commission arranged a tour for its members, one year inside Korea, lasting some ten days, and the next in the countries that it represented. I managed both, the first being the Korean tour. It had a memorable ending at Kyongju, a historic town in the centre of the country. There were some twenty of us on the tour, and one night we were all well and truly robbed.

I was sharing a room in a nice Korean hotel with my Turkish opposite number, and as usual put my wallet with money and identification papers etc. under my pillow; he left his in his coat pocket. Next morning we woke up to a considerable disturbance – the police were on us in force! Some expert thieves had 'done' the lot of us, including our general, whose brief-case contained a quantity of highly confidential papers. Luckily the robbers had not realised what they were and had thrown most of them over the balcony, where they were all recovered. The thieves had gone through ten rooms, all with two people sleeping in them, and no one had heard a thing until they woke up next morning. How could they have done it?

There were all sorts of theories, such as sleeping pills in our wine at dinner, but the Korean police gave us the answer. The burglars worked in teams of three to a room. One had a long bamboo tube through which he blew, very gently, what the dentists call 'laughing gas' (nitrous oxide) into the faces of the two occupants in their beds. While they were well and truly drugged the second man would rifle their pockets, and search under their pillows. The third man, who was the leader of the group, would merely watch the proceedings carefully to make sure the victims were still unconscious – the slightest stir and the team would withdraw.

It was all quite an experience, particularly when we were greeted at Kimpo Airport on our return that afternoon by a grinning Moon, who was brandishing the local newspaper and basking in the fame of being the servant of one of the distinguished characters who was involved in a famous case of robbery!

The overseas tour the following year included Thailand, Hong Kong, the Philippines and Taiwan, with a day on Okinawa. I could not make the Thailand or Philippines stops, but I was responsible for arrangements in Hong Kong, where Basil and Marcia Eugster were the kindest and most generous of hosts. Taiwan was perhaps the most interesting place of any I had seen, and as we were sponsored by the US Forces Mission, we were taken to many places that the ordinary tourist would never be allowed near. We were shown over General Chiang Kai Shek's personal residence, which took one's breath away with the riot and clashes of colour that the Chinese excel in, but which I found gave me a headache, and the National Museum's exquisite exhibits of artefacts, parchments and paintings brought across from mainland China.

At that time there were no diplomatic relations between Britain and Taiwan, and I therefore had to have a special form of passport, so that my own would not bear the so-called 'Chinese' stamp on it. I cannot think why the regulations were so stuffy about that, but 'Orders is Orders' and so I had to comply. The orders even went so far as to forbid me from asking the Taiwanese military attaché to my house in Seoul, together with his charming and talented wife, who was a great friend of Sylvia's. I rather fear I paid no attention to that particular order.

Okinawa was fascinating. It was then a major US Air Force base, and the whole time we were there we could hear the enormous B52s taking off and landing from their missions in faraway Vietnam. We were totally under Air Force hospitality, and though they drove us round parts of the island, there was really little chance of seeing anything of any historical or noteworthy interest. It was all one vast air base!

In March Sylvia started to feel unwell, and it was decided that she should go to Hong Kong to be looked at by the surgical specialists there. After a week's examination and tests they decided that something was not quite as it should be, that she should have a hysterectomy, and that they would check very thoroughly what the surgeons at 121 Evac in Seoul had done. I was given ten days' leave to go down after she had had her operation and bring her back.

All went very successfully. I arrived to find her in a sumptuous ward surrounded by flowers and bottles of all sorts and sizes. I asked where these had come from, and was told that it was Marcia Eugster's doing. Apparently when Sylvia was first installed in her room, Marcia came to visit her, and said in horrified tones: 'My dear – no bar! Nothing to give your friends when they come and see you! I shall put that right at once!'

On her return to the GOC's house she sent her driver back to the hospital with a choice selection of drinks and suitable mixers, and when I suggested some form of repayment she refused to discuss the matter. It was a small compensation for all the parties we had given her and Basil when they had visited Seoul the year before.

The BMH Hong Kong gave Sylvia a clean bill of health, and after some ten days I flew back with her to Seoul. Just before that Maggie passed through on her way to Australia. She had got herself a teaching post at the big Catholic convent at Kincoppal in Sydney, and the three of us had quite a celebration in Hong Kong ending with an enormous official dinner at the Eugsters', with Sylvia and Maggie resplendent in the lovely Korean silk dresses that one could pick up for a song over there.

It was now April, and I was due to be relieved in July, but there was a hiccup: my replacement's posting was changed at the last minute, and someone had to conjure up another replacement rather quickly, and that was not easy. This meant that I had no hope of returning to the UK by ship, the fast cargo/passenger liners that went through Panama. We had to be back home in time for the end of term at Downside, where Sandy was at school, and that would have meant leaving Korea in mid-June. My replacement would need five days' handover, which meant virtually a whole week before we ourselves could go, and our clothes and household goods had to be packed and listed ready to fly to Hong Kong by the Honour Guard plane, there to be put on a ship. (Little did we know that they would arrive in UK waters just as the dock labourers had declared a strike that shut all ports down, and our baggage would end up in Holland.)

In the midst of all this an inspector arrived from the Foreign Office to review the Embassy staff and their expenses. I was only under his eagle eye as far as my job of Defence Attaché was concerned, but there was the whole question of the house and its staff. He took exception to the fact that I had installed two extra air conditioners. It did not matter that I had bought them myself; for the size of the house and the cubic footage of the rooms they were outside the regulations, and there also was the question of the extra electricity that they consumed! He was a nice enough chap, but a typical example of the 'Babu' mentality, not that his findings would affect me, but what I said and what he decided would impinge on my successors. At that stage of the game I really could have done without him.

Before I left I had one last special trip, to the DMZ. Commanding the Third Battalion of the 23rd US Infantry was a great friend, Hugh McWhinnie, a distinguished and interesting soldier from Perthshire who had started life in the Black Watch, served with the Parachute Regiment in

North Africa, where he was severely wounded and taken prisoner, escaped from his camp in Italy, fought with the partisans there until life got too hot, and then managed to get into Switzerland. When the war ended he got back to Scotland, married Doris, and took off for America, where he joined the US Army and attained the rank of Lieutenant Colonel. Hugh invited me to spend three days with his battalion, which was on active duty on the DMZ. The Commanding General of Second Division, Lee Cagwin, was an old friend of mine from SHAPE days, and pretended not to know about my visit – at least he authorised it!

At this time reductions were going on in the British Army, and my regiment, the Argylls, were under threat. We were conducting a vigorous campaign to stop any disbandment or amalgamation, and we had a whole lot of posters printed, with SAVE THE ARGYLLS printed in the Regimental colours. On his latest trip on leave to Scotland, Hugh had collected a sheaf of them, and had pasted them on his battalion transport. His soldiers thought this was great fun, but his superiors looked on it with well-merited disfavour. Worse still, suspicion fell on me for encouraging this illicit recruiting drive.

Luckily General 'Mike' Michaelis, now UN Commander-in-Chief, and Lee Cagwin were friends who knew the regiment and turned a blind eye to this nonsense, and I was allowed to go up to what was literally the front line. We did not go over the wire into the DMZ itself – that would have been very rash and asking for trouble – but standing in the command post watchtower at night, hearing the occasional shot and watching the Verey lights go up, with Seoul just thirty miles behind us, gave me a good idea of just how tense the situation was in those days.

For the last time, or so I thought, I packed glass, silver and china, clothes, linen, pictures and all our possessions in our boxes, locked and screwed them down, stencilled names and destinations on them, typed out lists of contents for Customs and insurance, saw them loaded on one of our trucks, and wondered whether I should ever see them again. At the end of June my relief, Harry Edwardes, arrived with his wife. He had been at Wellington with me, but our paths had never crossed there, nor had we ever served together. I was very worried about him: he was clearly a very sick man, with some form of heart complaint, and he found difficulty in getting about. In the event he was to die of a heart attack before the year was out.

On Friday 26 June Sylvia and I sat surrounded by our sparse travel bags in the drawing room of the house, waiting for Moon to drive us to Kimpo. Isi, Ahn and Mrs Kim were almost in tears; they had become much more than mere servants, and it was a real wrench to leave them. We would never see their like again. Somehow we disengaged ourselves and got to Kimpo, where there was a sort of official send-off headed by Nigel Trench, our Ambassador. All sorts of friends were there, an assortment of many ranks and many races, and – most touching of all – a small party of the children from the school where Sylvia had lent a hand. The Korean ladies and girls were all dressed in their beautiful national costume, which gave a blaze of colour to the scene. Eventually the party had to end, and we got on the aircraft for Tokyo. We were making a leisurely trip via Japan, Taiwan, Hong Kong and Singapore, which was to take us the best part of two weeks.

The plane taxied down the runway, and turned into wind just by the spot where we had bivouaced with the Middlesex and 3RAR nearly twenty years before, in October 1950. We were slightly delayed while two ROK Air Force fighters took off for a routine patrol, and I had a good view of the tree-lined bank where we had had our bivouacs for the five days or so before we set off across the parallel to the far north. I scarcely recognised the place.

Just about 1 pm, on time, Flight CX451 took off for Haneda. There were patches of light cloud, and for some time I could see the Korean countryside gradually diminishing as we gained height. Finally there was a typical little village with its thatched roofs, surrounded by green *padi* fields, until the clouds took over and Korea disappeared for ever.

The Cathay girls produced their usual delectable appetisers, but somehow they tasted like cardboard. We both found it difficult to talk. This was the posting that Sylvia had dreaded, but she had fallen in love with the land and its people, and I think she knew somehow that she would never see any of it again. As for me, I knew it was the last job I was ever to do in the Army. Another chapter in the book was firmly closed for ever.

NOTES

1   The *Pueblo* was a US Navy Intelligence SIGINT gathering ship that was intercepted and captured by the North Koreans. This was the first time in history that a US Navy ship had been boarded by an enemy without firing a shot in defence. It is a fascinating story, and one that received worldwide publicity at the time.

ENVOI
Port and liqueurs

It used to be the custom when I was much younger that, at the end of a good dinner, the ladies would be led to the drawing room by their hostess, and the men would stay round the table to discuss things on their own. Sylvia disliked this, and although she went along with it, she would complain afterwards that it was uncivilised. Why should the ladies be so disposed of? Why could they not stay? But diplomatic protocol still held, and that was the way we ran things. It is all a bit different today.

So we have come to the end of the party, and there are a great many things to discuss and talk about with the port.

The Armed Services, for example, that were part and parcel of my life for so many years. They have changed out of all recognition from the days when I first knew them as a small boy in India, and as a newly commissioned officer. Their contraction means that less and less are they part of the scene in this country, and fewer and fewer have served in their ranks or have relatives serving. The days when the troops of Aldershot Command could fill Rushmoor Arena for that marvellous Tattoo are long gone, and now even the Royal Tournament has faded away. In country towns bandstands stand empty, barracks are replaced by new housing, and once famous regiments are left with perhaps one room in some local museum.

That is one side of the story. On the other hand television brings all sorts of up-to-the-minute pictures of operations in strange countries into millions of houses, and sometimes not so good and very slanted 'soaps' and documentaries of what producers think the public will want to see.

I would class myself as a sort of regimental dodo, a sole survivor of a species that is fast disappearing, but I do still have contact with the young of all ranks. From time to time they ask me to visit them and tell them something of how life was when I was their age, how we worked and how we fought, and sometimes I wonder if they really believe me (they are much too polite to say so!). I first joined a horse-drawn Army, with simple weapons that had not changed much since the Boer War, and communications that were based on the telephone line, heliograph and signal lamp. How different from today's computers and multiple weapon systems. Which means that the young soldier of today has to be far better trained in technical details than we ever possibly imagined, and air transport has meant that he can be moved at very short notice almost anywhere in the world, to deal with very tricky situations, sometimes of a highly political nature. I wonder how much longer we can afford to go on doing this.

Which brings me to the final subject for thought, the *bilan*, a French word that can mean two things – account, or perhaps balance sheet.

You have not read the complete account. This story ends in 1971, thirty years ago, and much has happened since. I remarried – Alison, an old friend, whose children and mine were practically brought up together – and so I inherited a second large family. Sadly Alison died four years ago after a series of strokes, so there is both a credit and a debit to be considered.

But on the whole I know I end up vastly in credit: all the places I have seen, the many friends I have made, and – more than that – the privilege of serving alongside those marvellous soldiers of the County regiments of this country. Royal Scots, Royal Berkshires, Royal Welch Fusiliers, Durham Light Infantry, Camerons, Gordons, Seaforths and many others – so many have all gone now, passed into history. Reductions and amalgamations have succeeded where the enemy could not.

Successive generations of statesmen and politicians have never really understood the British Army. They have dubbed us with all sorts of names – 'Chinless Wonders', 'Mercenaries', 'Contemptible' – and even the great Duke of Wellington once referred to us as 'Scum'! But just before the Battle of Waterloo he pointed out a British soldier in a square in Brussels, and said to his companion, Mr Creevey, 'It all depends on that article . . . give me enough of it and I am sure.'

Today we still depend on what the Duke called 'that article', and we have never had enough of him. But we watch with pride as he carries out his thankless tasks wherever he may be sent – Sierra Leone, Croatia, Bosnia, Kosovo, the Falklands, Kuwait. The list goes on and on.

The British soldier of today is a worthy descendant of his forebears, so well described in A.E. Housman's 'Epitaph on an Army of Mercenaries':

> These, in the days when heaven was falling,
> The hour when earth's foundations fled,
> Followed their mercenary calling
> And took their wages and are dead.
>
> Their shoulders held the sky suspended;
> They stood, and earth's foundations stay;
> What God abandoned, these defended,
> And saved the sum of things for pay.